Wide Angle

3

MILES CRAVEN

OXFORD
UNIVERSITY PRESS

OXFORD
UNIVERSITY PRESS

198 Madison Avenue
New York, NY 10016 USA

Great Clarendon Street, Oxford, OX2 6DP,
United Kingdom

Oxford University Press is a department of the University of Oxford. It furthers
the University's objective of excellence in research, scholarship, and education by
publishing worldwide. Oxford is a registered trade mark of Oxford University Press
in the UK and in certain other countries

ISBN: 978 019 452856 6   Wide Angle American 3 SB W/OP Pack
ISBN: 978 0 19 452832 0   Wide Angle American 3 SB
ISBN: 978 019 454665 2   Wide Angle American 3 OP

Printed in China

This book is printed on paper from certified and well-managed sources

ACKNOWLEDGEMENTS

Back cover photograph: Oxford University Press building/David Fisher

Illustrations by: 5W Infographics p. 52; A. Richard Allen/Morgan Gaynin Inc pp. 5, 140;
Michael Kirkham/Heart USA Inc p. 44; Shaw Nielsen pp. 13, 25, 37, 49, 61, 73, 85, 97,
109, 121, 133, 145; Aaron Sacco/Mendola Artists p. 109.

Video Stills: pp. Mannic Productions: pp.12, 24, 36, 48, 60, 72, 84, 96, 108, 120, 132,
144. People's Television: 103, 124, 136.

*The Publishers would like to thank the following for their kind permission to reproduce
photographs and other copyright material*: **123rf:** pp. 21 (terracotta soldiers/王 学典
), 42 (tourists on segways/flaperval), 50 (whale watching/Konrad Mostert), 68 (3/
jakobradlgruber),68 (7/Kampee Patisena), 69 (B/Sergio Delle Vedove), 79 (futuristic
city/algolonline), 100 (job interview/Antonio Diaz), 104 (hotel manager/Dmitry
Kalinovsky), 113 (surveillance camera/sablevector), 114 (Data/carloscastilla),
114 (knowledge/Setsiri Silapasuwanchai), 125 (airport line/Ufuk Uyanik); **Alamy:**
pp. 4 (office/Bertrand Gardel), 6 (3/East Fence Images), 6 (5/Vadym Drobot), 11 (social
event/ZUMA Press), 23 (Mysterious place of historical interest/Chris Willson),
33 (Ray Kurzweil/Splash News), 41 (parkour/Radius Images), 43 (gallo pinto/
RosaIreneBetancourt 10), 46 (4/Image Source), 46 (8/Sirayot Bunhlong), 55 (beach/
PCJones), 55 (bedroom/David Williams), 58 (packing/Lev Dolgachov), 59 (Somalia/
robertharding), 62 (Jackson, Wyoming/Niebrugge Images), 74 (bike riding/Wig
Worland), 77 (Julie/Mint Images Limited), 77 (man grey shirt/Image Source),
77 (Mateo/Joana Lopes), 77 (Sarah/40260.com), 77 (Steve/Cultura RM), 77 (Susie/
Hero Images Inc.), 79 (hologram phone/Dmitry SHISHKIN), 82 (escalator sign/Ira
Block), 88 (fashion/Juliane Thiere), 93 (gold car/amer ghazzal), 95 (someone on
phone/MIKA Images), 103 (police officer/Hemis), 104 (check in/Cultura Creative
(RF), 106 (Google tricycle mapper/Jamie Pham), 142 (worried woman/Kobryn
Andrii), 143 (marshmallow/Still Curved), **Annie Hudson.** p. 107 (Annie Hudson/
Annie Hudson); **Blink:** Cover, Edu Bayer, pp. 3 (security officer in museum/Edu
Bayer), 8 (family with horse/Gianni Cipriano), 15 (cowgirl eating ice cream/Krisanne
Johnson), 19 (walking beach/Krisanne Johnson), 27 (cooking class/Gianni Cipriano),
33 (man with brain activity monitor/Edu Bayer), 39 (woman singing in road/Krisanne
Johnson), 47 (man on phone/Quinn Ryan Mattingly), 51 (man and baby/Nadia
Shira Cohen), 54 (dark bedroom/Nadia Shira Cohen), 63 (man's reflection/Quinn
Ryan Mattingly), 67 (selfie stick/Nadia Shira Cohen), 75 (boy/Nadia Shira Cohen),
77 (girls laughing/Krisanne Johnson), 87 (man adjusting tie/Gianni Cipriano),
92 (eating noodles/Quinn Ryan Mattingly), 99 (harvest salt /Quinn Ryan Mattingly),
102 (Representatives talking/Quinn Ryan Mattingly), 111 (Cosplays/Gianni Cipriano),
119 (wifi at museum/Edu Bayer), 123 (hot air balloon/Nadia Shira Cohen), 128 (man
magnifying glass/Gianni Cipriano), 135 (woman waiting/ Krisanne Johnson),
138 (women dancing/Krisanne Johnson); **Bridgeman:** p. 66 (Van Gogh/Gogh,
Vincent van (1853-90)/National Gallery of Art, Washington DC, USA); **Data Cuisine:**
pp. 114 (Taste of Migration/Dish: Eleonora Ivanova, Susanne Jaschko, Moritz
Stefaner — Data Cuisine (http://data-cuisine.net/data-dishes/taste-of-migration/),
116 (Sea Change/Lynn Cherny, Alex Dorsk, Susanne Jaschko, Moritz Stefaner —
Data Cuisine (http://data-cuisine.net/data-dishes/sea-change/); **David McCandless:**
p. 115 (David McCandless /David McCandless), 115 (David McCandless visualisation/
David McCandless@informationisbeautiful.net); **Encyclopaedia of Aesthetics:**
p. 116 (measuring cup/Measuring Cup (Sydney 1859-2009) 2010, Mitchell Whitelaw);
Eugene Minogue: p. 40 (Eugene Minogue/Eugene Minogue); **Getty:** pp. 5 (ping
pong table/Bloomberg), 6 (4/Anna Pekunova), 7 (fake smile/drbimages), 7 (woman
frowning/Tim Graham), 14 (women talking/Hero Images), 16 (abandoned residential
area/ApMadoc), 16 (Detroit 1920s/Popperfoto), 16 (Detroit 1950s/Underwood
Archives), 18 (Eagleman's experiment/John B. Carnett), 20 (people playing volleyball/
Angelo Merendino), 21 (Gobekli Tepe/Mark Daffe), 21 (Nazca lines/Chris Beall),
22 (Rosetta Stone/Michael Ochs Archives), 26 (family on beach/Education Images),
28 (job interview/Steve Debenport), 31 (man loading washing machine/RoBeDeRo),
31 (man running on treadmill/Katarina Premfors), 32 (Google car/KAREN BLEIER),
32 (Nick Bostrom/The Washington Post), 32 (robot hotel receptionist/Bloomberg),
38 (Indian shop owner/Christian Augustin), 42 (ferry/Photographer's Choice
RF), 43 (Tortuguero river/The Image Bank), 46 (3/Utah-based Photographer Ryan
Houston), 46 (5/Juanmonino), 57 (house or apartment with 'for rent' sign/ejs9),
59 (Medecins Sans Frontieres doctors/Patrick Robert - Corbis), 65(astronaut eating in
space /Space Frontiers), 66 (Rembrandt/DEA/G. NIMATALLAH), 68 (1/Jordan Siemens),
69 (A/Stephen J Boitano), 69 (C/UniversalImagesGroup), 70 (Hideo/Dan Dalton),
70 (Raymond/Stella Kalinina), 83 (man giving speech/Viorika), 90 (elderly lady eating/
SilviaJansen), 95 (handbags/Peter Dazeley), 95 (jewelled phonecase/Franck Prevel),
95 (sneakers/Edward Berthelot), 103 (teacher/Hill Street Studios), 129 (The Wild
Bunch/Movie Poster Image Art), 137 (man painting/Alyson Aliano), 139 (satisfied
man/Westend6), 139 (waiting in line/Chesnot), 140 (Joshua/Nick Clements),
(shopping bags/Britt Erlanson); **iStock:** p. xvi, (phone/lvcandy), (tablet/RekaReka),
pp. 6 (1/RistoArnaudov), 6 (6/NicolasMcComber), 16 (modern Detroit/tomprout),
31 (diabled girl talking to friend/Tashi-Delek), 45 (casual woman/alvarez), 50 (tourist/
JordiRamisa), 139 (curious child/Romrodinka);

Newscom: p. 69 (D/Zuma/Newscom); **OUP:** pp. 77 (blonde woman/Gareth Boden),
126 (Fantasy Stories/Oxford University Press), 126 (Grimm's Tales/Oxford University
Press), 126 (Science Fiction Stories/Oxford University Press), 126 (Treasure Island/
Oxford University Press), 127 (The Three Strangers/Oxford University Press); **REX:**
pp. 129 (Braveheart/Icon/Ladd Co/Paramount/Kobal), 129 (Fast & Furious 6/Universal/
Kobal), 129 (Les Miserables/Working Title Films/Kobal), 129 (Love Actually/Universal/
Dna/Working Title/Kobal), 129 (Sprited Away/Studio Ghibli/Kobal), 129 (The
Hunger Games Mockingjay/Color Force/Lionsgate/Kobal), 130 (Jennifer Lawrence
as Katniss/Snap Stills), 130 (mockingjay pin/Michael Buckner/Variety), 134 (Ernest
Hemingway/SNAP); **Shutterstock:** pp. 7 (real smile/eurobanks), 7 (woman
looking disgusted/Michal Kowalski), 9 (Sydney /BkBook), 16 (man/AJR_photo),
21 (Stonehenge/Nicholas E Jones), 22 (hieroglyphics/ Fedor Selivanov), 22 (papyrus/
Jerry Lin), 31 (man buying ticket/illpax), 42 (cable cars on street/Luciano Mortula),
43 (man in jungle/GaudiLab), 45 (smart woman/Monkey Business Images), 46 (1/Felix
Mizioznikov), 46 (2/AJR_photo), 46 (6/pixelheadphoto digitalskillet), 46 (7/Nakoff),
46 (9/katfox.art), 68 (2/Sergey Novikov), 68 (4/Koldunov), 68 (5/Zeeker2526), 68 (6/
stockfour), 68 (8/7th Son Studio), 70 (Julie/The Art of Pics), 70 (Miguel/cheapbooks),
71 (unusual building/VDV), 76 (texting/urbazon), 77 (Eva/Michae Allen), 77 (Simon/
Dragon Images), 79 (hologram man/kurhan), 79 (medical pod/Ociacia), 80 (flying
car/Costazzurra), 86 (basketball player/bbernard), 91 (organic food/Rawpixel.
com), 95 (sound system/Pavel L Photo and Video), 98 (man on phone/LStockStudio),
98 (phone/Quality Stock Arts), 98 (woman with headset/Pro Image Content),
104 (globe/Kalamurzing), 104 (hotel entrance/Dutourdumonde Photography),
104 (Stephania/Mettus), 112 (identify theft/frank_peters), 114 (information/
Khakimullin Aleksandr), 117 (women whispering/jesadaphorn), 122 (black camera/
jocic), 122 (pink camera/Roman Samokhin), 134 (aunt and niece/Asia Images Group),
143 (Jordan Davis/Asier Romero), 146 (balalaika/SergSmass);

Superstock: pp. 6 (2/Erickson Productions Inc), 16 (Detroit circa 1900/Circa
Images/Glasshouse Images), 35 (drawing/Ian Cook/Image Source), 64 (Earth/NASA),
103 (nurse/Caia Images), 104 (bed and breakfast/Otto Stadlero/imageBROKER);
Tinkersbubble.org: p. 54 (Tinker's Bubble/David Spero).

Authentic Content Provided by Oxford Reference

The publisher is grateful to those who have given permission to use the following extracts and adaptations of copyright material:

p.7 adapted from "facial expression." In *The Oxford Companion to the Body*, edited by Blakemore, Colin, and Jennett, Sheila.: Oxford University Press, 2001. http://www.oxfordreference.com/view/10.1093/acref/9780198524038.001.0001/acref-9780198524038-e-360

p.19 adapted from "déjà vu." In *The Oxford Companion to the Mind*, edited by Richard L. Gregory.: Oxford University Press, 2004. http://www.oxfordreference.com/view/10.1093/acref/9780198662242.001.0001/acref-9780198662242-e-239

p.38 selected from "Henry Miller." In *Oxford Dictionary of Quotations*, edited by Knowles, Elizabeth.: Oxford University Press, 2014. http://www.oxfordreference.com/view/10.1093/acref/9780199668700.001.0001/q-author-00010-00002298

p.54 adapted from "Climate Control." In *Encyclopedia of Climate and Weather*, edited by Schneider, Stephen H., Root, Terry L., and Mastrandrea, Michael D..: Oxford University Press, 2011. http://www.oxfordreference.com/view/10.1093/acref/9780199765324.001.0001/acref-9780199765324-e-0084

p.65 adapted from "Space Food." In *The Oxford Encyclopedia of Food and Drink in America* edited by Andrew F. Smith.: Oxford University Press, 2012. http://www.oxfordreference.com/view/10.1093/acref/9780199734962.001.0001/acref-9780199734962-e-0832

p.82 adapted from "Loanword." In *Concise Oxford Companion to the English Language*, edited by McArthur, Tom.: Oxford University Press, 1998. http://www.oxfordreference.com/view/10.1093/acref/9780192800619.001.0001/acref-9780192800619-e-737

p.91 adapted from "Organic Food." In *The Oxford Encyclopedia of Food and Drink in America* edited by Andrew F. Smith.: Oxford University Press, 2012. http://www.oxfordreference.com/view/10.1093/acref/9780199734962.001.0001/acref-9780199734962-e-0621

p.101 adapted from "interviews." In *The Oxford Companion to the Mind*, edited by Richard L. Gregory.: Oxford University Press, 2004. http://www.oxfordreference.com/view/10.1093/acref/9780198662242.001.0001/acref-9780198662242-e-465

p.116 adapted from "Information Theory." In *Encyclopedia of Aesthetics*, edited by Michael Kelly.: Oxford University Press, 2014. http://www.oxfordreference.com/view/10.1093/acref/9780199747108.001.0001/acref-9780199747108-e-107

p.134 adapted from "Hemingway, Ernest." In *The Oxford Encyclopedia of American Literature* edited by Jay Parini and Phillip W. Leininger.: Oxford University Press, 2004. http://www.oxfordreference.com/view/10.1093/acref/9780195156539.001.0001/acref-9780195156539-e-0117

p.142 adapted from "Prisoner's Dilemma." In *Dictionary of the Social Sciences*, edited by Craig Calhoun: Oxford University Press, 2002. http://www.oxfordreference.com/view/10.1093/acref/9780195123715.001.0001/acref-9780195123715-e-1338

p.147 selected from "Ralph Waldo Emerson." In *Oxford Essential Quotations*, edited by Ratcliffe, Susan.: Oxford University Press, http://www.oxfordreference.com/view/10.1093/acref/9780191843730.001.0001/q-oro-ed5-00004155

p.148 selected from "Georgia O'Keeffe." In *The Oxford Dictionary of American Quotations*, edited by Rawson, Hugh, and Margaret Miner.: Oxford University Press, 2006. http://www.oxfordreference.com/view/10.1093/acref/9780195168235.001.0001/q-author-00008-00001232

p.149 selected from "Education." In *Oxford Essential Quotations*, edited by Ratcliffe, Susan.: Oxford University Press, http://www.oxfordreference.com/view/10.1093/acref/9780191843730.001.0001/q-oro-ed5-00003970

p.150 selected from "Robert Maynard Hutchins." In *The Oxford Dictionary of American Quotations*, edited by Rawson, Hugh, and Margaret Miner.: Oxford University Press, 2006. http://www.oxfordreference.com/view/10.1093/acref/9780195168235.001.0001/q-author-00008-00000812

p.151 selected from "Louisa May Alcott." In *The Oxford Dictionary of American Quotations*, edited by Rawson, Hugh, and Margaret Miner.: Oxford University Press, 2006. http://www.oxfordreference.com/view/10.1093/acref/9780195168235.001.0001/q-author-00008-00000025

p.152 selected from "Jean-Luc Godard." In *Oxford Dictionary of Quotations*, edited by Knowles, Elizabeth.: Oxford University Press, 2014. http://www.oxfordreference.com/view/10.1093/acref/9780199668700.001.0001/q-author-00010-00001361

p.153 selected from "Albert Einstein." In *Oxford Dictionary of Quotations*, edited by Knowles, Elizabeth.: Oxford University Press, 2014. http://www.oxfordreference.com/view/10.1093/acref/9780199668700.001.0001/q-author-00010-00001079

p.154 selected from "Shopping." In *Oxford Dictionary of Humorous Quotations*, edited by Sherrin, Ned.: Oxford University Press, 2012. http://www.oxfordreference.com/view/10.1093/acref/9780199570034.001.0001/q-subject-00002-00000200

p.155 selected from "Diane Ravitch." In *Oxford Essential Quotations*, edited by Ratcliffe, Susan.: Oxford University Press, http://www.oxfordreference.com/view/10.1093/acref/9780191843730.001.0001/q-oro-ed5-00017763

p.156 adapted from "Wikipedia." In *A Dictionary of Journalism* by Tony Harcup.: Oxford University Press, 2014. http://www.oxfordreference.com/view/10.1093/acref/9780199646241.001.0001/acref-9780199646241-e-1488

p.156 selected from "Neil Gaiman." In *Oxford Essential Quotations*, edited by Ratcliffe, Susan.: Oxford University Press, http://www.oxfordreference.com/view/10.1093/acref/9780191843730.001.0001/q-oro-ed5-00017943

p.157 adapted from "fan fiction." In *The Oxford Companion to Children's Literature* edited by Hahn, Daniel..: Oxford University Press, 2015. http://www.oxfordreference.com/view/10.1093/acref/9780199695140.001.0001/acref-9780199695140-e-1106

p.157 selected from "Oscar Wilde." In *Oxford Dictionary of Quotations*, edited by Knowles, Elizabeth.: Oxford University Press, 2014. http://www.oxfordreference.com/view/10.1093/acref/9780199668700.001.0001/q-author-00010-00003431

p.158 adapted from "emotional appeal." In *A Dictionary of Business and Management*, edited by Law, Jonathan.: Oxford University Press, 2016. http://www.oxfordreference.com/view/10.1093/acref/9780199684984.001.0001/acref-9780199684984-e-2172

p.158 selected from "LAUGH and the world laughs with you; weep and you weep alone." In *Oxford Dictionary of Proverbs*, edited by Speake, Jennifer.: Oxford University Press, 2015. http://www.oxfordreference.com/view/10.1093/acref/9780198734901.001.0001/acref-9780198734901-e-1226

p.127 Extract from Oxford Bookworms Factfiles, Stage 2: John F. Kennedy by Anne Collins, © Oxford University Press 2014. Reproduced by permission.

The publisher and author would like to thank the following for their time and assistance:

Annie Hudson

David McCandless

Eugene Minogue

With special thanks to:

Robert Campbell

Lindsay Clandfield

Cover photo by Edu Bayer.
El Cogul, Spain, 2015.

Marc Serena and Edu Bayer in a vintage Volkswagen van tour some of the tiniest villages in their homeland of Catalonia while researching a book about contemporary rural life. Their book, *Microcatalunya*, was published in 2015.

Contents

ENGLISH FOR REAL	GRAMMAR	VOCABULARY	PRONUNCIATION	REVIEW
▶ Starting and ending a conversation	Simple present and present continuous Questions forms: *Do*, *did*, and *be* Tag questions in the present tenses: *Be* and *do*	Communication Body language and emotions Adverbs of manner	Using intonation to show interest	see page 147
▶ Apologizing	Simple past: *Be* Simple past and past continuous *Used to*	Describing change Phrases with *time*	Word stress	see page 148
▶ Getting clarification	Present perfect simple with *for* and *since* Present perfect and simple past Present perfect with *just*, *already*, *yet*, *ever*, *never*, and *still*	Verbs and nouns from adjectives Useful verbs Education	Contractions with *'s* and *'ve*	see page 149
▶ Being a customer	*Will* versus *going to* Simple present in future time clauses Present tenses for future plans and schedules	Phrasal verbs: Separable and inseparable Traveling	Intonation for asking for and giving directions	see page 150
▶ Making an invitation ▶ Accepting and rejecting invitations	Making comparisons Using two or more adjectives *-ed* and *-ing* adjectives	Expressions with *make* Nouns and prepositions Phrasal verbs	Weak sounds	see page 151
▶ Giving compliments ▶ Accepting compliments	Quantifiers: *Both*, *several*, *most*, and *all* Quantifiers: *Too much/ too many, a little/ a few, a lot, enough* Verbs with two objects	Agent nouns Photography	Adding focus	see page 152

GRAMMAR FOCUS 159–170

Acknowledgments

AUTHOR

Miles Craven has worked in English language education since 1988, teaching in schools, colleges, and universities around the world. He has a wide range of experience as a teacher, teacher-trainer, examiner, course designer, and textbook writer. He is the author or co-author of over thirty textbooks for adults and young adults. He has written many articles and online materials, and regularly presents at conferences and workshops. He also acts as an advisor for Executive Education programs at The Møller Centre for Continuing Education Ltd., Churchill College, University of Cambridge. His research focuses on developing skills and strategies to help learners become more confident communicators, as well as improve their exam performance.

SERIES CONSULTANTS

PRAGMATICS Carsten Roever is Associate Professor in Applied Linguistics at the University of Melbourne, Australia. He was trained as a TESOL teacher and holds a PhD in Second Language Acquisition from the University of Hawai'i at Manoa. His research interests include interlanguage pragmatics, language testing, and conversation analysis.

Naoko Taguchi is an Associate Professor of Japanese and Second Language Acquisition at the Dietrich College of Modern Languages at Carnegie Mellon University. She holds a PhD from Northern Arizona University. Her primary research interests include pragmatics in Second Language Acquisition, second language education, and classroom-based research.

PRONUNCIATION Tamara Jones is an instructor at the English Language Center at Howard Community College in Columbia, Maryland.

INCLUSIVITY & CRITICAL THINKING Lara Ravitch is a senior instructor and the Intensive English Program Coordinator of the American English Institute at the University of Oregon.

ENGLISH FOR REAL VIDEOS Pamela Vittorio acquired a BA in English/Theater from SUNY Geneseo and is an ABD PhD in Middle Eastern Studies with an MA in Middle Eastern Literature and Languages from NYU. She also designs ESL curriculum, materials, and English language assessment tools for publishing companies and academic institutions.

MIDDLE EAST ADVISORY BOARD Amina Saif Al Hashami, Nizwa College of Applied Sciences, Oman; **Karen Caldwell**, Higher Colleges of Technology, Ras Al Khaimah, UAE; **Chaker Ali Mhamdi**, Buraimi University College, Oman.

LATIN AMERICA ADVISORY BOARD Reinaldo Hernández, Duoc, Chile; **Mauricio Miraglia**, Universidad Tecnológica de Chile INACAP, Chile; **Aideé Damián Rodríguez**, Tecnológico de Monterrey, Mexico; **Adriana Recke Duhart**, Universidad Anáhuac, Mexico; **Inés Campos**, Centro de Idiomas, Cesar Vallejo University, Peru.

SPAIN ADVISORY BOARD Alison Alonso, EOI Luarca, Spain; **Juan Ramón Bautista Liébana**, EOI Rivas, Spain; **Ruth Pattison**, EOI, Spain; **David Silles McLaney**, EOI Majadahonda, Spain.

We would like to acknowledge the educators from around the world who participated in the development and review of this series:

ASIA **Ralph Baker**, Chuo University, Japan; **Elizabeth Belcour**, Chongshin University, South Korea; **Mark Benton**, Kobe Shoin Women's University, Japan; **Jon Berry**, Kyonggi University, South Korea; **Stephen Lyall Clarke**, Vietnam-US English Training Service Centers, Vietnam; **Edo Forsythe**, Hirosaki Gakuin University, Japan; **Clifford Gibson**, Dokkyo University, Japan; **Michelle Johnson**, Nihon University, Japan; **Stephan Johnson**, Rikkyo University, Japan; **Nicholas Kemp**, Kyushu International University, Japan; **Brendyn Lane**, Core Language School, Japan; **Annaliese Mackintosh**, Kyonggi University, South Korea; **Keith Milling**, Yonsei University, Korea; **Chau Ngoc Minh Nguyen**, Vietnam – USA Society English Training Service Center, Vietnam; **Yongjun Park**, Sangi University, South Korea; **Scott Schafer**, Inha University, South Korea; **Dennis Schumacher**, Cheongju University, South Korea; **Jenay Seymour**, Hongik University, South Korea; **Joseph Staples**, Shinshu University, Japan; **Greg Stapleton**, YBM Education Inc. – Adult Academies Division, South Korea; **Le Tuam Vu**, Tan True High School, Vietnam; **Ben Underwood**, Kugenuma High School, Japan; **Quyen Vuong**, VUS English Center, Vietnam

EUROPE **Marta Alonso Jerez**, Mainfor Formación, Spain; **Pilar Álvarez Polvorinos**, EOI San Blas, Spain; **Peter Anderson**, Anderson House, Italy; **Ana Anglés Esquinas**, First Class Idiomes i Formació, Spain; **Keith Appleby**, CET Services, Spain; **Isabel Arranz**, CULM Universidad de Zaragoza, Spain; **Jesus Baena**, EOI Alcalá de Guadaira, Spain; **José Gabriel Barbero Férnández**, EOI de Burgos, Spain; **Carlos Bibi Fernandez**, EIO de Madrid-Ciudad Lineal, Spain; **Alex Bishop**, IH Madrid, Spain; **Nathan Leopold Blackshaw**, CCI, Italy; **Olga Bel Blesa**, EOI, Spain; **Antoinette Breutel**, Academia Language School, Switzerland; **Angel Francisco Briones Barco**, EOI Fuenlabrada, Spain; **Ida Brucciani**, Pisa University, Italy; **Julie Bystrytska**, Profi-Lingua, Poland; **Raul Cabezali**, EOI Alcala de Guadaira, Spain; **Milena Cacko-Kozera**, Profi-Lingua, Poland; **Elena Calviño**, EOI Pontevedra, Spain; **Alex Cameron**, The English House, Spain; **Rosa Cano Vallese**, EOI Prat Llobregate, Spain; **Montse Cañada**, EOI Barcelona, Spain; **Elisabetta Carraro**, We.Co Translate, Italy; **Joaquim Andres Casamiquela**, Escola Oficial d'Idiomes – Guinardó, Spain; **Lara Ros Castillo**, Aula Campus, Spain; **Patricia Cervera Cottrell**, Centro de Idiomas White, Spain; **Sally Christopher**, Parkway S.I., Spain; **Marianne Clark**, The English Oak Tree Academy, Spain; **Helen Collins**, ELI, Spain; **María José Conde Torrado**, EOI Ferrol, Spain; **Ana Maria Costachi**, Centro de Estudios Ana Costachi S.I., Spain; **Michael Cotton**, Modern English Study Centre, Italy; **Pedro Cunado Placer**, English World, Spain; **Sarah Dague**, Universidad Carlos III, Spain; **María Pilar Delgado**, Big Ben School, Spain; **Ashley Renee Dentremont Matthäus**, Carl-Schurz Haus, Deutch-Amerikanisches-Institute Freiburg e.V., Germany; **Mary Dewhirst**, Cambridge English Systems, Spain; **Hanna Dobrzycka**, Advantage, Poland; **Laura Dolla**, E.F.E. Laura Dolla, Spain; **Paul Doncaster**, Taliesin Idiomes, Spain; **Marek Doskocz**, Lingwista Sp. z o.o., Poland; **Fiona Dunbar**, ELI Málaga, Spain; **Anna Dunin-Bzdak**, Military University of Technology, Poland; **Robin Evers**, l'Università di Modena e Reggio Emilia, Italy; **Yolanda Fernandez**, EOI, Spain; **Dolores Fernández Gavela**, EOI Gijón, Spain; **Mgr. Tomáš Fišer**, English Academy, Czech Republic; **Juan Fondón**, EOI de Langreo, Spain; **Carmen Forns**, Centro Universitario de Lenguas Modernas, Spain; **Ángela Fraga**, EOI de Ferrol, Spain; **Beatriz Freire**, Servicio de Idiomas FGULL, Spain; **Alena Fridrichova**, Palacky University in Olomouc, Faculty of Science, Department of Foreign Languages, Czech Republic, **Elena Friedrich**, Palacky University, **JM Galarza**, Iruñanko Hizkuntz Eskola, Spain; **Nancie Gantenbein**, TLC-IH, Switzerland; **Gema García**, EOI, Spain; **Maria Jose Garcia Ferrer**, EOI Moratalaz, Spain; **Josefa García González**, EOI Málaga, Spain; **Maria García Hermosa**, EOI, Spain; **Jane Gelder**, The British Institute of Florence, Italy; **Aleksandra Gelner**, ELC Katowice, Bankowa 14, Poland; **Marga Gesto**, EOI Ferrol, Spain; **Juan Gil**, EOI Maria Moliner, Spain; **Eva Gil Cepero**, EOI La Laguna, Spain; **Alan Giverin**, Today School, Spain; **Tomas Gomez**, EOI Segovia, Spain; **Mónica González**, EOI Carlos V, Spain; **Elena González Diaz**, EOI, Spain; **Steve Goodman**, Language Campus, Spain; **Katy Gorman**, Study Sulmona, Italy; **Edmund Green**, The British Institute of Florence, Italy; **Elvira Guerrero**, GO! English Granada, Spain; **Lauren Hale**, The British Institute of Florence, Italy; **Maria Jose Hernandez**, EOI de Salou, Spain; **Chris Hermann**, Hermann Brown English Language Centre, Spain; **Robert Holmes**, Holmes English, Czech Republic; **José Ramón Horrillo**, EOI de Aracena, Spain; **Laura Izquierdo**, Univerisity of Zaragoza, Spain; **Marcin Jaśkiewicz**, British School Żoliborz, Poland; **Mojmír Jurák**, Albi – jazyková škola, Czech Republic; **Eva Kejdová**, BLC, Czech Republic; **Turlough Kelleher**, British Council, Callaghan School of English, Spain; **Janina Knight**, Advantage Learners, Spain; **Ewa Kowalik**, English Point Radom, Poland; **Monika Krawczuk**, Wyższa Szkoła Finansów i Zarządzania, Poland; **Milica Krisan**, Agentura Parole, Czech Republic; **Jędrzej Kucharski**, Profi-lingua, Poland; **V. Lagunilla**, EOI San Blas, Spain; **Antonio Lara Davila**, EOI La Laguna, Spain; **Ana Lecubarri**, EOI Aviles, Spain; **Lesley Lee**, Exit Language Center, Spain; **Jessica Lewis**, Lewis Academy, Spain; **Alice Llopas**, EOI Estepa, Spain; **Angela Lloyd**, SRH Hochschule Berlin, Germany; **Helena Lohrová**, University of South Bohemia, Faculty of Philosophy, Czech Republic; **Elena López Luengo**, EOI Alcalá de Henares, Spain; **Karen Lord**, Cambridge House, Spain; **Carmen Loriente Duran**, EOI Rio Vero, Spain; **Alfonso Luengo**, EOI Jesús Maestro Madrid, Spain; **Virginia Lyons**, VLEC, Spain; **Anna Łętowska-Mickiewicz**, University of Warsaw, Poland; **Ewa Malesa**, Uniwersytet SWPS, Poland; **Klara Małowiecka**, University of Warsaw, Poland; **Dott. Ssa Kim Manzi**, Università degli Studi della Tuscia – DISTU – Viterbo, Italy; **James Martin**, St. James Language Center, Spain; **Ana Martin Arista**, EOI Tarazona, Spain; **Irene Martín Gago**, NEC, Spain; **Marga Martínez**, ESIC Idiomas Valencia, Spain; **Kenny McDonnell**, McDonnell English Services S.I., Spain; **Anne Mellon**, EEOI Motilla del Palacar, Spain; **Miguel Ángel Meroño**, EOI Cartagena, Spain; **Joanna Merta**, Lingua Nova, Poland; **Victoria Mollejo**, EOI San Blas-Madrid, Spain; **Rebecca Moon**, La Janda Language Services, Spain; **Anna Morales Puigicerver**, EOI TERRASSA, Spain; **Jesús Moreno**, Centro de Lenguas Modernas, Universidad de Zaragoza, Spain;

Emilio Moreno Prieto, EOI Albacete, Spain; **Daniel Muñoz Bravo**, Big Ben Center, Spain; **Heike Mülder**, In-House Englishtraining, Germany; **Alexandra Netea**, Albany School of English, Cordoba, Spain; **Christine M. Neubert**, Intercultural Communication, Germany; **Ignasi Nuez**, The King's Corner, Spain; **Guadalupe Núñez Barredo**, EOI de Ponferrada, Spain; **Monika Olizarowicz-Strygner**, XXII LO z OD im. Jose Marti, Poland; **A. Panter**, Oxford School of English, Italy; **Vanessa Jayne Parvin**, British School Florence, Italy; **Rachel Payne**, Academia Caledonian, Cadiz, Spain; **Olga Pelaez**, EOI Palencia, Spain; **Claudia Pellegrini**, Klubschule Migros, Switzerland; **Arantxa Pérez**, EOI Tudela, Spain; **Montse Pérez**, EOI Zamora, Spain; **Esther Pérez**, EOI Soria, Spain; **Rubén Pérez Montesinos**, EOI San Fernando de Henares, Spain; **Joss Pinches**, Servicio de Lenguas Modernas, Universidad de Huelva, Spain; **Katerina Pitrova**, FLCM TBU in Zlin, Czech Republic; **Erica Pivesso**, Komalingua, Spain; **Eva Plechackova**, Langfor CZ, Czech Republic; **Jesús Porras Santana**, JPS English School, Spain; **Adolfo Prieto**, EOI Albacete, Spain; **Sara Prieto**, Universidad Católica de Murcia, Spain; **Penelope Prodromou**, Universitá Roma Tre, Italy; **Maria Jose Pueyo**, EOI Zaragoza, Spain; **Bruce Ratcliff**, Academia Caledonian, Spain; **Jolanta Rawska**, School of English "Super Grade," Poland; **Mar Rey**, EOI Del Prat, Spain; **Silke Riegler**, HAW Landshut, Germany; **Pauline Rios**, Rivers, Spain; **Laura Rivero**, EOI La Laguna, Spain; **Carmen Rizo**, EOI Torrevieja, Spain; **Antonio F. Rocha Canizares**, EOI Talavera de la Reina, Spain; **Eva Rodellas Fontiguell**, London English School; **Sara Rojo**, EOI Elche, Spain; **Elena Romea**, UNED, Spain; **Ann Ross**, Centro Linguistico di Ateneo, Italy; **Tyler Ross**, Ingliese for you, Italy; **Susan Royo**, EOI Utebo, Spain; **Asuncion Ruiz Astruga**, EOI Maria Molinar, Spain; **Tamara Ruiz Fernandez**, English Today, Spain; **Soledat Sabate**, FIAC, Spain; **Maria Justa Saenz de Tejad**, ECI Idiomas Bailen, Spain; **Sophia Salaman**, University of Florence, Centro Linguistico de ATENEO, Italy; **Elizabeth Schiller**, Schillers Sprachstudio, Germany; **Carmen Serrano Tierz**, CULM, Spain; **Elizabeth R. Sherman**, Lexis Language Centre, Italy; **Rocio Sierra**, EOI Maspalomas, Spain; **David Silles McLaney**, EOI Majadahonda, Spain; **Alison Slade**, British School Florence, Italy; **Rachael Smith**, Accademia Britannica Toscana, Italy; **Michael Smith**, The Cultural English Centre, Spain; **Sonia Sood**, Oxford School Treviso, Italy; **Monika Stawska**, SJO Pigmalion, Poland; **Izabela Stępniewska**, ZS nr 69, Warszawa / British School Otwock, Poland; **Rocío Stevenson**, R & B Academia, Spain; **Petra Stolinova**, Magic English s.r.o., Czech Republic; **Hana Szulczewska**, UNO (Studium Języków Obcych), Poland; **Tim T.**, STP, Spain; **Vera Tauchmanova**, Univerzita Hradec Kralove, Czech Republic; **Nina Terry**, Nina School of English, Spain; **Francesca R. Thompson**, British School of East, Italy; **Pilar Tizzard**, Docklands Idiomes, Spain; **Jessica Toro**, International House Zaragoza, Spain; **Christine Tracey**, Università Roma Tre, Italy; **Loredana Trocchi**, L'Aquila, Italy; **Richard Twiggl**, International House Milan, Italy; **Natàlia Verdalet**, EOI Figueres, Spain; **Sergio Viñals**, EOI San Javier, Spain; **Edith von Sundahl-Hiller**, Supernova Idiomes, Spain; **Vanda Vyslouzilova**, Academia, Czech Republic; **Helen Waldron**, ELC, Germany; **Leslie Wallace**, Academia Language School, Switzerland; **Monika Wąsowska-Polak**, Akademia Obrony Narodowej, Poland; **Melissa Weaver**, TLC-IH, Switzerland; **Maria Watton**, Centro Lingue Estere CC, Italy; **Dr. Otto Weihs**, IMC FH Krems, Austria; **Kate Williams**, Oxford House Barcelona, Spain; **June Winterflood**, Academia Language School, Switzerland; **Ailsa Wood**, Cooperativa Babel, Italy; **Irene Zamora**, www.speakwithirene.com, Spain; **Coro Zapata**, EOIP Pamplona, Spain; **Gloria Zaragoza**, Alicante University, Spain; **Cristina Zêzere**, EOI Torrelavega, Spain

LATIN AMERICA **Fernando Arcos**, Santo Tomás University, Chile; **Ricardo Barreto**, Bridge School, Brazil; **Beth Bartlett**, Centro Cultural Colombo Americano, Cali, Colombia; **Julie Patricia Benito Lugo**, Universidad Central, Colombia; **Ana Luisa Bley Soriano**, Universidad UCINF, Chile; **Gabriela Brun**, I.S.F.D N 129, Argentina; **Talita Burlamaqui**, UFAM, Brazil; **Lourdes Leonides Canta Lozano**, Fac. De Ciencias Biolgicas UANL, Mexico; **Claudia Castro**, Stratford Institute – Moreno-Bs.As, Argentina; **Fabrício Cruz**, Britanic, Brazil; **Lisa Davies**, British Council, Colombia; **Adriana de Blasis**, English Studio Ciudad de Mercedes, Argentina; **Nora Abraira de Lombardo**, Cultural Inglesa de Mercedes, Argentina; **Bronwyn Donohue**, British Council, Colombia; **Andrea C. Duran**, Universidad Externado de Colombia; **Phil Elias**, British Council, Colombia; **Silvia C. Enríquez**, Escuela de Lenguas. Universidad Nacional de La Plata, Argentina; **Freddy Espinoza**, Universidad UCINF, Chile; **Maria de Lourdes Fernandes Silva**, The First Steps School, Brazil; **Doris Flores**, Santo Tomás English Program, Chile; **Hilda Flor-Páez**, Universidad Catolica Santiago de Guayaquil, Ecuador; **Lauriston Freitas**, Cooplem Idiomas, Brazil; **Alma Delia Frias Puente**, UANL, Mexico; **Sandra Gacitua Matus**, Universidad de la Frontera, Chile; **Gloria Garcia**, IPI Ushuaia-Tierra del Fuego, Argentina; **Alma Delia Garcia Lnsastegui**, UALM, Mexico; **Karina Garcia Gonzalez**, Universidad Panamericana, Mexico; **Miguel García Rojas**, UNMSM, Peru; **Macarena González Mena**, Universidad Tecnológica de Chile, Inacap, Chile; **Diana Granado**, Advanced English, Colombia; **Paul Christopher Graves**, Universidad Mayor, Chile; **Mabel Gutierrez**, British Council, Colombia; **Niamh Harnett**, Universidad Externado de Colombia, Colombia; **Elsa Hernandez**, English Time Institute, Argentina; **Reinaldo Hernández Sordo**, DUOC UC, Chile; **Eduardo Icaza**, CEN, Ecuador; **Kenel Joseph**, Haitian-American Institute, Haiti; **Joel Kellogg**, British Council, Colombia; **Sherif Ebrahim Khakil**, Chapingo Universidad Autonoma Chapingo, Mexico; **Cynthia Marquez**, Instituto Guatemalteco Americano, Guatemala; **Aaron McCarroll**, Universidad Sergio Arboleda, Colombia; **Milagro Machado**, SISE Institute, Peru; **Marta de Faria e Cunha Monteiro**, Federal University of Amazonas – UFAM, Brazil; **Lucía Murillo Sardi**, Instituto Británico, Peru; **Ricardo A. Nausa**, Universidad de los Andes, Colombia; **Andrea Olmos Bernal**, Universidad de Guadalajara, Mexico; **M. Edu Lizzete Olvera Dominguez**, Universidad Autonoma de Baja California Sur, Mexico; **Blanca Ortecho**,

Universidad Cesar Vallejo Centro de Idiomas, Peru; **Jim Osorio**, Instituto Guatemalteco Americano, Guatemala; **Erika del Carmen Partida Velasco**, Univam, Mexico; **Mrs. Katterine Pavez**, Universidad de Atacama, Chile; **Sergio Peña**, Universidad de La Frontera, Chile; **Leonor Cristina Peñafort Camacho**, Universidad Autónoma de Occidente, Colombia; **Tom Rickman**, British Council, Colombia; **Olga Lucia Rivera**, Universidad Externado de Colombia, Colombia; **Maria-Eugenia Ruiz Brand**, DUOC UC, Chile; **Gabriela S. Eguiarte**, London School, Mexico; **Majid Safadaran**, Instituto Cultural Peruano Norteamericano, Peru; **María Ines Salinas**, UCASAL, Argentina; **Ruth Salomon-Barkmeyer**, UNILINGUAS – UNISINOS, Brazil; **Mario Castillo Sanchez Hidalgo**, Universidad Panamericana, Mexico; **Katrina J. Schmidt**, Universidad de Los Andes, Colombia; **Jacqueline Sedore**, The Language Company, Chile; **Lourdes Angelica Serrano Herrera**, Adler Schule, Mexico; **Antonio Diego Sousa de Oliveira**, Federal University of Amazonas, Brazil; **Padraig Sweeney**, Universidad Sergio Arboleda, Colombia; **Edith Urquiza Parra**, Centro Universitario México, Mexico; **Eduardo Vásquez**, Instituto Chileno Britanico de Cultura, Chile; **Patricia Villasante**, Idiomas Católica, Peru; **Malaika Wilson**, The Language Company, Chile; **Alejandra Zegpi-Pons**, Universidad Católica de Temuco, Chile; **Boris Zevallos**, Universidad Cesar Vallejo Centro de Idiomas, Peru; **Wilma Zurita Beltran**, Universidad Central del Ecuador, Ecuador

THE MIDDLE EAST Chaker Ali Mhamdi, Buraimi University College, Oman; **Salama Kamal Shohayb**, Al-Faisal International Academy, Saudi Arabia

TURKEY M. Mine Bağ, Sabanci University, School of Languages; **Suzanne Campion**, Istanbul University; **Daniel Chavez**, Istanbul University Language Center; **Asuman Cincioğlu**, Istanbul University; **Hatice Çelikkanat**, Istanbul Esenyurt University; **Güneş Yurdasiper Dal**, Maltepe University; **Angeliki Douri**, Istanbul University Language Center; **Zia Foley**, Istanbul University; **Frank Foroutan**, Istanbul University Language Center; **Nicola Frampton**, Istanbul University; **Merve Güler**, Istanbul University; **H. Ibrahim Karabulut**, Dumlupınar University; **Catherine McKimm**, Istanbul University; **Merve Oflaz**, Dogus University; **Burcu Özgül**, Istanbul University; **Yusuf Özmenekşe**, Istanbul University Language Center; **Lanlo Pinter**, Istanbul University Language Center; **Ahmet Rasim**, Amasya University; **Diana Maria Rios Hoyos**, Istanbul University Language Center; **Jose Rodrigues**, Istanbul University; **Dilek Eryılmaz Salkı**, Ozyegin University; **Merve Selcuk**, Istanbul Kemerburgaz University; **Mehdi Solhi Andarab**, Istanbul Medipol University; **Jennifer Stephens**, Istanbul University; **Özgür Şahan**, Bursa Technical University; **Fatih Yücel**, Beykent University

UNITED KINGDOM Sarah Ali, Nottingham Trent International College, Nottingham; **Rolf Donald**, Eastbourne School of English, Eastbourne, East Sussex; **Nadine Early**, ATC Language Schools, Dublin, Ireland; **Dr. Sarah Ekdawi**, Oxford School of English, Oxford; **Glynis Ferrer**, LAL Torbay, Paignton Devon; **Diarmuid Fogarty**, INTO Manchester, Manchester; **Ryan Hannan**, Hampstead School of English, London; **Neil Harris**, ELTS, Swansea University, Swansea; **Claire Hunter**, Edinburgh School of English, Edinburgh, Scotland; **Becky Ilk**, LAL Torbay, Paignton; **Kirsty Matthews**, Ealing, Hammersmith & West London's college, London; **Amanda Mollaghan**, British Study Centres London, London; **Shila Nadar**, Twin ECL, London; **Sue Owens**, Cambridge Academy of English, Girton, Cambridge; **Caroline Preston**, International House Newcastle, Newcastle upon Tyne; **Ruby Rennie**, University of Edinburgh, Edinburgh, Scotland; **Howard Smith**, Oxford House College, London; **Yijie Wang**, The University of Edinburgh, Scotland; **Alex Warren**, Eurotraining, Bournemouth

UNITED STATES Christina H. Appel, ELS Educational Services, Manhattan, NY; **Nicole Bollhalder**, Stafford House, Chicago, IL; **Rachel Bricker**, Arizona State University, Tempe, AZ; **Kristen Brown**, Massachusetts International Academy, Marlborough, MA; **Tracey Brown**, Parkland College, Champaign, IL; **Peter Campisi**, ELS Educational Services, Manhattan, NY; **Teresa Cheung**, North Shore Community College, Lynn, MA; **Tyler Clancy**, ASC English, Boston, MA; **Rachael David**, Talk International, Miami, FL; **Danielle De Koker**, ELS Educational Services, New York, NY; **Diana Djaboury**, Mesa Community College, Mesa, AZ; **Mark Elman**, Talk International, Miami, FL; **Dan Gauran**, EC English, Boston, MA; **Kerry Gilman**, ASC English, Boston, MA; **Heidi Guenther**, ELS Educational Services, Manhattan, NY; **Emily Herrick**, University of Nebraska-Lincoln, Lincoln, NE; **Kristin Homuth**, Language Center International, Southfield, MI; **Alexander Ingle**, ALPS Language School, Seattle, WA; **Eugenio Jimenez**, Lingua Language Center at Broward College, Miami, FL; **Mahalia Joeseph**, Lingua Language Center at Broward College, Miami, FL; **Melissa Kaufman**, ELS Educational Services, Manhattan, NY; **Kristin Kradolfer Espinar**, MILA, Miami, FL; **Larissa Long**, TALK International, Fort Lauderdale, FL; **Mercedes Martinez**, Global Language Institute, Minneapolis, MN; **Ann McCrory**, San Diego Continuing Education, San Diego, CA; **Simon McDonough**, ASC English, Boston, MA; **Dr. June Ohrnberger**, Suffolk County Community College, Brentwood, NY; **Fernanda Ortiz**, Center for English as a Second Language at the University of Arizona, Tuscon, AZ; **Roberto S. Quintans**, Talk International, Miami, FL; **Terri J. Rapoport**, ELS, Princeton, NJ; **Alex Sanchez Silva**, Talk International, Miami, FL; **Cary B. Sands**, Talk International, Miami, FL; **Joseph Santaella Vidal**, EC English, Boston, MA; **Angel Serrano**, Lingua Language Center at Broward College, Miami, FL; **Timothy Alan Shaw**, New England School of English, Boston, MA; **Devinder Singh**, The University of Tulsa, Tulsa, OK; **Daniel Stein**, Lingua Language Center at Broward College, Miami, FL; **Christine R. Stesau**, Lingua Language Center at Broward College, Miami, FL; **David Stock**, ELS Educational Services, Manhattan, NY; **Joshua Stone**, Approach International Student Center, Allston, MA; **Maria-Virginia Tanash**, EC English, Boston, MA; **Noraina Vazquez Huyke**, Talk International, Miami, FL

Overview

A REAL-WORLD VIEWPOINT

Whatever your goals and aspirations, *Wide Angle* helps you use English to connect with the world around you. It empowers you to join any conversation and say the right thing at the right time, with confidence.

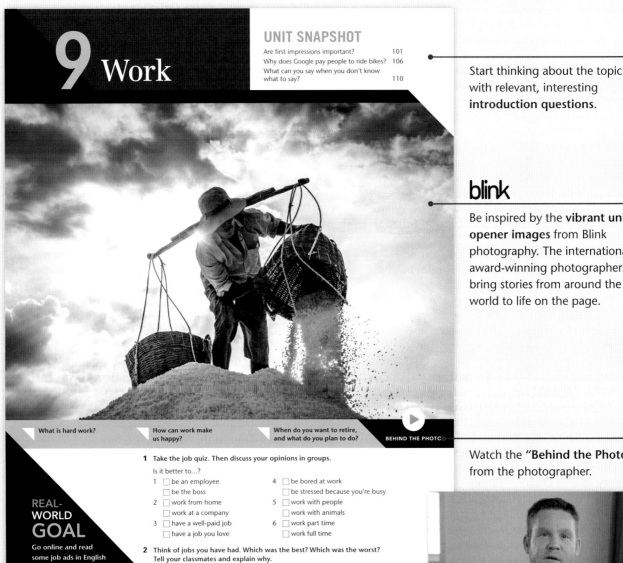

9 Work

What is hard work?

How can work make us happy?

When do you want to retire, and what do you plan to do?

BEHIND THE PHOTO

REAL-WORLD GOAL

Go online and read some job ads in English

1 Take the job quiz. Then discuss your opinions in groups.

Is it better to...?

1 ☐ be an employee
☐ be the boss
2 ☐ work from home
☐ work at a company
3 ☐ have a well-paid job
☐ have a job you love

4 ☐ be bored at work
☐ be stressed because you're busy
5 ☐ work with people
☐ work with animals
6 ☐ work part time
☐ work full time

2 Think of jobs you have had. Which was the best? Which was the worst? Tell your classmates and explain why.

Start thinking about the topic with relevant, interesting **introduction questions**.

blink

Be inspired by the **vibrant unit opener images** from Blink photography. The international, award-winning photographers bring stories from around the world to life on the page.

Watch the **"Behind the Photo"** video from the photographer.

"Salt is harvested by flooding a shallow pool with ocean water and waiting for the water to evaporate and the salt to dry. This man was collecting the salt for a company he works for. He was part of a team, as it takes many people to harvest salt."

Quinn Ryan Mattingly

Apply learning to your own needs with **Real-World Goals**, instantly seeing the benefit of the English you are learning.

Enjoy learning with the huge variety of **up-to-date, inventive, and engaging audio and video.**

Understand what to say and how to say it with **English For Real.**

These lessons equip you to choose and adapt appropriate language to communicate effectively in any situation.

9.4 Let Me Get That for You

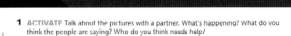

1 ACTIVATE Talk about the pictures with a partner. What's happening? What do you think the people are saying? Who do you think needs help?

2 INTERACT Do you always ask for help when you need it? Tell a partner and explain your reasons.

REAL WORLD ENGLISH Offering to help

When you offer to help, the language you use depends not only on your relationship to the person but also if the person has let you know if they want help. People may not want to ask for help because it can suggest they are not capable. Their facial expressions or body language can sometimes tell you if they want help. You can also say something about the difficulty of the task to let the other person know why you are offering. This gives the other person a chance to let you know if they do or do not want help. People often refuse an offer of help at first but accept if the offer is repeated.

3 ▶ ANALYZE Watch the video and answer the questions.

	Andy	Jenna	Sam
1 Who offers to help?	☐	☐	☐
2 Who refuses any offer of help?	☐	☐	☐
3 Who accepts help immediately?	☐	☐	☐
4 Who accepts help in the end?	☐	☐	☐

4 ▶ IDENTIFY Watch the video again. Complete the offers you hear. Some offers may be completed in more than one way.

1 Let me...	a get those.
2 Do you want me to...	b this on the table?
3 Would you like	c sort those for you.
4 I can...	d get the door.
	e me to take one?
	f get that for you.
	g help you sort?

108

5 ASSESS Study the expressions for offering help in Exercise 4. What is the difference in use between them?

REAL-WORLD ENGLISH
Accepting and rejecting offers

The way you accept or reject an offer often depends on the difficulty of the task and your relationship to the person. For accepting help with a difficult task or from someone you don't know, more complex expressions are polite because they show you are grateful. For accepting help with a simple task or from someone you know well, shorter expressions are common. For rejections, the length of the expression also shows politeness, but it is important to pay attention to the tone used. A serious tone can indicate a genuine refusal of an offer.

6 EXPAND Read this extract from the video. What expressions does Sam use to reject Andy's offers? Why do you think he finally accepts?

Andy: Do you want me to take one?
Sam: No. It's OK. Um, I got it.
Andy: Are you sure? I mean...They look...
Sam: It's all right, thank you. I got it.
Andy: Can I help you?
Sam: OK. Thanks.

7 INTEGRATE Label the conversation in Exercise 6 with the functions below.

Accept	Offer to help	Refuse again
Comment about the task	Refuse	Offer again

8 ASSESS Work in pairs. Look at the situations. Which people would you offer to help? Tell your partner and explain your reasons. What expressions would you use?

1 You go to the train station to meet a friend. Your friend arrives with lots of baggage.
2 You're at school. You see your teacher carrying lots of books.
3 You're at the bus stop. An elderly man you don't know has dropped his wallet.
4 Your roommate is trying to wrap a gift.

ENGLISH FOR REAL

Comment about the task
Refuse again
Offer again
Accept/refuse

GO ONLINE
to create your own version
of the English For Real video.

Step into the course with **English For Real videos** that mimic real-life interactions. You can record your voice and respond in real time for out-of-class practice that is relevant to your life.

109

COMPREHENSIVE SYLLABUS

Ensure progress in all skills with a pedagogically consistent and appropriately leveled syllabus.

5 He *would* / *wouldn't* like to be an actor.
6 Hassan is a good taxi driver because he is *calm* / *a careful driver*.

4 WHAT'S YOUR ANGLE? Do you think you could do Hassan's job? Why or why not?

5 VOCABULARY Match each adjective with a definition.

3

1 artistic   a able to work without help
2 confident   b strong, never giving up
3 capable   c not shy or timid
4 enthusiastic   d excited and eager
5 determined   e able to do something
6 independent   f creative and imaginative
Oxford™ 3000

6 USE Choose three adjectives from Exercise 5. Write example sentences to show their meaning.

8 WHAT'S YOUR ANGLE? What personal skills do you have? Use the words in Exercise 5 or talk about other skills you have.

I think I'm hardworking and confident.

103

▼ VOCABULARY

The Oxford 3000™ is a word list containing the most important words to learn in English. The words are chosen based on frequency in the Oxford English Corpus and relevance to learners of English. Every word is aligned to the CEFR, guiding you on the words you should know at each level.

If you practice interviews, you improve.
First conditional:
You might not get the job if you're nervous in the interview.
If you prepare well, you'll feel more confident.

GRAMMAR IN CONTEXT Zero and first conditional

To form the zero conditional, we use:
If + simple present and _____ or an imperative.
To form the first conditional, we use:
If + simple present and *will* or _____ + infinitive without *to*.
We use the zero conditional to ___ and ___.
We use the first conditional to ___.

a talk about events and the results that always follow
b talk about a possible action or situation in the future and the result that follows
c give instructions

See Grammar focus on page 167.

not understand you.
7 Show you're interested
Ask questions! If you _____ ask questions, the interviewer might think you don't want the job.

4 WHAT'S YOUR ANGLE? Which tips are the most useful for you? Why? Choose three and explain your reasons to a partner. Use the zero or first conditional when you can.

5 INTERACT Discuss these questions in groups. Use the zero and first conditional.

1 What will an interviewer think:
- if you wear nice clothes?
- if you smile a lot?
- if your hair is a mess?
- if you look worried?
- if your clothes are too casual?

2 How can these things give the interviewer a good or bad impression?
- looking at the floor or wall
- speaking very quietly
- moving your hands
- looking directly at the interviewer
- changing position in your seat

▼ GRAMMAR

The carefully graded grammar syllabus ensures you encounter the most relevant language at the right point in your learning.

 First Impressions Count

Research has shown clearly that people form impressions of each other very quickly. For example, many people think that if someone wears glasses, they are intelligent and thoughtful. Similarly, in an interview, if you are anxious, the interviewer might have a negative opinion of you. Even very small things can create a big impression.

However, did you know that interviewers often look for reasons not to select a candidate? This is understandable because they need to reject most of the applicants, but it means the first impression you give is even more important. Interviewers are quick to reach an early negative impression, and this is difficult to change, whereas an early positive impression is not so easy to make but can change later.

Interestingly, it is clear that if the interviewer talks for a long time, the candidate might get the job. One possibility is that the interviewer has made a quick decision and wants the candidate to be interested in the position.

Nonverbal factors also affect the impression you give. These include your general appearance, clothes, and facial expression as well as eye contact, body movements, and how loud your voice is.

If you want to be good at interviewing, preparation and experience are valuable. Practicing using video can be useful if you want detailed feedback on your weaknesses.

—adapted from *The Oxford Companion to the Mind*, 2nd ed., by Richard L. Gregory

Oxford Reference is a trusted source of over two million authentic academic texts.

Free access to the Oxford Reference site is included with Student Books 4, 5, and 6.

9.3 You Do What?

1 ACTIVATE Look at the photograph and read the text. What does a Google tricycle mapper do?

2 WHAT'S YOUR ANGLE? Would you leave your current job to be a tricycle mapper or think of becoming one in the future? Why or why not?

3 VOCABULARY Write each word in the correct place.

executive   candidate   employment   qualified

1 potential / unlikely _____
2 temporary / permanent _____
3 fully / highly _____
4 senior / junior _____
🕮 Oxford™ 3000

4 USE Complete these sentences using each word in Exercise 3.

1 I am looking for a _____ job, so something just over the summer.
2 Being an airline pilot is a _____ skilled job that requires years of training.
3 The only _____ problem with this candidate is they live overseas.
4 It's a very _____ position, but you should be able to work your way up.
5 After successfully completing your training, you will be a _____ qualified teacher.
6 Martine started the company and is a _____ partner in the business.
7 All _____ employees receive free health care, paid vacations, and sick leave.
8 It is _____ they will offer me the job after that terrible interview.

5 INTERACT Work in groups. Think of at least three examples of each of the following, with reasons why you think so: potential careers for you; unlikely careers for you; temporary jobs you would like to try; jobs you are highly qualified for.

Did you know that Google introduced the Street View Trikes in 2009 to get images of locations that are difficult to reach by car? Would you like to be a tricycle mapper? You have to be in good shape. The Google Trike weighs about 250 pounds and is nine feet high, but you'll earn around $60,000 a year and stay in shape!

LISTENING SKILL Predicting while listening

While you are listening, you can use the information you hear to help you make predictions. Think about what you have already heard, the topic, and the context, and try to guess what you will hear next. Checking if your prediction is correct will help you know if you have understood. If you don't hear what you expect, you may have misunderstood. You can make a new prediction and listen to check if it's correct

6 IDENTIFY You are going to listen to an interview with Annie Hudson about an unusual career. What might the career be? What words might you hear? Why? Listen and check your predictions.

I think the career will be…
I think I might hear…

106

7 ASSESS What is Annie's job? What kind of information or words and phrases do you think you will hear next? Make predictions for what you might hear in the next part of the interview.

8 ◀) DEVELOP Listen and check your predictions from Exercise 7.

9 ASSESS Make predictions about the next part of the interview: what words, phrases, and information might you hear?

10 ◀) EXPAND Listen to the final part of the interview and check your predictions from Exercise 9.

11 ◀) INTEGRATE Now listen to the complete interview and answer the questions.

1 Why does Annie love her job?
2 Where can you see Annie's work?
3 Who does she work with?
4 How does she travel to work?
5 Where did she train?

12 WHAT'S YOUR ANGLE? Do you ever take photos of food you cook? When? Tell a partner.

GRAMMAR IN CONTEXT Reflexive pronouns

We use reflexive pronouns (*myself, yourself, herself, himself, itself, ourselves, yourselves, themselves*) when the person who does the action (the subject) is also the person affected by the action. The reflexive pronoun is the object of the verb or preposition. It agrees with the subject.
It's really fun, and we enjoy ourselves
I might not treat all the final myself
We sometimes use *themselves* instead of *himself/herself* to talk about a person when we don't say or don't know if the person is male or female.
Anyone can call themselves an expert.

See Grammar focus on page 167.

13 APPLY Complete the list of reflexive pronouns.

Subject pronoun	Object pronoun
I	myself
you (singular)	
he	
she	
it	
we	
you (plural)	
they	

14 INTEGRATE Complete the sentences with reflexive pronouns.

1 Annie buys all the ingredients _____ for the dishes she makes.
2 I never thought of _____ as having an unusual job.
3 Please help _____ to some more cake.
4 The last time he cooked a meal, Gary burned _____ badly.
5 You have to be very experienced before you can call _____ a food stylist.
6 Anyone who works for _____ has to be prepared to work hard.
7 We grow all the fruit and vegetables we need _____.
8 The oven Annie uses at home can clean _____.

15 EXPAND Put the phrases in order to complete the questions.

1 think of yourself / do you / creative person / as a / ?
2 changing / can you / careers / see yourself / ?
3 or on / by yourself / would you / a team / rather work / ?
4 for yourself / want to work / one day / do you / ?
5 yourself / you see / where do / in a year / ?

16 INTERACT Work with a partner. Ask and answer the questions in Exercise 15.

17 PREPARE Think of an unusual job. Take notes and prepare to talk about it.
Job: _____
Description: _____

18 INTEGRATE Tell the class about the job you chose, but *do not* say what it is. When you finish your description, your classmates can ask questions for more information. Can they guess your job?

19 WHAT'S YOUR ANGLE? Which of the unusual jobs would you like to do? Are there any you *wouldn't* want?

107

Build confidence with the **activation-presentation-practice-production** method, with activities moving from controlled to less controlled, with an increasing level of challenge.

▼ READING AND LISTENING

Explicit reading and listening skills focus on helping you access and assimilate information confidently in this age of rapid information.

WRITING SKILL Giving reasons

You can support your ideas and opinions with reasons. Phrases for giving reasons are:

The main reason is / One reason is
We can use these phrases before *that* clauses; *that* is often left out in informal writing.
The main reason is (that) I want to travel.

Because and *because of*
We use *because* and *because of* when we give the reader new information or a reason they don't know.
because + subject + verb:
I want to be an actor **because I love** performing.
because of + noun / pronoun:
I'd like to be a pilot **because of the travel opportunities**.

As / Since
We use *as / since* when the reader probably knows the reason already. They are more formal than *because* and are normally used at the beginning of sentences.
As / Since acting is a very glamorous job, it's a very _____

1 If _____ (you / have) (you / want) to work abroad
2 Do you think _____ (you / speak) p _____
3 If _____ (you / earn) _____ (you / move) h
4 _____ (you / apply) fo (it / involve) a lot of driving?
5 If _____ (you / not be job, _____ (you / try) _____ (you / leave)?

13 INTERACT Ask and answer th Exercise 12 with a partner.

14 PREPARE Prepare to write ab to have. Read the questions be your answers; include your rea to present your ideas. Use the help you.
Presentation
■ What job would you like to

▼ WRITING

The writing syllabus focuses on the writing styles needed for today, using a **process writing approach** of **prepare-plan-draft-review-correct** to produce the best possible writing.

SPEAKING Explaining words you don't know

Sometimes when you are talking, you realize that you don't know or remember the word you need to use. To keep the conversation going, let the person you are speaking to know you are looking for a word. They might be able to help you. Try to define the word you need or use a similar word to help them understand. Use these phrases:
What's the word in English? It means "go down."
What's another word for "cook," you know like "cook a cake"?
How do you say it in English?
What's the word I'm looking for? It's part of your car, you put gas in it…Gas trunk? Gas tank? Yes, gas tank!

4 ◀) APPLY Listen again to Ariel and Manish each explain a word they don't know. Decide who uses each strategy.

	Ariel	Manish
1 uses *you know* to ask for help	☐	☐
2 defines the word	☐	☐

8 ◀) APPLY Listen to the sentences. I sounds.

1 I'll do everything by the end of th
2 We are going to Italy on vacation
3 Who are you meeting in the after
4 It will be all over before you arrive
5 Please go and get three extra tick
6 I might be able to help you after I

9 ◀) USE Listen and repeat.

10 PREPARE Prepare to talk about way life influences your free time. First, ta your work/school life.
Is it very busy and stressful, or do you you sit down a lot or do you get a lot see lots of people or are you on your

11 DEVELOP Now think about the thir free time. Take notes.
How do you like to relax? Why do yo things?

▼ SPEAKING

Speaking and **pronunciation skills** build the functional language you need outside of class.

XV

A BLENDED LEARNING APPROACH

Make the most of *Wide Angle* with opportunities for relevant, personalized learning outside of class.

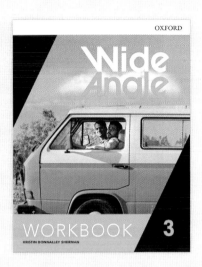

ONLINE PRACTICE

When you see this icon in your Student Book, go online to extend your learning.

With Online Practice you can:

- Review the skills taught in every lesson and get **instant feedback**.

- Practice grammar and vocabulary through **fun games**.

- Access **all audio and video** material. Use the Access Code in the front of this Student Book to log in for the first time at wideangle.oxfordonlinepractice.com.

WORKBOOK

Your Workbook provides additional practice for every unit of the Student Book.

Each unit includes:

- An entirely new reading with skill practice linked to **Oxford Reference**.

- Support for the **Discussion Board**, helping students to master online writing.

- Listening comprehension and skill practice using the **Unit Review Podcast**.

- Real-life English practice linked to the **English For Real** videos.

- **Grammar** and **vocabulary** exercises related to the unit topic.

Use your Workbook for homework or self-study.

FOCUS ON THE TEACHER

The Teacher's Resource Center at wideangle.oxfordonlinepractice.com saves teachers time by integrating and streamlining access to the following support:

- **Teacher's Guide**, including fun **More to Say** pronunciation activities, and **professional development** materials.

- **Easy-to-use** learning management system for the student Online Practice, **answer keys**, **audio**, lots of **extra activities**, **videos**, and so much more.

The **Classroom Presentation Tool** brings the Student Book to life for heads-up lessons. Class audio, video, and answer keys, as well as teaching notes, are available online or offline, and are updated across your devices.

1 Interactions

Can you communicate through art?

Are you a "people person," or do you prefer time on your own?

How important is technology in your relationships?

BEHIND THE PHOTO

REAL-WORLD GOAL

Organize a social event online

1 Choose the top five ways you communicate with other people. Number them 1–5 (1 = most important). Tell your partner which you prefer, and give your reasons.

email ___	tweet ___	blogs ___
phone call ___	video chat ___	face-to-face ___
social networking site ___	Internet forum ___	letter ___
online gaming ___	text message ___	other: _____

2 Think about how you interact with these groups of people. Is there a difference in the way you communicate with each group? Discuss with a partner.

friends   family   classmates   neighbors   co-workers

1.1 The New Office

1 ACTIVATE Do you know anyone who works in an office? What is their job? What kind of things do they do?

2 VOCABULARY Match each phrase with its meaning.

1	look forward to	a	manage (a difficult situation)
2	keep in touch with	b	admire
3	have an influence on	c	stay in contact with someone
4	look up to someone	d	affect someone or something
5	deal with	e	find a solution
6	work something out	f	be excited about

🔑 Oxford 3000™

3 BUILD Complete the sentences using the words from Exercise 2.

1 Somebody I really admire is my boss. I _____ up to him a lot.
2 We sometimes disagree, but we always _____ it out in the end.
3 In my job, I need to _____ with some difficult customers.
4 I _____ forward to meeting next week.
5 Facebook and other social media have an _____ on how we communicate.
6 Technology can help family members living away from each other to _____ in touch.

4 USE Work in pairs. Make sentences about yourself using the phrases in Exercise 2. Ask each other for more information.

A: I keep in touch with some of my friends from school.
B: Oh yes? Who do you keep in touch with?

5 ASSESS You are going to hear a radio show about CityWorks. First, read the ad. What kind of place is CityWorks? Who do you think goes there?

CITYWORKS provides a comfortable and friendly working environment where you can hang out with other professionals, make friends, and become part of the local business community.

Membership

Friend:	$80 per month. Access to a workspace 4 days per month. 9 a.m.–6 p.m.
Associate:	$190 per month. Access to a workspace weekdays. 9 a.m.–6 p.m.
Partner:	$250 per month. Access to a workspace 24/7.

LISTENING SKILL Guessing meaning from context

Sometimes speakers use words you don't know. You can use the context—the words around another word—to help you guess what a word means. You can also listen for any examples that help explain the meaning. Identify the part of speech, and try to think of another word or phrase that could replace it.

For example, you hear: *There are more than 100 desks here. This place is enormous!* You can guess that the speaker is talking about an office because there are *desks*, and *enormous* is an adjective that might mean "very big" because there are many desks there.

6 INTEGRATE Listen to the extracts from a radio show. Think about the context and try to guess the part of speech and meaning of these words and phrases. Compare your answers with a partner.

Word/phrase	Part of speech	Possible meaning
1 bargain		
2 get to know		
3 alternative		
4 convenient		

7 EXPAND Listen again and note the context clues that help you identify the meaning of each word or phrase in Exercise 6.

Facilities
- Fast Internet and a variety of business support services
- Coffee shop, monthly social events, and games to relax
For big office facilities and amazing co-workers at small prices, come to CityWorks!

✉ *Contact us today for more information*

8 🔊 **IDENTIFY** Listen to the radio show. Match the people with how often they go to CityWorks and why they go there.

1	Alex	once a week	to meet co-workers
2	Jonathan	every day	for fast Internet
3	Grace	two to three times a week	to make friends

9 **INTEGRATE** Look again at the ad in Exercise 5. What membership does each person probably have?

10 🔊 **EXPAND** Listen to the radio show again and answer the questions.

1 What is Alex's job?
2 Who gets bored because they work on their own?
3 How do the games help Jonathan?
4 What does Grace look forward to?
5 Why does Grace love email and the Internet?

11 **WHAT'S YOUR ANGLE?** Has technology changed where you work or study? How?

12 **IDENTIFY** Look at the sentences from the radio show. Then read the Grammar box and complete the rules.

I <u>work</u> for myself.
We <u>meet</u> here once a week.
Today, I'<u>m visiting</u> CityWorks.
I'<u>m waiting</u> for a co-worker to arrive.

GRAMMAR IN CONTEXT
Simple present and present continuous

We use the _____ to talk about routines and things that are always true.

We use the _____ to talk about things happening now or around now.

We don't usually use the present continuous with verbs that describe feelings, thoughts, states, and senses.

See Grammar focus on page 159.

13 **APPLY** Choose the correct answers to complete the text.

How we communicate always ¹*shapes / is shaping* the way we interact with each other. Digital devices ²*have / are having* a huge influence on the way we work, learn, spend our leisure time, and communicate with each other. Research ³*shows / is showing* that, as a result, our sense of identity ⁴*is changing / changes*. These days, we all ⁵*are having / have* an online identity as well as our real identity. At times, it can feel like our digital self is even more "real" than real life. Perhaps this is one reason why now some people ⁶*start / are starting* to question the role of technology in our lives. They ⁷*are choosing / choose* to reject technology. What ⁸*are you thinking / do you think*? Could you live without the Internet?

14 **EXPAND** Complete the questions using the verbs in the box in the simple present or present continuous tense.

think	send	carry	prefer	use	spend

1 _____ you _____ text messages every day?
2 _____ you _____ of getting a new cell phone?
3 _____ you _____ too much time on the Internet during the week?
4 _____ you _____ to check your email on your cell phone or tablet?
5 _____ you _____ any electronic devices with you right now?
6 In general, _____ you _____ social media sites like Facebook a lot?

15 **INTERACT** Work with a partner. Ask and answer the questions in Exercise 14.

16 **WHAT'S YOUR ANGLE?** Discuss the question. Give reasons for your answer.

> *Does **technology** keep people apart more than it brings them together?*

1.2 Talking Without Words

1 ACTIVATE Read the quote. What gestures and expressions do people often use in your country?

"Body language is a very powerful tool. We had body language before we had speech, and apparently, 80 percent of what you understand in a conversation is read through the body, not the words."
—Deborah Bull, dancer

2 VOCABULARY Match each gesture with a photograph.

bow to someone	cross your arms	hug someone
kiss someone	~~point at something~~	wave goodbye

🔑 Oxford 3000™

point at something
fear

_____

_____

_____
_____

_____
_____

_____
_____

3 BUILD Which emotions can you see in the photographs? Match the words in the box with the images in Exercise 2.

anger	calm	enjoyment	~~fear~~	happiness	sadness

🔑 Oxford 3000™

4 INTERACT Work in pairs. Try using gestures and expressions to communicate the ideas below. Can your partner guess what you are "saying"?

be quiet	I don't agree	hurry up
good luck	you're crazy	come here

READING SKILL Skimming

Skimming means reading a text quickly to understand the main ideas. It is useful when you want to get the general idea of a text rather than details. When you skim, you do not need to read every word. Focus on the important words (usually nouns, verbs, and adjectives), and don't stop if you see a word you don't know. Keep reading until you reach the end.

5 APPLY Skim the article.

Facial Expressions

Can we really understand how someone is feeling by the expression on the person's face? Do people all around the world share the same facial expressions? Is it possible to lie using our expressions?

Charles Darwin looks at some of these questions in his book *The Expression of the Emotions in Man and Animals* (1872). According to Darwin, there are facial expressions of some emotions that people everywhere share: anger, fear, sadness, disgust, and enjoyment. Today, a lot of research supports Darwin's theory.

So, does this mean we can always understand what people are feeling by looking at their faces? Well, modern research shows that we can learn to control our facial expressions when we need to. For example, people who lose a competition may try to hide their disappointment. The country or culture you are living in can also be important. Studies show that Japanese people often smile to hide negative emotions but that Americans do not. This is because in Japan many people prefer not to show negative emotions.

We can also express emotions that we don't feel— for example, you may try to look happy when you are disappointed at a gift you don't like. However, when we use our faces to hide the truth, these "false expressions" are usually easy to notice—so be careful!

—adapted from *The Oxford Companion to the Body* by Colin Blakemore and Sheila Jennett

Disgust

Frowning means sadness in some cultures.

6 IDENTIFY Choose the three main ideas.

- [ ] Researchers today disagree with Darwin's theory.
- [ ] Most facial expressions people use are negative.
- [ ] We can use our faces to hide our emotions.
- [ ] Some facial expressions are the same everywhere.
- [ ] How you use expressions depends on the country you are from.

7 EXPAND Read the article again carefully and answer the questions.

1 Which book is the article about?
2 Which five emotions did Darwin think everyone could recognize?
3 How do Americans differ from Japanese people in their use of facial expressions?
4 When do people try to hide their disappointment? Find an example.
5 What is a false expression?

8 WHAT'S YOUR ANGLE? In what situations do you try to control *your* emotions? How do you hide your feelings?

9 ASSESS Read the text. Can you identify which smile is false?

Did you know... we have 43 muscles in our face and can make 10,000 facial expressions? We usually hide our feelings with a smile, but a false smile is easy to identify. When we smile, the corners of our mouth move up, and our eyes become narrow. We can move the muscles around the mouth easily, but the muscles around the eyes are very difficult to control. So, if someone's mouth is smiling, but their eyes are not, then you know it's a false smile!

Real [ ]   False [ ]   Real [ ]   False [ ]

GRAMMAR IN CONTEXT
Question forms: *Do, did,* and *be*

We usually form *yes/no* questions for most verbs with *do, does,* or *did.*

Do you use a lot of facial expressions? Yes, I do. / No, I don't.
Does your face show what you are feeling? Yes, it does. / No, it doesn't.
Did he smile? Yes, he did. / No, he didn't.

We form *wh-* questions with the question word first followed by *do, does,* or *did.*

Why do people use facial expressions?
When does someone control his or her expression?

With the verb *be,* we don't need *do, does,* or *did.*

Is she angry with him? Yes, she is. / No, she isn't.
Were they disappointed? Yes, they were. / No, they weren't.

In *wh-* questions, the question word comes before the *be* verb.

Why are gestures important?

See Grammar focus on page 159.

10 INTEGRATE Complete the questions using *do* or *is.*

How do you know when people are lying? Here are some signs to look for. If you can answer *yes* to five or more of these questions, then the person you are speaking with is probably lying!

1 ___ their hand in front of their mouth when they are speaking?
2 ___ they look you in the eye?
3 ___ they turn their body away from you?
4 ___ their eyes move to the right?
5 ___ they use any unusual gestures?
6 ___ their face or neck red?
7 ___ they scratch their nose?

11 EXPAND Choose the correct words to complete the questions.

1 When *did / are* you last shake hands with someone?
2 How *are / do* you usually greet your friends?
3 Why *is / does* a smile better than a frown?
4 Who *does / is* the calmest person you know?
5 What *do / are* you look like when you are angry?
6 *Does / Is* it OK to greet people with a kiss in your country?

12 INTERACT Ask and answer the questions from Exercise 11 with a partner.

13 DEVELOP Complete the sentences with the words in the box.

were	was	does	is	do	did

1 Why _____ Anne so upset last night?
2 Who _____ you see at the party?
3 _____ animals understand our expressions?
4 _____ you able to explain how you felt?
5 Look at this photo. Who _____ it remind you of?
6 Tom looks well. How _____ his health these days?

14 WHAT'S YOUR ANGLE? Which do you think are more important in communicating meaning: the gestures people use or their facial expressions? Discuss your ideas with a partner and give examples to support your opinion.

Children in Torretta, a village in Palermo, Italy

1.3 Making Connections

1 ACTIVATE Match each type of friend with a definition.

1 a **long-lost** friend   a   a friend for many years

                   b   a friend who does not help you in difficult times

2 a **close** friend

                   c   a friend from the past you are no longer in contact with

3 an **old** friend

                   d   a friend that you have in common with someone else

4 a **mutual** friend

5 a **fair-weather** friend   e   someone who is friends with all of your family

6 a **family** friend   f   a very good friend

2 WHAT'S YOUR ANGLE? Choose three types of friends from Exercise 1. For each type of friend, think of someone you know. Tell your partner about them.

Gabriella is a close friend. She helps me a lot, and when I have a problem, I always ask her for advice.

From: gailconner@mailinator.com

To: tina.brice@mailinator.com

Date: Wednesday, June 28

Subject: Time to meet?

Hey Tina,

How are things? I hope you're having fun and enjoying life in Sydney. Did you come back because you missed the beach? It's amazing that we're living in the same city again after ten years! I hope you're gradually starting to feel at home again. I'm so happy my long-lost friend is back!

Anyway, I'm writing because I'm having some friends over for dinner tomorrow night at my place. You remember Carol, don't you? She's coming, and a few people from my office. I'm sure you'll like them. Do you think you can come? Let me know. It would be great to see you!

Lots of love,

Gail

---

3 INTEGRATE Read the emails and answer the questions.

1 What is the purpose of Gail's email?
   a   to share some news
   b   to make an invitation
   c   to ask for help

2 Where is the event taking place?
   a   a hotel
   b   at Gail's home
   c   in an office

3 What is Gail and Tina's relationship?
   a   They are co-workers.
   b   They are neighbors.
   c   They are old friends.

From: tina.brice@mailinator.com

To: gailconner@mailinator.com

Date: Wednesday, June 28

Subject: Re: Time to meet?

Hi Gail,

Great to hear from you. Yes, things are going well, thanks. I really like Rose Bay—it's so beautiful, isn't it? I'm working hard, but I'm really enjoying it.

Thank you for the invitation. I'd love to come tomorrow. It's always good to make new friends, but nothing is better than seeing old friends! What time should I get there? I work until six, but I could be there by seven. That's not too late, is it?

Do you want me to bring anything? Dessert, maybe?

Best wishes,

Tina

PS: You don't know anyone who has an apartment to rent, do you? I'm staying in a hotel. It's good because I can get to the office easily, but I'd rather find a place of my own soon. 😃

4 IDENTIFY Read the emails again. Decide if the statements are true (T), false (F), or not given (NG).

1 Gail and Tina have a mutual friend. ____
2 They both have jobs. ____
3 The event is taking place on Saturday. ____
4 Gail and Tina are old friends. ____
5 Gail is inviting Tina to dinner at a restaurant. ____
6 Tina is looking for a house to rent. ____

5 WHAT'S YOUR ANGLE? Where do you like to go when you meet your friends? What do you do?

6 ASSESS Read the Grammar box and study the examples of questions tags in the emails. Complete the rules.

> **GRAMMAR IN CONTEXT**
> **Tag questions in the present tenses: Be and do**
>
> We use tag questions to turn statements into questions, to check information, or to ask people if they agree with us.
>
> *It's fun here, isn't it?*
> *You don't know anyone who has an apartment to rent, do you?*
>
> We use a *positive/negative* tag question after a positive statement.
>
> We use a *positive/negative* tag question after a negative statement.

See Grammar focus on page 159.

7 IDENTIFY Look again at the emails. How many tag questions can you find?

8 APPLY Turn these statements into questions by adding tag questions.

1 Gail lives in Sydney, _____?
2 Tina and Gail aren't old friends, _____?
3 Tina knows Carol, _____?
4 They both like Sydney, _____?
5 Tina's working until seven tomorrow, _____?
6 Tina and Gail don't live together, _____?

9 INTERACT With a partner, ask and answer the questions in Exercise 8. Look at the emails again to help you.

> **VOCABULARY DEVELOPMENT** Adverbs of manner
>
> Adverbs of manner explain how something happens. They help the writer describe a scene in more detail. To make an adverb, we usually add *-ly* to the adjective.
> *calm* → **calmly**
> *gradual* → **gradually**
>
> The spelling can change for adjectives ending in *-y*, *-le*, *-ic*, and *-ll*.
> *angry* → **angrily**
> *simple* → **simply**
> *enthusiastic* → enthusiastically
> *full* → **fully**
>
> There are some irregular adverbs of manner. The adverb for *good* is *well*. A small number of adverbs of manner have the same form as the adjective like *early*, *fast*, *hard*, and *late*.
>
> 🜲 Oxford 3000™

10 BUILD Write the adverbs for these adjectives.

1 happy _____
2 loud _____
3 dangerous _____
4 fast _____
5 good _____
6 painful _____
7 gentle _____

11 USE Complete the text. Change the adjectives in parentheses into adverbs.

To have good friends, you need to be a good friend. You need to take your friendship ¹_____ (serious) and work ²_____ (hard) to support each other through good times and bad. It is a two-way relationship, where you give your time ³_____ (willing) and ⁴_____ (generous). Exchanging gifts is a way to thank your friends and to show you appreciate them. Giving a ⁵_____ (beautiful) wrapped gift allows you to connect and can ⁶_____ (great) strengthen your relationship. What's more, research also shows that giving a gift makes you feel happier!

WRITING SKILL
Using informal expressions in emails

When we write emails to people we know well, such as friends and family, we use informal expressions. You can appear angry, rude, or upset if you use expressions that are too formal.

Informal expressions are usually shorter, and can often be used in speech as well as writing.

Hello! / Hi!
How are you?

12 APPLY Write each word or phrase below the correct heading.

Hi
How's it going?
Kind regards
Dear
Hey
Lots of love
I would like to ask if…
Well, that's all for now.
Best wishes
I hope this email finds you well.
I'm writing because…
Please get in touch at your earliest convenience.
Hope to hear from you soon.
Just a quick note to…
How are things?

Greeting	Formal or informal?

Opening	Formal or Informal?

Reason for writing	Formal or informal?

Closing	Formal or informal?

Saying goodbye	Formal or informal?

13 IDENTIFY Look again at the expressions in Exercise 12. Write *F* (formal) or *I* (informal) next to each expression. Some expressions can be both formal and informal.

14 ASSESS Look at the emails again. Which expressions can you find?

15 WRITE Choose one type of friend from Exercise 1. Think of a person you know, and write an informal email to invite this person to an event. Use the expressions in Exercise 12 to help you.

16 DEVELOP Exchange emails with a partner. Read your partner's email. Identify the type of friend your partner is writing to, and then use the checklist to help you review their work.

☐ Is the email well organized?

☐ Is the invitation clear?

☐ Is the language appropriate?

☐ Are there any grammar, vocabulary, or punctuation errors?

17 IMPROVE Ask your partner to suggest improvements to your email. Then write your email again, making any necessary changes.

18 WHAT'S YOUR ANGLE? Think about an invitation you received. Who was it from? What was the invitation? Did you accept it?

1 ACTIVATE Talk about the pictures with a partner. What's happening? Where are the people? In what ways are the situations the same or different?

2 ▶ IDENTIFY Watch the video and answer the questions.

1 What reason does Kevin give for leaving?
2 Why is Max surprised to see Andy?
3 What is causing the bad smell?
4 Where is Professor Lopez going next?
5 Why is Andy worried?

3 ANALYZE Think about Max's relationship with the people in the video. With a partner, choose your answers to these questions.

	Very well			Not at all	
a How well does Max know Andy and Kevin?	1	2	3	4	5
b How well does he know Professor Lopez?	1	2	3	4	5

	Relaxed			Formal	
c How does Max feel speaking with Kevin and Andy?	1	2	3	4	5
d How does he feel speaking with Professor Lopez?	1	2	3	4	5

REAL-WORLD ENGLISH Starting and ending a conversation

Conversations often begin with a greeting and a question about how the other person is. Asking how the other person is helps to build the conversation or keep it short if the person has no time to chat. How you respond to this lets the other person know the direction you would like the conversation to take.

To finish a conversation, it is polite to let the other person know you have to go before you say goodbye. People often give a reason for wanting or needing to go.

Well, it's getting late, so…

4 ▶ **INTEGRATE** Watch the video again. Who says each expression?

Scene 1

To start the conversation

		Max	Andy	Kevin
1	How's it going?	☐	☐	☐
2	What's up?	☐	☐	☐

To end the conversation

		Max	Andy	Kevin
1	I'll catch up with you later.	☐	☐	☐
2	See you.	☐	☐	☐
3	Bye.	☐	☐	☐

Scene 2

To start the conversation

		Max	Andy	Professor Lopez
1	Good afternoon.	☐	☐	☐
2	How are you?	☐	☐	☐

To end the conversation

		Max	Andy	Professor Lopez
1	Have a nice weekend.	☐	☐	☐
2	Take care.	☐	☐	☐
3	Nice to see you.	☐	☐	☐

5 **ANALYZE** With a partner, compare the two scenes. How is the language different? Why? In what way are the conversations similar?

6 **DEVELOP** Which expressions below would you use with these people? Why? Discuss your answers with a partner.

a co-worker	a neighbor	your teacher
a close friend	a family member	your boss

Hello. How are you?

Hey. How's it going?

What's up?

It was great to see you, but it's getting late. I really should go.

Got to go. See you around.

a co-worker I don't know well: Hello. How are you?
a co-worker I know well: Hey. How's it going?

7 **EXPAND** Match each expression in Exercise 6 with a reply.

1 A: _____
   B: Sure. Take it easy.

2 A: _____
   B: Of course. It was nice to see you.

3 A: _____
   B: It's going OK, thanks.

4 A: _____
   B: Nothing much.

5 A: _____
   B: I'm very well, thank you.

8 **INTERACT** Practice each dialogue with a partner.

9 **INTEGRATE** With a partner, prepare to role-play a short conversation between two people. Use the questions to help you decide the context.

1 Who are the speakers? (What are their names?)
2 What is the relationship between them?
3 How well do they know each other?
4 Where does the conversation take place?
5 Should the language be careful and polite or relaxed and informal?
6 How can you start and end the conversation?

10 **INTERACT** Role-play your conversation for the class. Your classmates can refer to the questions in Exercise 9 to analyze the context.

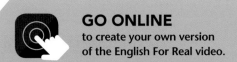

GO ONLINE
to create your own version
of the English For Real video.

1.5 Making Small Talk

1 🔊 **ACTIVATE** Look at this list of topics people often talk about when they first meet. Then listen to the questions. Write the number of each question (1–8) next to the correct topic.

___ hometown ___ weather ___ work ___ sports
___ school ___ family ___ free time ___ vacation

2 🔊 **IDENTIFY** Listen again and complete each question.

1 It's very _____ today, don't you think?
2 So, what do you _____ exactly?
3 Where are you _____?
4 Are you going anywhere on _____?
5 Do you have any _____ or _____?
6 What _____ do you like?
7 Are you a _____?
8 Do you have any _____ for the weekend?

3 **ASSESS** Read the definition of *small talk*. Why is small talk important?

> **small talk** *noun* [U] polite conversation, for example at a party, about unimportant things

4 🔊 **IDENTIFY** Listen to Pippa and Grace make small talk at a community barbecue. Which topics from Exercise 1 do they talk about?

SPEAKING Showing interest

When speaking with people, showing interest in what they are saying will encourage them and help keep the conversation going. Use these expressions to show you are interested in what the other person is saying:

Really? *Wow.* *That's great.* *How exciting!*
Amazing! *Oh yeah?* *Incredible!* *That's interesting.*

5 🔊 **IDENTIFY** Listen to the conversation again. Which expressions for showing interest do you hear?

6 **APPLY** With a partner, practice responding to each statement using an expression from the box.

1 My sister lives in Malaysia
2 I'm studying economics at Oxford.
3 I like playing soccer on weekends.
4 I'm thinking of traveling around Europe for three months.
5 My best friend and I share the same birthday.

PRONUNCIATION SKILL
Using intonation to show interest

The way you use your voice is an important part of showing someone you are interested in what they are saying. Often, the more your voice rises and falls, the more interested you sound.

7 🔊 **NOTICE** Listen to these sentences. You will hear each sentence twice. Which sounds more interested: A or B?

1 What are you doing here in Los Angeles? A / B
2 So, you have three brothers and a sister. A / B
3 What do you study? A / B
4 You're going on vacation to Mexico. A / B
5 Where in England are you from? A / B
6 Do you play tennis a lot? A / B
7 Yes, it's really hot today. A / B
8 Photography sounds like an interesting hobby. A / B

8 🔊 **APPLY** Listen and repeat. Practice making your voice rise and fall to sound interested.

9 **WHAT'S YOUR ANGLE?** Do you find it easy or difficult to make small talk with people you don't know? What do you usually talk about?

10 **INTERACT** Imagine you are at a party where you don't know anyone. Stand up and make small talk with your classmates.

- Start the conversation and introduce yourself.
- Make small talk and ask questions to develop the conversation.
- Show you are interested by reacting to what you hear.
- Use intonation to sound interested.
- End the conversation. Say goodbye.

Now go to page 147 for the Unit 1 Review.

2 Time

Why do people miss "the old days"?

Why is time important?

What's your favorite time of day?

BEHIND THE PHOTO

Ask and answer the questions in pairs.

1 Are you a patient person?
2 Do you manage your time well?
3 Would you rather be busy or take things easy?
4 Are you good at meeting deadlines?
5 In what ways do you waste time?

REAL-WORLD GOAL

Make time to do three fun things this weekend

2.1 Changing Times

1 ACTIVATE Think about the area you live in. What has changed in the last five years?

2 VOCABULARY Match the words that have a similar meaning. Use a dictionary to help you.

1	abandon (v)	a	advantage (n)
2	benefit (n)	b	decline (n)
3	decrease (n)	c	rise (n)
4	growth (n)	d	improve (n)
5	recover (v)	e	leave (v)
6	replace (v)	f	take the place of (phr.)
7	reverse (v)	g	undo (v)

🔑 Oxford 3000™

3 INTERACT Work in pairs. Look at the photographs of Detroit, Michigan. How did the city change? What do you think caused its growth and decline?

1900
The _____ of the West

1920s
The _____ capital of the world

1950s
The _____ largest city in the United States

1960s
a long period of _____

2014
population fell to _____

4 **IDENTIFY** Listen to the first part of a podcast and choose the correct answers.

1 Detroit had a successful *building / car / job* industry.
2 The population *grew / decreased / stayed the same* in the 1950s.
3 By 2014, Detroit was *successful / growing / in decline*.

5 🔊 **EXPAND** Listen again. Complete the missing information in the timeline from Exercise 3.

6 WHAT'S YOUR ANGLE? Detroit is famous for car manufacturing. With a partner, think of at least three cities in your country that are famous for something.

LISTENING SKILL Previewing

You can improve your comprehension by trying to predict what you might hear before you listen. Use information such as the title, headings, and any photographs to help you focus on the topic. Ask yourself what you know about the topic, and think of any key words and phrases you might hear.

7 APPLY Before you listen, study the headings and the photograph. What do they tell you about Detroit today? What do you think the next part of the podcast is about?

City Matters
Episode 16: A New Hope

↻ add to station

via https://www.thep...
1 hour ago

Call in   ⭐ Favorite   < Share

8 🔊 **ASSESS** Listen to the second half of the podcast. Were your predictions in Exercise 7 correct?

9 🔊 **IDENTIFY** Listen again and answer the questions.

1 When did Clara move back to Detroit?
2 What are residents of Detroit called?
3 What is Clara's job?
4 Which type of companies are moving to Detroit?
5 What benefit of living in Detroit does Clara *not* mention?

low cost of living	great art scene
good restaurants	sports
cheap property	support for businesses

10 **WHAT'S YOUR ANGLE?** What are residents of your hometown called? What are the advantages of living there?

11 **ASSESS** Study the Grammar box and complete the rules.

> **GRAMMAR IN CONTEXT** Simple past: *Be*
>
> _____ and _____ are the past forms of *is*, *isn't*, *am*, and *am not*.
>
> _____ and _____ are the past forms of *are* and *aren't*.
>
> We often use *was/were* with past time expressions like *last week, in 2003, 500 years ago*, or *yesterday*.
>
> *In the nineteenth century, Detroit* **was** *an important business center.*
>
> We also use *there was/wasn't* and *there were/weren't* to talk about things in the past.
>
> *There* **were** *lots of jobs in the car industry.*
> *People left the city because* **there wasn't** *a future for them there.*

See Grammar focus on page 160.

12 **APPLY** Complete the text using *there was/wasn't* or *there were/weren't*.

I grew up in a small village. ¹_____ only 4,000 people! It was a friendly place, and I liked it, but I remember ²_____ a lot to do after school or on weekends. ³_____ any big stores, for example, and ⁴_____ a movie theater either. When I went back recently, I was surprised. It was so different! ⁵_____ a huge shopping center, a new sports stadium, and even a hotel. ⁶_____ lots of new houses and people everywhere. To be honest, I don't think I like it anymore!

13 **EXPAND** Use the words and phrases in the box to complete the text.

was	were	there was	there were
wasn't	weren't	there wasn't	there weren't

My family lived in Taiwan when I ¹_____ younger. We ²_____ in the south for three years, and I really enjoyed my time there. Our apartment ³_____ very large, but ⁴_____ a small field nearby. I remember ⁵_____ some banana trees in the field. They ⁶_____ large trees, but they had lots of bananas. We lived in a city, and ⁷_____ many places to play, so all the children from the neighborhood went to this field. Then one summer, the owner of the field cut down all the trees and built a parking lot. We were sad because ⁸_____ anywhere to play.

> **PRONUNCIATION SKILL** Word stress
>
> All words have syllables. A syllable is a sound; for example, *water* has two syllables. For words with two or more syllables, one syllable is stressed more than the others. It is often louder than the other syllables: for example, *TOpic, CApital, imPORtant*. Stressing the correct syllable in a word is very important. If you stress the wrong syllable, then the word can be difficult to understand.

14 🔊 **NOTICE** Listen and find the stressed syllable in each word.

1 abandon
2 advantages
3 benefit
4 improve
5 million
6 recovering
7 replace
8 reverse

15 🔊 **APPLY** Listen and repeat.

16 **IDENTIFY** Work in pairs. Find the stressed syllable in these words.

1 apartment
2 important
3 business
4 company
5 industry
6 manufacturing
7 impossible
8 neighborhood
9 property

17 🔊 **APPLY** Listen and check. Then listen and repeat.

18 **WHAT'S YOUR ANGLE?** Think of a town or city you know well. How was it different in the past? Do you think the changes are good or bad?

2.2 Is Time Playing Tricks on Us?

1 ACTIVATE Read the text. When do you feel that time goes quickly? When does it go slowly?

"I was ten years old, and it was the last day of school before the summer vacation. I was studying math, and I couldn't concentrate. The time was going so slowly! I was falling asleep at my desk when the bell rang, and everyone cheered! Now I can't even remember the vacation, but I remember that last day of school."—Rick

2 INTEGRATE Study these sentences from the text in Exercise 1. Then choose the correct tenses to complete the rules in the Grammar box.

It was the last day of school.

Time was going so slowly!

I was falling asleep at my desk when the bell rang.

> **GRAMMAR IN CONTEXT**
> **Simple past and past continuous**
>
> We use the ¹*simple past / past continuous* to talk about completed actions, the order of events, repeated actions, and past states.
>
> We use the ²*simple past / past continuous* to talk about actions in progress in the past or to describe a scene.
>
> We use the past continuous and simple past with *when* to talk about one action interrupting another action in the past. We use the past continuous for the ³*shorter / longer* action and the simple past for the ⁴*shorter / longer* action.

See Grammar focus on page 160.

3 IDENTIFY Write *simple past* or *past continuous* for each sentence.

1 I went to sleep early last night. _____
2 In the morning, I woke up, got up, and opened the window. _____
3 The sun was shining, but it was raining. _____
4 I looked at my watch three times. _____
5 I couldn't believe it was 9 a.m.! _____
6 At 10 a.m., I was still getting ready for work. _____

4 APPLY Write the number of each sentence in Exercise 3 next to the correct use.

a things that happened one after the other ___
b completed actions in the past ___
c repeated actions ___
d to describe a scene ___
e actions in progress in the past ___
f to describe past states ___

5 EXPAND Complete the text using the verbs in parentheses in the simple past or past continuous.

Can our emotions affect our perceptions of time? Dr. David Eagleman, from Stanford University, ¹_____ (study) time and ²_____ (invent) a test to find out if time really does slow down when we are in danger. Volunteers ³_____ (fall) backward from a height of 15 stories. While they ⁴_____ (fall), they ⁵_____ (try) to read numbers flashing in front of them on two screens. The results? Well, they couldn't read the numbers, so time ⁶_____ (not / slow) down for them. However, the fall ⁷_____ (take) only three seconds, but afterward volunteers said it ⁸_____ (feel) much longer. Dr. Eagleman's test ⁹_____ (prove) that time doesn't slow down, but our *memory* of time slows down when we feel in danger. Time can go quicker or slower in our minds!

A test of time perception

6 INTEGRATE Read the text. There are six mistakes with simple past and past continuous. Find them and correct them.

In a different experiment, Dr Eagleman was asking people to look at a computer screen. While they looked at the screen, lots of images were appearing. They needed to click a button when an image was appearing, and again when it disappeared. Most images were being of the same brown shoe, but sometimes there was an image of a flower – the "oddball". All the images were on the screen for the same length of time, but after the test, more than 70 percent of people were saying the oddball images were on the screen longer. The "oddball effect" happens when the brain experiences something new, unusual, or interesting, and this can affect how we experience time passing.

Scanning means quickly looking through a text to find the information you want. This is useful when you want to find answers to specific questions rather than understand the whole text. You do not need to read every word. Only look for the information you need to find.

7 APPLY Scan the article to find answers to these questions.

1 What is déjà vu?

2 At what events do people usually experience déjà vu?

3 What does déjà vu mean in English?

4 How long does it last?

8 IDENTIFY Now read the article. Decide if the statements are true (T), false (F), or not given (NG).

1 Déjà vu is when you have the same experience twice. ___

2 Most people experience déjà vu only once. ___

3 There are different explanations for déjà vu. ___

4 There are different types of déjà vu. ___

5 We remember emotional events more easily. ___

9 EXPAND How many explanations for déjà vu are there in the article? Which one do you believe?

Déjà Vu

"It happened on my first visit to Paris. As I was walking along the street, I suddenly had the feeling that this wasn't my first time in the city. I felt that I recognized the place. It was all happening again!"

This is a typical example of déjà vu. The phrase comes from French and literally means "already seen" in English. Déjà vu is the feeling that someplace or something is very familiar to you, but you know it can't be true. It lasts only for a few seconds, but most people experience déjà vu at least once in their lives.

So, are we remembering something that happened in the past? It's certainly possible that we are remembering a similar event that did happen and are confusing the two. Alternatively, some people say it's because the left and right sides of the brain lose connection for a moment, so one side of the brain receives the messages a short time after the other. However, another explanation is that our long-term memory changes over time. Each time we remember an event, we change it. This gives us false memories. When we are in a situation that we are certain is "new"—and especially when our emotions are involved—these false memories can come to the surface. This is why people experience déjà vu most often when they go to new places or to events such as weddings, job interviews, and funerals.

—adapted from *The Oxford Companion to the Mind*, 2nd ed., by Richard L. Gregory

Strandfontein Beach in Cape Town, South Africa

We can use the noun *time* with different parts of speech.

adjective + *time*: *the first / next / last time, a short / long time, this / that time*

preposition + *time*: *over time, through time, in time, on time*

verb + *time*: *have time, spend time, waste time, make time, run out of time*

10 **APPLY** Scan the article again to find all the examples of phrases with *time*. What parts of speech are they used with?

11 **BUILD** Read the sentences and decide which part of speech is missing: adjective, preposition, or verb.

1 Some people are always late. They find it very hard to be _____ time.

2 The _____ time I went skiing, I broke my leg. I'm not going again!

3 _____ time doing things you enjoy will make time pass more quickly.

4 My brother _____ time playing computer games instead of studying, so he failed his exams.

5 It took scientists a _____ time to discover DNA.

6 Things such as the cost of living and property prices increase _____ time.

7 Happy people _____ time to exercise, eat healthily, and do fun things like see friends.

8 The _____ time I go on vacation, I'm going somewhere hot. The weather here is so cold!

12 **INTEGRATE** Complete the sentences in Exercise 11 with the correct words. Check that you used the correct form of the verbs.

13 **WHAT'S YOUR ANGLE?** Have you or any of your classmates ever experienced déjà vu? When? Share your stories.

1 ACTIVATE Write the name of each discovery under the correct photograph.

Stonehenge   Nazca Lines   Terracotta Warriors   Göbekli Tepe

1 _____

2 _____

3 _____

4 _____

2 IDENTIFY Where in the world are these discoveries? Match each country with a discovery from Exercise 1.

1 England   a Göbekli Tepe
2 China   b Nazca Lines
3 Peru   c Terracotta Warriors
4 Turkey   d Stonehenge

3 INTERACT Work in groups. Make notes on anything you know about these discoveries. Then share your ideas with the class.

4 WHAT'S YOUR ANGLE? Which discovery is most mysterious to you? Why?

We use *used to* to talk about regular actions that we did in the past but don't do now.

We form positive sentences with *used to* + infinitive.
*In ancient Egypt, people **used to** write in hieroglyphics.*

We form negative sentences with *didn't* + *use to* + infinitive.
*We **didn't use to** understand hieroglyphics.*

We form questions with *Did* + subject + *use to* + infinitive?
***Did the Eyptians use to** speak all three languages?*

See Grammar focus on page 160.

5 IDENTIFY Choose the correct form of *used to* to complete the sentences.

1 People *used to / didn't use to* be able to touch the Stonehenge stones. Now, they can't.
2 The emperor *use to / used to* be buried with terracotta warriors.
3 The Nazca Lines *used to / used* be well preserved, but now they are damaged.
4 People *didn't use to / used to* live on Easter Island. No one knows what happened to them.
5 What did people *used to / use to* do at Göbekli Tepe? It's a mystery!

6 INTEGRATE Complete the sentences with the correct form of *used to* and the verbs in the box.

be	build	build	use	write

The Incan Empire is famous for its impressive architecture. They ¹_____ complex cities that worked well with the surrounding land. One example is Machu Picchu. Machu Picchu means "old peak." It is on a tall mountain. There ²_____ 140 buildings there, and people think the city is in the shape of a bird. One of the mysteries of Machu Picchu is how the Incans built the city. We know the Incans ³_____ (not) the wheel, but did you know they ⁴_____ (not) either? How ⁵_____ (they) such complex cities without writing?

7 EXPAND Skim the article. What links the Rosetta Stone and hieroglyphics?

8 ASSESS Read the article again and answer the questions.

1 What did the ancient Egyptians use for paper?
2 What else did the Egyptians use to write on?
3 What is the Rosetta Stone?
4 Who found it?
5 When did they find it?
6 Where did they find it?
7 Who translated it?
8 Why is it an important discovery?

Home	About	Articles		Search

The Rosetta Stone

In ancient Egypt, people used to write in hieroglyphics. They used pictures, or hieroglyphs, to represent words, syllables, or sounds. The word *hieroglyph* comes from two Greek words: *hieros* (holy) and *glyphe* (writing). So, *hieroglyph* means "holy writing." At that time, ancient Egyptians used to write on papyrus. They used to dry papyrus reeds to make paper. They also used to paint the hieroglyphs on walls or carve them onto stone.

We didn't use to understand hieroglyphics until the discovery of the Rosetta Stone. In July 1799, French soldiers were exploring El-Rashid, Egypt, a small town also called Rosetta, when they found a strange stone. Three types of writing were on the stone: Greek, Egyptian, and hieroglyphics.

In 1822, Frenchman Jean-François Champollion made an important breakthrough. While he was studying the stone, he realized that the writing was the *same* passage, repeated in each type of writing. Using his knowledge of Greek and Egyptian, he translated the hieroglyphics.

Did the Egyptians use to speak all three languages? Whoever made the stone did. Thanks to the stone, the world had the key to three thousand years of Egyptian history! It unlocked the mysteries of ancient Egypt.

An example of hieroglyphics

Papyrus plants

The Rosetta Stone

WRITING SKILL Using time expressions

We often use time expressions when we write in the past to show when things happened, for example: *last week/year*, *five years ago*, *in the summer*, and *on June 20*. Using time expressions helps readers to follow the order of events.

9 APPLY Complete the lists with the time expressions in the box.

meanwhile	until	afterward
later	at that time	during

1 Time expressions for events happening at different times:

previously	_____	then
after	_____	finally
_____	as soon as	before

2 Time expressions for a period of time in the past:

back then _____ a long time ago

3 Time expressions for events happening together:

_____	at the same time	while
when	_____	as

10 IDENTIFY Look at the article on the Rosetta Stone again. How many time expressions can you find?

11 APPLY Choose the correct time expression to complete each statement.

1 French soldiers found the Rosetta Stone *in / on* July 15, 1799.
2 *While / During* they were knocking down an old wall, they saw the stone hidden inside.
3 *After / Afterward* they removed the stone from the wall, they noticed the writing.
4 They knew it was an important discovery *until / as soon as* they saw it.
5 The stone *later / previously* became known as the Rosetta Stone because of the name of the town.
6 Experts believe ancient Egyptians wrote on the stone at *the same time / a long time ago*—in 196 BCE!

12 WHAT'S YOUR ANGLE? Work with a partner. Think of a discovery you would like to learn more about. Choose one of the discoveries in Exercise 1 or something else.

13 PREPARE Research the discovery online to find facts and information. Take notes to answer these questions:

1 What is it?
2 Who discovered it?
3 When did they find it?
4 Where did they find it?
5 Why is it an important discovery?
6 How did life use to be before the discovery?

14 PLAN Look at your notes and decide how to organize a short article about the discovery. Make sure you answer the questions from Exercise 13.

15 WRITE Write your article. Use no more than 200 words.

Use the checklist to help you:
☐ Add photographs or pictures.
☐ Use time expressions.
☐ Answer the questions in Exercise 13.

16 SHARE Exchange articles with a partner. Read your partner's article. Does it answer the questions in Exercise 13? Is the order of events clear?

17 IMPROVE Look again at your partner's article and make suggestions for improvements.

18 WHAT'S YOUR ANGLE? Post your article online. Add it to your social media page or blog. Ask your friends for their opinions!

Divers explore the mysterious Yonaguni Monument off the coast of Yonaguni, Japan

ENGLISH FOR REAL

1 **ACTIVATE** How important do you think it is to be on time? Take the punctuality quiz to find out!

Punctuality Quiz			
For each situation, decide when you should typically arrive.	early	on time	late
1 a job interview	☐	☐	☐
2 English class	☐	☐	☐
3 meeting friends	☐	☐	☐
4 a party	☐	☐	☐
5 visiting relatives	☐	☐	☐
6 the doctor or dentist	☐	☐	☐

2 **INTERACT** Work in groups. Share your answers from the quiz. What does it mean to be "on time"? How many minutes is "early" or "late"? Who is the most punctual person in your group?

3 ▶ **IDENTIFY** Watch the video and answer the questions.

1   What was Andy doing when Max called?
2   Why did Max call Andy?
3   Who did Andy meet on his way out of the building?
4   How late was Andy when he finally arrived?

REAL-WORLD ENGLISH Apologizing

The language you use to apologize to someone often depends on how serious the mistake is and your relationship to the person. If the mistake is big or you do not have a close relationship with the person, you may need to apologize directly by taking responsibility and explaining why it happened. If the mistake is small or with someone you know well, you may not need to be as direct or take as much responsibility for the mistake.

It is common to use words like *really* or *so* to emphasize how sorry you are. The number of times you apologize is also important. You can also repeat *very* or *really* for emphasis.

I'm really, really sorry.   *I'm so sorry.*

It is often a good idea to offer to fix the problem and promise to avoid making the same mistake in the future.

4 **INTERACT** How important is it in your culture to apologize? Do you always apologize when you are late?

5 **DEVELOP** Write each function in the correct place.

Give an explanation   Promise to do better
Say you're sorry   Take responsibility
Offer to fix the problem

Functions of an apology

1 _____

Sorry.
I'm really/so sorry.
I'm very sorry about…
I (do) apologize.

2 _____

My mistake.
I'm always late.
I'm so forgetful.
It's all my fault.

3 _____

My train was late.
I saw James and stopped to chat.
The traffic is terrible!
I totally forgot!

4 _____

Let me buy another one for you.
I'll help you clean this up.

5 _____

This won't happen again.
I'll definitely finish this tomorrow.

6 **APPLY** Look at these sentences from the video. With a partner, decide who Andy was apologizing to, and then match each sentence with a function from the box above.

1 Here, let me help you.
2 I promise to be on time next week.
3 I ran into Professor Jackson!
4 It was completely my fault.
5 I'm late for a meeting, so I was in a hurry.

7 ▶ **INTEGRATE** Watch the video again. Note the expressions Andy uses to apologize.

1 To apologize to Max: _____
2 To apologize to Professor Jackson: _____
3 To apologize to the study group: _____

8 **ANALYZE** Compare the way Andy apologizes to each person. Why does he apologize differently each time? Think about the context for each apology, and discuss these questions with a partner.

1 How serious was Andy's mistake?
2 How well does Andy know the person?
3 What is their relationship?

9 **ANALYZE** With a partner, prepare to role-play these short conversations. Discuss the context. How serious is being late in each situation? How much does it affect the other person? Also think about how well the people know each other and what their relationship is. Choose which functions to include in your apology and which expressions to use.

1 A: You are a teacher. You didn't have time to grade your student's homework from the last class.
  B: You are a student. Ask your teacher for your homework.

2 A: You are a store manager. You went to a meeting that lasted longer than expected. You return to your office 30 minutes late to interview a job applicant.
  B: You are the job applicant. You are worried about picking up your kids after school.

3 A: You are a customer in a restaurant. You asked the server for the check 20 minutes ago. You are still waiting.
  B: You are the server. You forgot to bring the check because the restaurant is busy.

4 A: You are working with a classmate on an important assignment. You agree to meet one evening to complete it together, but your classmate arrives very late.
  B: You are the classmate. Explain why you are late.

10 **INTERACT** In groups, take turns role-playing your conversations. Decide if the apology and the language is appropriate. Discuss why.

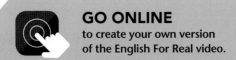

GO ONLINE
to create your own version
of the English For Real video.

25

4 **IDENTIFY** Listen again. How does Sally introduce her story? What adjectives does she use to bring her story alive?

5 **EXPAND** Listen once more. Write two questions Anna uses to move the story forward.

6 **APPLY** Listen to the sentences. Mark how Sally varies her voice.

1 I'll always remember the last time.
2 My mom said she wanted to talk.
3 I didn't want to leave my friends.
4 That's how I started taking photos.
5 The rest is history!

1 **ACTIVATE** Describe the picture with a partner. Who are the people? Where are they? What's happening?

2 **WHAT'S YOUR ANGLE?** What did you use to do with your family as a child?

3 **APPLY** Listen to Sally tell her friend Anna a story about her childhood. Answer the questions.

1 What did Anna use to do with her family?
2 What did her mother tell her?
3 What gift did her mother give her?
4 What two places did Anna use to live?
5 In what way did this day influence her?

7 **WHAT'S YOUR ANGLE?** Think of an important event in your life. Choose one of the ideas below, or use your own idea.

first job interview	trip to…
first day at school	the day I met…
first apartment	when I got…

8 **PREPARE** Prepare to tell your story. Follow the outline below and make notes.

Introduce your story	Describe how you felt
Say what happened	Explain why the story is important

9 **DEVELOP** Practice telling your story. Use time expressions where needed, and remember to vary your intonation.

10 **INTERACT** Work in groups. Tell your stories to each other, and ask questions to help to keep the stories moving forward.

I'll never forget my first day at college. I was…

SPEAKING Telling and responding to a story

When you tell a story, start by giving some background information, like where and when it took place.
Use adjectives to describe how you felt. This can help your story come alive.

I was so scared!   It was really funny.   I felt so happy.

If there are several steps, use time expressions (*first, then, next, after that*) to show the structure of the story. Remember to vary your intonation to keep the listener interested.

She never said things like that.

When listening to someone tell a story, you can ask questions to keep the story moving forward.

What did you do then? How did that make you feel?

Now go to page 148 for the Unit 2 Review.

3 Learning

How are the women learning?

Can we ever be too old to learn something new?

Are you a quick learner?

BEHIND THE PHOTO

1 How do you prefer to learn? Why? Compare your answers with a partner.

- ☐ blogs
- ☐ websites
- ☐ online courses
- ☐ books and magazines
- ☐ TV programs
- ☐ videos
- ☐ games
- ☐ teacher
- ☐ family
- ☐ friends

2 What is the first thing you remember learning? Work in groups and compare your answers. Share your memories with a partner.

REAL-WORLD GOAL

Go online to watch a video about something

3.1 As You Can See from My Résumé…

1 ACTIVATE Read the text. Choose the statements that are correct.

An application for a job or further studies needs a good cover letter. It is an opportunity to highlight your skills and experience and to encourage the employer to read your résumé. It answers the question, "Why should I interview you?"

The purpose of a cover letter is…

☐ to give as much information as possible.
☐ to emphasize key points in your application.
☐ to answer difficult questions.
☐ to help you get an interview.

2 APPLY Read the email cover letters.

From: rav33@mailinator.com

To: humanresources@mailinator.com

Subject: Application

Dear Hiring Manager,

I would like to apply for the position of Marketing Manager. I feel I have the suitable creative skills and experience for the role and would be delighted to come for an interview. Please find attached my résumé, which I hope will be of interest.

If you need any further information, please do not hesitate to contact me.

Yours faithfully,

Raoul Alvarez

From: mika.endo@mailinator.com

To: humanresources@mailinator.com

Subject: Marketing Manager vacancy

Dear Mr. McKenna,

I'm writing to express my interest in the position of Marketing Manager, as advertised on the website jobsnow.com. Please find my résumé attached.

As you can see, I have a bachelor's degree in business administration from Tokyo University, and I have worked in marketing since 2016. I am currently working at Stenton Graphics, Inc., where I have been a Marketing Assistant for two years. I have a strong track record in marketing and sales. In addition, I am reliable and can work equally well as part of a team or on my own.

I am now looking for a fresh challenge. Not only is KL Pharma a large company, but it also has a very good reputation. I believe I have the right mix of skills to be a valuable addition to your company and am available for an interview immediately.

Thank you for considering my application. I look forward to hearing from you in the near future.

Yours sincerely,

Mika Endo

---

5 WHAT'S YOUR ANGLE? Who would you interview for the position? Why? Compare the two email cover letters with a partner.

3 IDENTIFY Answer the questions.

1 What job are Raoul and Mika applying for?
2 Where did Mika see the ad for the job?
3 What have both applicants attached to their emails?

4 EXPAND Read the emails again. Decide if the statements are true (T), false (F) or not given (NG).

1 Raoul and Mika have both applied for the same job. ___
2 Raoul is not working at the moment. ___
3 Mr. McKenna is the Marketing Manager. ___
4 Mika is a graduate of Tokyo University. ___
5 Mika hasn't worked in marketing before. ___

6 **INTEGRATE** What makes a good cover letter? Study the emails and choose your answers.

JOBS NOW.com

Cover Letters
Eight Tips for Success

1. *Do / Don't* address the right person.

2. *Do / Don't* be short and to the point.

3. *Do / Don't* show you have the right skills and experience.

4. *Do / Don't* show you have a positive and professional attitude.

5. *Do / Don't* send the same cover letter to all employers.

6. *Do / Don't* say why you are interested in the job.

7. *Do / Don't* make spelling or grammar mistakes.

8. *Do / Don't* say why you want to work for the company.

7 **ASSESS** Whose email follows the tips for success? How would you improve the other applicant's cover letter?

8 **WHAT'S YOUR ANGLE?** Have you written a cover letter for a job or further studies? What was it for? Why did you want the position? Were you successful? Tell a partner.

GRAMMAR IN CONTEXT
Present perfect simple with *for* and *since*

We use the present perfect to talk about present activities and states that started in the past.

We use *for* to talk about the period of time up to the present, e.g., *for four years, for two days.*

I have worked as a Marketing Assistant for two years.

We use *since* to talk about the time when an activity started. This can be a date, a day, a month, a time, or an event, e.g., *since 1903, since yesterday, since May, since 8 a.m., since my birthday, since I was ten years old.*

I have worked in marketing since 2016.

See Grammar focus on page 161.

9 **APPLY** Complete each sentence with *for* or *since*.

1. Yasmin hasn't had a full-time job _____ she had a baby.
2. Jason has worked at this company _____ four months.
3. Unemployment has fallen _____ the last financial quarter.
4. I haven't heard anything _____ the interview.
5. I've been head of HR here _____ ten years.
6. How many jobs have you applied for _____ your graduation?
7. _____ I was ten years old, I've wanted to be an architect.
8. Tom has been absent from work _____ three days now.
9. The president has been on vacation _____ a week.
10. We've had 20 applications _____ we placed the ad last week.

10 **INTERACT** Make true sentences about yourself using *for* and *since*. Share with a partner.

I've worked at my current job since…

I've been interested in…for…

I haven't had a vacation since…

VOCABULARY DEVELOPMENT
Verbs and nouns from adjectives

Many adjectives have a verb and noun form. To avoid using too many adjectives when you write, you can change them to nouns and verbs. This will give your writing more variety and interest.

To change an adjective to a noun, you need to change the suffix. Common suffixes for nouns are *-ence*, *-ness*, and *-ity*.

confident → **confidence**
kind → **kindness**
responsible → **responsibility**

To turn an adjective into a verb, sometimes you need to take a suffix away. Common suffixes you take away are *-able*, *-ing*, and *-ive*.

acceptable → **accept**
understanding → **understand**
active → **act**

Ⓧ Oxford 3000™

11 APPLY Look in the emails to find the adjective form of these words.

1   suit (v) _____ (adj)
2   create (n) _____ (adj)
3   rely (v) _____ (adj)
4   value (v) _____ (adj)
5   availability (n) _____ (adj)

12 EXPAND Work with a partner to complete the two charts. Use a dictionary if necessary.

Adjective	Verb
approving	
challenging	
enjoyable	

Adjective	Noun
ambitious	
capable	
committed	

WRITING SKILL Using addition linking words

When you want to make several points, using addition linking words helps show that the points are related. This will make your writing clearer and easier to follow. Study these words and phrases you can use.

As well as / In addition to *having a degree, I have three years' experience.*
I have a degree. ***In addition / Moreover / Furthermore****, I have three years' experience.*
Not only *do I have a degree,* ***but I also*** *have three years' experience.*

---

13 IDENTIFY Look at Mika's email. Which words and phrases from the box can you find?

14 INTEGRATE Rewrite the sentences using the words in parentheses.

1   I have a degree in computing. I've worked in IT for five years. (furthermore)

_____

_____

2   I am an effective communicator. I work well on a team. (not only…but also…)

_____

_____

3   Jason is adaptable. He is hardworking. (moreover)

_____

_____

4   Your company has a good reputation. It is a world leader in its field. (as well as)

_____

_____

5   Helen has a strong track record in sales. She has a marketing diploma. (in addition)

_____

_____

6   You should have good communication skills. You should be a quick learner. (in addition to)

_____

_____

15 WHAT'S YOUR ANGLE? What is your dream job? What would you write about in your cover letter?

16 PREPARE Study Mika Endo's email. How is it organized? Write each stage (1–7) next to the correct paragraph.

Structure:

1   First paragraph
2   Second paragraph
3   Third paragraph
4   Last paragraph

Structure:

a   say why you are interested in the job
b   thank the employer and say you look forward to hearing from them soon
c   summarize your personal strengths
d   state the position you're applying for
e   outline your relevant experience and skills
f   say where you heard about the position
g   explain why the company attracts you

17 WRITE Prepare to write a cover email in support of an application for a job or further studies. Use the structure above, and follow the tips for success in Exercise 6. Be sure to use appropriate language.

18 IMPROVE Exchange cover letters with a partner. Read your partner's letter and make suggestions for improvements. Then write your letter again, making any changes necessary.

3.2 Machines Are Taking Over!

1 ACTIVATE Look at the photos and discuss the ways machines help us in our daily lives. Are there other ways machines help us?

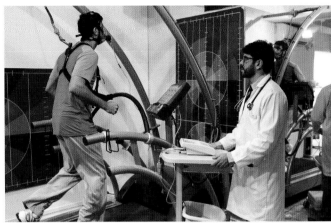

2 WHAT'S YOUR ANGLE? Think about what you did yesterday. How many times did you use technology or a machine? What did you use it for?

3 VOCABULARY Match each verb with a word or phrase.

1	announce	a	a plan
2	recognize	b	to work
3	refuse	c	someone's face
4	perform	d	a problem
5	realize	e	something is wrong
6	solve	f	an operation

🔑 Oxford 3000™

4 BUILD Complete the sentences using verbs from Exercise 3.

1 Some robots can _____ very difficult tasks that humans can't do.

2 Excon is pleased to _____ the winner of this year's Robot Awards.

3 Would you _____ if you were talking to a robot online?

4 I saw a video of a robot that can _____ different objects.

5 Robots can _____ puzzles more quickly than we can.

6 I _____ to believe that one day a robot will be in every home.

5 ASSESS Which is the best heading for the article?

Study finds machines are better workers.

Could a robot do your job?

Are machines stealing from us?

Perfect for some jobs, not for others.

6 IDENTIFY Read the article. Identify the part of speech and find a synonym for each word in bold.

	Part of speech	Synonym
1 claim		
2 suggests		
3 progressed		
4 error		
5 view		
6 threat		

READING SKILL
Recognizing and understanding synonyms

Synonyms are words that have similar meanings. A writer may use a synonym to avoid repeating a word in a text or to help explain what it means. When you see a word you don't know, it can be useful to look for a synonym in the text. This can help you understand the meaning.

7 EXPAND Read the article again. Find synonyms for these words.

1 identify (v) _____ (para 2)

2 suggest (v) _____ (para 2)

3 incredible (adj) _____ (para 3)

4 able (adj) _____ (para 3)

5 rest (n) _____ (para 4)

6 concerned (adj) _____ (para 4)

*Some people **claim** that machines have become too powerful. They argue we have taught them too much and intelligent, thinking machines are a danger to us. But is this true? Professor Nick Bostrom at the Future of Humanity Institute in Oxford certainly thinks so. His research **suggests** that machine learning has **progressed** far more quickly than we expected. He proposes that as robots have developed, so has the possibility of **error**. In his **view**, a fault in robot design is a bigger **threat** to the planet than climate change, disease, or nuclear disaster. Many well-known scientists support his opinion.*

Like it or not, machines are learning. Computers have become an essential part of our personal lives. They have learned not only to understand what we say but to recognize our faces and our voices. They have learned so much about us that they can recommend movies to watch, tell us what products to buy, and choose what advertisements to show us. But have things gone too far?

As computers have become more advanced, they have learned to do an amazing number of tasks, from picking fruit to flying planes. They already work as tour guides, accountants, office clerks, receptionists, reporters, pharmacists, waiters, and security guards. They are even capable of performing operations in hospitals.

One study by Carl Frey and Michael Osborne found that almost 50 percent of jobs in the United States and the United Kingdom could be done by machines. Remember—once a computer has learned to solve a problem or do a task, it will never forget. They never get sick, need a break, or refuse to work. Aren't you worried a robot might steal your job?

Henn na Hotel opened in Japan in 2015. It has become famous as the world's first robot hotel. Almost all the staff are robots. ▲

Not only can robots make our cars, they've learned to drive them! There are more and more self-driving cars on our roads. By 2030, experts say a quarter of all cars will be driverless. ▼

8 IDENTIFY Read the article again. Find four reasons why robots are good workers.

9 WHAT'S YOUR ANGLE? Work in groups. Do you agree with the reasons listed in the article? Are there any jobs that humans do better than robots?

GRAMMAR IN CONTEXT
Present perfect and simple past

We use the *simple past* to talk about a specific time in the past.

*Henn na Hotel **opened** in Japan in 2015.*

We use the *present perfect* to talk about an action or situation in the past when we don't know the exact time or if it isn't important.

*It **has become** famous as the world's first robot hotel.*

See Grammar focus on page 161.

---

10 USE Choose the correct options.

1 Where *did you buy / have you bought* that robot vacuum cleaner?

2 I *watched / have watched* a great program about robots on TV last night.

3 *Did / Have* you ever seen a robot dance?

4 In what ways *did / have* robots influenced our lives?

5 Technology such as cash machines *made / have made* our lives more convenient.

6 In 1996, world chess champion Garry Kasparov *beat / has beaten* the computer Deep Blue at chess. In 1997, Deep Blue *beat / has beaten* Kasparov.

7 What jobs *did / have* machines already taken?

8 Scientists *developed only / have only developed* "narrow intelligence" for robots so far—only humans possess "general intelligence."

11 APPLY Complete the text using the verbs in the box in the present perfect or simple past.

make	reach	read	write	predict

I ¹_____ an interesting article last week about Ray Kurzweil. He's an expert on machine learning and ²_____ several books on the subject. He ³_____ many accurate predictions about the future of technology. In 1990, he ⁴_____ the huge growth in the Internet in his book *The Age of Intelligent Machines*. However, despite rapid progress, computers ⁵_____ (not) what Kurzweil calls "singularity"—the point where they become more intelligent than humans. He says that'll be in 2045!

12 WHAT'S YOUR ANGLE? Do you agree that machines will one day become more intelligent than humans? What are the benefits? Are there any dangers?

A man tests new brain sensor technology in New York City, USA

3.3 It's Free!

1 ACTIVATE Which of these online courses interest you? Why? Tell a partner.

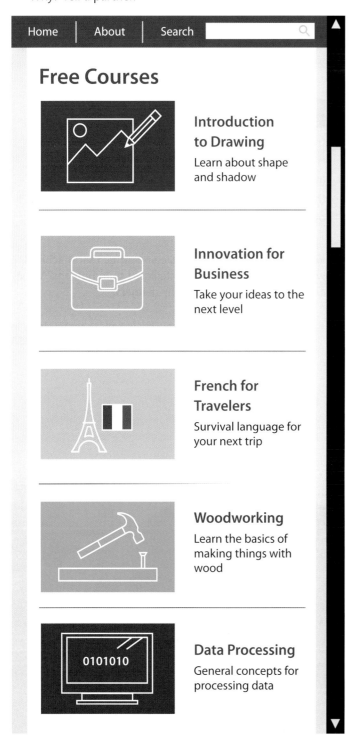

Free Courses

Introduction to Drawing
Learn about shape and shadow

Innovation for Business
Take your ideas to the next level

French for Travelers
Survival language for your next trip

Woodworking
Learn the basics of making things with wood

Data Processing
General concepts for processing data

2 WHAT'S YOUR ANGLE? In what ways is learning online different from learning in a class? Which do you think is better? Does it depend on what you are learning?

3 VOCABULARY Complete the phrases using words from the box.

attend (v)	certificate (n)	degree (n)	educate (v)
essay (n)	presentation (n)	register (v)	

🔑 Oxford 3000™

1 _____ for a course
2 give a short _____
3 _____ someone about something
4 receive a(n) _____ of achievement
5 _____ a lecture
6 write a(n) _____
7 earn a bachelor's, master's, or doctoral _____

4 BUILD Complete the sentences with the words from Exercise 3.

1 Students have to give a(n) _____ as part of their course work.
2 You receive a(n) _____ when you complete your studies.
3 All foreign language students need to submit one _____ every week.
4 Did you know you can _____ online to be in this class?
5 At the end of the semester, everyone who passes the exam gets a(n) _____ .
6 This company needs to _____ its workers about health and safety.
7 I was unable to _____ last week's lecture because I was sick.

5 ◀ ASSESS Listen to the first part of a conversation. Which course from Exercise 1 are they talking about?

> **LISTENING SKILL**
> **Understanding a speaker's purpose**
>
> When you listen to what someone is saying, think about why they are saying it. A speaker's purpose can often be to persuade, inform, or entertain.
>
> *Persuade:* The speaker wants you to agree with them and often focuses on benefits or why you need to do something.
>
> *Inform:* The speaker wants to share information with you and often focuses on facts or details.
>
> *Entertain:* The speaker wants to interest or amuse you and often focuses on humor or interesting stories.
>
> Whether you are listening to a news item, a speech, an informal discussion, or a friend talking to you, identifying the speaker's purpose will give you a better understanding and help you decide how to respond to what you hear.

6 🔊 **APPLY** Listen to the whole conversation and complete the summary with the words in the box.

> benefits   information   interested   reasons   persuade

Mandy shows Nick an ad for an online course in order to ¹_____ him to sign up. She gives him ²_____ about the course and describes the ³_____—for example, they will get help with their business plan. At first, Nick is not ⁴_____, but Mandy gives him some good ⁵_____ why he should do it.

7 🔊 **EXPAND** Listen again. Choose the correct answer.

1 Nick and Mandy are at *work / home.*
2 Nick *has / hasn't* heard of a MOOC.
3 He prefers to learn *alone / with other people.*
4 Mandy *persuades / doesn't persuade* Nick to join her.
5 At the end of the conversation, Nick feels *surprised / excited.*

8 **WHAT'S YOUR ANGLE?** Think about the last time you persuaded someone to do something. What was it, and what did you say?

9 **ASSESS** Look at these sentences from the conversation. Then complete the rules in the Grammar box.

Has that show ended yet?
I've just found this great site.
Have you ever thought about starting your own company?
A MOOC? I've never heard of it.
We still haven't made a business plan.
I've already decided.

GRAMMAR IN CONTEXT Present perfect with
just, already, yet, ever, never, and still

We use _____ in positive sentences to talk about very recent news.

We use _____ in negative sentences and questions to talk about actions we expect to happen.

We use _____ in positive sentences to talk about news and events that happened before now or earlier than expected.

We use _____ in negative sentences to talk about actions that we expected to happen before now.

When we talk about life experiences, we can use _____ for "at any time in the past" in questions, and _____ meaning "at no time in the past."

See Grammar focus on page 161.

---

10 **APPLY** Choose the correct answer to complete each item.

1 I've *already / still / yet* read more than 50 books using my e-reader.
2 Have you *still / ever / yet* used your cell phone to study English?
3 Have you finished that online course *ever / still / yet?*
4 Tina's *yet / just / ever* shown me how to use Excel. It's amazing!
5 We've *never / yet / still* had so much homework to do.
6 I *already / never / still* haven't received your written assignment.

11 **INTEGRATE** Complete the text with *just, already, yet, ever, never,* and *still.*

I've ¹_____ signed up for an Introduction to Drawing course online. I'm really excited because I've ²_____ done an online course before. I've ³_____ bought a sketch pad and special drawing pencils, but I ⁴_____ haven't bought an easel and some other equipment. I emailed the tutor and asked her if she's ⁵_____ taught an online course before, and she said no! I did a lot of drawing when I was younger, but I've ⁶_____ shown anyone my work. I promised to send the tutor some drawings, but I haven't done it ⁷_____—I'm a bit nervous. She said she's ⁸_____ sold some of her paintings, and she can give us advice on becoming professional artists. What a great idea!

12 **WHAT'S YOUR ANGLE?** Have you ever taken an online course? Would you like to take a MOOC? Why or why not?

What Was That?

1 **ACTIVATE** Work in pairs. Discuss why it is sometimes necessary to ask someone to clarify what they said. Can you add more reasons to this list?

Sometimes people…

- speak too quickly.
- use a word I don't understand.
- speak at the same time.
- talk about a topic I don't know.
- speak too quietly.

2 **EXPAND** Choose the *three* most important reasons why you sometimes don't understand what people say in English. Tell a partner and give examples.

3 **INTERACT** What do you do when you don't understand what someone has said? What do you say? Work in groups and share your strategies.

4 ▶ **IDENTIFY** Watch the video and answer the questions.

Scene 1

1   What did Max ask his teacher to clarify?
2   What did Dave ask Max?

Scene 2

1   Why couldn't Max understand Andy?
2   What will Max buy from the supermarket?

REAL-WORLD ENGLISH Getting clarification

When you are listening to someone, you can show you understand by saying things like *I see, Got it!, OK,* and *Uh-huh.*

When you don't hear or understand something, you can let the other person know you need clarification. The language you use can depend on the amount of clarification you need and the situation. For example, shorter and more direct expressions like *What?* or *Huh?* can be used when you need a simple clarification. When you need a bigger explanation or are with people you don't know well, you need to ask in a less direct and more polite way. You can use longer expressions like, *Could you go over that again, please?*

Adding *please* and *sorry* makes your question more polite and respectful: *I'm sorry, but would you mind explaining that? / Do you think you could say that again, please?*

5 ▶ **INTEGRATE** Watch the video again. Complete the expressions Max uses to ask for clarification.

1 with his teacher:
  Sorry, so I _____ quite _____ what pages?

2 with his classmate Dave:
  _____ did you _____?

3 with his roommate Andy:
  _____ was that?

6 **ANALYZE** Match each situation (1–4) with a list of appropriate expressions to use (A–D).

1 You didn't hear what a friend said.
2 You didn't hear what your boss said.
3 You didn't understand what a classmate said.
4 You didn't understand what your teacher said.

A Could you repeat that, please?
  Could you say that again?
  Sorry, I didn't quite catch that.

B Can you go over that again?
  Sorry, I'm not sure I understand.
  Do you mind explaining that?

C Huh?
  Sorry?
  What?

D What are you trying to say?
  What's your point exactly?
  What do you mean?

7 **DEVELOP** With a partner, think of at least *five* different ways to make these expressions less direct and more polite.

1 Say that again.

  _____
  _____
  _____
  _____
  _____

2 I don't understand.

  _____
  _____
  _____
  _____
  _____

8 **APPLY** In groups, prepare a role play asking for clarification. Use some of the ideas in Exercise 1 to help you.

  What is the situation?
  Who are the characters?
  What is their relationship?
  Who asks for clarification? Why?
  What expressions should you use?

9 **ANALYZE** Role-play your conversation to the class. Do your classmates think you used the appropriate expressions for the context?

GO ONLINE
to create your own version
of the English For Real video.

37

3.5 Learning the Hard Way

1 ACTIVATE Discuss this quote with a partner. What do think it means? Do you agree?

"In this age, which believes that there is a shortcut to everything, the greatest lesson to be learned is that the most difficult way is, in the long run, the easiest."

—Henry Miller, selected from *Oxford Dictionary of Quotations*, 8th ed., edited by Elizabeth Knowles

> ### PRONUNCIATION SKILL
> ### Contractions with *'s* and *'ve*
>
> ◀) When we speak, we often join words together using contractions. For example, as an auxiliary, *has* contracts to *'s*.
>
> After an unvoiced sound, *'s* is pronounced as /s/.
> *Life's taught me to be kind.*
>
> After a voiced sound, *'s* is pronounced as /z/.
> *He's learned many things.*
>
> The auxiliary *have* contracts to /v/ after a vowel sound.
> *I've learned to be patient.*

2 NOTICE Find the contractions. How is each contraction pronounced: /s/, /z/, or /v/?

1 We've just started a new business.
2 Pat's disagreed with everything I've said.
3 Henry's always given me lots of good advice.
4 So you've never lived in another country?
5 It's been a long time since they've seen each other.

3 ◀) APPLY Listen and check your answers from Exercise 2.

4 ◀) APPLY Listen to the sentences again, and then repeat.

5 ◀) IDENTIFY Read the life lessons. Then listen to Ajeet. Which life lesson do you think he's learned?

☐ Work makes you happier.
☐ Money isn't everything.
☐ Work isn't the only thing in life.
☐ To be successful, you have to work hard.
☐ There's nothing more important than family.

6 ◀) EXPAND Listen again and answer the questions.

1 When did Ajeet start his company?
2 What did he do in his 20s?
3 Was his business successful?
4 Why did he decide to change his life?
5 What two new hobbies has Ajeet started?
6 Is Ajeet's life better now?

> ### SPEAKING Describing experiences and events
>
> When you want to refer to a specific event or experience, it's a good idea to use a specific time phrase to describe when it happened.
>
> *I was 25 when I started my company.*
> *I got married five years ago.*
>
> When you want to describe a longer experience, or talk more generally, you can use time phrases such as:
>
> *In my 20s, I spent a lot of time working.*
> *Over the last few years, I've learned a lot.*
> *I've had a lot of fun recently. I've joined a dance class, and I go every week.*
>
> Be sure to use the correct tense:
>
> *Over the last few months, I did a lot of thinking / I've done a lot of thinking about my future.*

7 PREPARE Think of an important life lesson you have learned. Make notes and prepare to talk about it.

A life lesson I've learned: _____
Describe the situation. (When was it? Where were you?)
Say what happened.
How did you feel?
How has the experience changed you?

8 SHARE Work in groups and talk about your life lessons.

9 WHAT'S YOUR ANGLE? Who have you learned most from in your life? A family member, friend, teacher? Tell your classmates, and explain what you learned from this person.

Now go to page 149 for the Unit 3 Review.

4 Movement

How does the woman feel?

How does the way you move express who you are?

Do you prefer to relax, or do you like to be "on the move"?

BEHIND THE PHOTO

1 Work in groups. List at least *three* benefits of regular exercise. Which is the most important?

2 Ask and answer these questions. Who is the most active person in your group?

1 Do you belong to a fitness club or sports team?
2 How long do you spend sitting at a desk every day?
3 How many hours of TV do you watch per week?
4 How often do you walk or bike somewhere?
5 Do you have an active hobby or interest like gardening or dancing?
6 Do you take the stairs or the elevator?

REAL-WORLD GOAL

Try a new physical activity or sport

4.1 Get Moving!

1 ACTIVATE Have you ever joined a gym or started to exercise and then stopped? Why did you stop?

VOCABULARY DEVELOPMENT
Phrasal verbs: Separable and inseparable

A phrasal verb is a verb followed by a preposition, an adverb, or both. The preposition or adverb can change the meaning of the verb.

Some phrasal verbs cannot be separated. The preposition or adverb must stay next to the verb.

*Kevin's going to **go out** at lunch to run.*

Some phrasal verbs can be separated. The preposition or adverb can be separated from the verb.

*You need to **take off** your shoes to do yoga.*
*You need to **take** your shoes **off** to do yoga*

2 BUILD Match each phrasal verb with a phrase.

1	end up	a	a new membership
2	bring up	b	going to the gym
3	throw away	c	your old gym shoes
4	put off	d	a topic for discussion
5	look into	e	staying home
6	try out	f	socks from the floor
7	pick up	g	an old team photo
8	put up	h	a new sport
9	watch out	i	your hand to ask a question
10	come across	j	for any danger

🔑 Oxford 3000™

3 IDENTIFY Find six phrasal verbs from Exercise 2 that can be separated. Use a dictionary to help you.

4 USE Work in pairs. Make two sentences for each phrasal verb in Exercise 3.

Please put up your hand when you have a question.
Please put your hand up when you have a question.

5 ASSESS You are going to hear an interview about parkour. Look at the image on page 41 and discuss the questions.

1 What is parkour?
2 Where can you do it?
3 How can you learn to do it?

LISTENING SKILL Recognizing reductions with *to*

🔊 In informal speech, native speakers often leave out certain sounds to combine two words. This is called a reduction. It is very common for phrases like *going to* and *have to*. Learning to recognize this will help you understand spoken English.

going to → /ɡonə/
*Where (are) you **going to** go?*

want to → /wonə/
*What do you **want to** do?*

got to → /gotə/
*I('ve) **got to** go.*

Listen and notice how the schwa sound /ə/ in *to* helps to join these words.

have to → /haevtə/
*You **have to** practice hard.*

has to → /haestə/
*She **has to** work weekends.*

need to → /nidtə/
*We **need to** be careful.*

6 🔊 APPLY Here are some sentences from the first part of the interview. Decide if you hear the full form (F) or the reduction (R).

1	How many of you need to get in shape?	F / R
2	We are going to hear about parkour.	F / R
3	You're going to see the city differently.	F / R
4	But it has to be dangerous?	F / R
5	Rule one is you need to be safe.	F / R

7 🔊 EXPAND Listen to the first part of the interview. Check your answers to Exercise 6.

8 🔊 IMPROVE Listen to the second part of the interview. How many reductions of *going to* (/ɡonə/) do you hear?

Eugene Minogue

9 🔊 **IDENTIFY** Listen to the whole interview and complete the statements.

1 Another name for parkour is _____.
2 The most important rule in parkour is _____.
3 Learning how to climb, run, jump, and _____ is easy.
4 You need _____ of hours of experience to become an expert.
5 Children as young as _____ are learning parkour at school.
6 Parkour is a good option for people who don't like _____ sports.

10 **WHAT'S YOUR ANGLE?** Do you want to try out parkour?

11 **ASSESS** Study these sentences from the interview. Then complete the rules in the Grammar box with *will / won't* or *going to*.

1 I signed up last week. I**'m going to** try parkour for myself!
2 The course is free, so it**'s going to** be popular.
3 You **won't be** disappointed. You**'ll have** a great time!
4 It's a lovely day. I think I**'ll practice** some jumps!

@ **GRAMMAR IN CONTEXT** *Will* versus *going to*

For decisions

We usually use _____ when we make a decision at the moment of speaking.

We usually use _____ when we have already made a decision for plans and intentions.

For predictions

We usually use _____ to make predictions based on personal feelings or opinions.

We usually use _____ when there is some evidence in the present to support the prediction.

See Grammar focus on page 162.

12 **INTEGRATE** Match each sentence in Exercise 11 with a rule from the Grammar box.

13 **USE** Choose the correct options.

1 I saw a great racing bike online last week and *I'll/ I'm going to* buy it!
2 I feel really out of shape. I think *I'll / I'm going to* join a gym.
3 Jason told me he *will/ is going to* start biking to work.
4 *Will you/ Are you going to* go for a walk at lunchtime?
5 I heard Sharon say *we'll/ we're going to* have free yoga lessons.
6 Oh no! I missed my bus. I guess *I'll/ I'm going to* walk.

14 **WHAT'S YOUR ANGLE?** How can you be more active in your free time? Make notes of at least three things to do. Share your ideas with a group.

A: Next month I'm going to start swimming once a week.
B: Really? That'll be great. You'll definitely get in shape.
C: Yes. Maybe you can join a fitness center. It'll be cheaper.
A: That's a good idea. I'll look into that.

4.2 Are You a Traveler or a Tourist?

1 ACTIVATE Describe the pictures with a partner. How are these people traveling? What city or country do you think they are in?

1 _____

2 _____

3 _____

2 🔊 **IDENTIFY** Listen and write the name of each city next to the correct picture.

3 WHAT'S YOUR ANGLE? Think of a city you have visited that you really enjoyed. What did you do there? How did you travel around the city? Tell a partner.

4 VOCABULARY Complete the collocations with the words in the box.

security	economy	sights	bargain
reservation	forecast	baggage	

🔖 Oxford 3000™

1 go through _____
2 look for a _____
3 check the _____
4 carry lots of _____
5 make a _____
6 fly _____
7 see the _____

5 USE Complete the questions with the collocations from Exercise 4.

1 When you _____ for a hotel, do you do it by phone, online, or through a travel agent?

2 Have you ever flown business class or do you always _____?

3 Do you ever _____ before you leave to see if the weather will be good?

4 For your last trip, did you _____ to get the best value?

5 When you want to look around a city and _____, do you use a guidebook to help you?

6 Did it take you a long time to _____ on your last trip?

7 Do you _____, or do you only pack essential items?

6 INTERACT Work in pairs. Ask and answer the questions in Exercise 5.

7 WHAT'S YOUR ANGLE? Do you plan your vacations a long time in advance or book just before you go away? When do you usually pack: the week before or the night before?

8 IDENTIFY Read the blog. How many different forms of transportation does Michael mention?

| Home | About | Articles | | Search | 🔍 |

Travels around Central America: Day 28

Gallo pinto *is a traditional dish in Costa Rica. It's rice with black beans, eggs or cheese. Delicious!*

Well, it's the end of my time here in Costa Rica. As soon as I get up tomorrow, I'll go to the airport and then it's on to Nicaragua…It's been a great three weeks. I'll never forget the people I've met, but the best part was Tortuguero National Park…Spending five days deep in the rain forest on my own was amazing. I miss sleeping under the stars and waking up with all the animals and plants!

I'm flying to Managua, but I want to escape the crowds, so when I arrive, I'll take the bus to Jinotega—a small city in the north. I found a room in a hostel for just $15 a night—bargain! After I spend a day seeing the sights, I'll start to explore outside the city. I plan to bike everywhere, but the forecast isn't looking good! I'll go to Miraflor before I leave—a beautiful national park. I read about it online and made a reservation to stay for a week with a family and help them on their farm.

Anyway, I'll post some photos if I get online, so you guys can take a look!

Taking a boat up the river in Tortuguero.

READING SKILL Separating fact and opinion

When you read a text, it is important to be able to tell the difference between what is a fact and what is the writer's opinion.

A fact is something that is true:
Gallo pinto *is a traditional dish in Costa Rica.*

An opinion is a thought or feeling about something:
It's delicious.

To separate facts from opinions, look for evidence to support statements, and ask yourself:
"Is this always true?" and "Is it a thought or opinion"?

9 APPLY Read the text again. Answer the questions.
1 Where is Michael flying to tomorrow?
2 Did he enjoy his time in Costa Rica?
3 Where did he sleep outdoors?
4 What did he think about sleeping outdoors?
5 How does Michael plan to travel around Jinotega?

10 INTEGRATE Which questions from Exercise 9 are about Michael's opinions, and which are about facts? How do you know?

11 INTERACT Write five sentences about your country. Mix facts and opinions. Then swap your sentences with a partner. Can you separate the facts from opinions?

12 EXPAND Read the travel advice. What tips did Michael follow?

Six Travel Tips You Really Should Know
1 Read ahead—it's important to plan.
2 Get to know the locals—they can help you!
3 Look for a bargain—maybe there's a special deal?
4 Stay healthy—you don't want to get sick.
5 Get insurance—you never know when you'll need it.
6 Eat the local food—it's your window to the culture.

13 WHAT'S YOUR ANGLE? Which tips do you think are most useful? Discuss with a partner. Do you have any travel tips to add?

Simple present in future time clauses

We use the simple present to talk about the future after the words *when, if, as soon as, before,* and *after.* We usually use a future clause with *will* before or after the simple present clause. Notice that we add a comma after the simple present clause if it comes first.

As soon as I get up tomorrow, **I'll go** to the airport.
When I arrive, I'll take the bus to Jinotega.
After I spend a day seeing the sights, **I'll start** to explore outside the city.
I'll go to Miraflor **before I leave**.
I'll post some photos **if I get** online.

See Grammar focus on page 162.

14 APPLY Find the error in each sentence and correct it.

1 When we go to Europe, we visit France, Italy, and Spain in seven days.
2 Paul will take a Spanish course before he'll go to Colombia.
3 As soon as you'll get to the city, try the food at the local night market there!
4 If I save enough money I'll go hiking across Cambodia next summer.
5 The driver will collect your baggage when you'll finish packing.

15 DEVELOP Complete each gap using the simple present or *will* and the verb in parentheses.

1 Before I _____ (go) to Peru, I _____ (buy) a tourist map.
2 The manager _____ (greet) you when you _____ (arrive) at the hotel.
3 If you _____ (speak) the local language, people _____ (be) more helpful.
4 After we _____ (get on) the plane , we _____ (watch) as many movies as we can!
5 As soon as I _____ (get) home, I _____ (start) packing.
6 We _____ (collect) shells for souvenirs when we _____ (go) to the beach.

16 INTEGRATE Study the profiles of a traveler and a tourist. For each statement in Exercise 14, decide who it refers to. Write *Traveler* or *Tourist*.

A traveler

Likes	Dislikes
meeting people	tourist attractions
exchanging stories	organized tours
local food	hurrying
speaking the native language	hotels
traveling alone	tourists

A tourist

Likes	Dislikes
good hotels	insects
gift shops	bad weather
organized tours	unusual food
English speakers	wasting time
looking for a bargain	carrying baggage

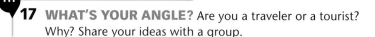

17 WHAT'S YOUR ANGLE? Are you a traveler or a tourist? Why? Share your ideas with a group.

18 INTERACT Think about your next trip. What will you do? Work in groups to talk about your plans. Are your classmates travelers or tourists? How do you know?

1 ▪)) **ACTIVATE** Listen to two voicemail messages, A and B. Match the photos to the messages. How do you know who left each message?

2 ▪)) **IDENTIFY** Listen again and match each person with a statement.

1	Nicki	a	has a singing lesson in the afternoon.
2	Mr. Wilkins	b	is meeting a friend for lunch.
3	Lisa	c	is going to make travel arrangements.
4	Tina	d	is flying to Seattle soon.

3 **ASSESS** Study these sentences from the voicemail messages. Is each sentence a schedule or a plan?

		Schedule	Plan
1	The next train leaves at ten.	☐	☐
2	I'm seeing Helen later for lunch.	☐	☐
3	I'm going to book your flight to Seattle.	☐	☐
4	What time does your presentation finish?	☐	☐

GRAMMAR IN CONTEXT
Present tenses for future plans and schedules

We use the present continuous or *be going to* to talk about future plans.

When the plan has a fixed time and/or place, we usually use the present continuous.

We usually use *be going to* when we talk about plans or intentions with no time or place.

We use the simple present with a future meaning to talk about schedules, such as bus or train schedules or somebody's personal schedule.

See Grammar focus on page 162.

4 **USE** Choose the correct option to complete the sentences.

1 What day *do / are* you going to the dentist's next week?
2 Joe and Emily are *playing / going* tennis this evening.
3 The bus to the airport *leaves / leaving* at 2 p.m.
4 We *going to meet / are meeting* some friends at a restaurant tonight.
5 When *does / is* the library close on Sundays?
6 What time is this train *going / go* to leave for Euston?
7 The school holidays *start / going to start* soon.
8 Are your parents *coming / come* here this New Year?

5 INTEGRATE Read the text messages below. Answer the questions.

1 When does the library close?
2 Who is exercising in the afternoon?
3 What is Jenny going to do in the morning?
4 What starts at 6 p.m.?
5 Why does Kim need the sales figures?
6 Who is Dan meeting later?

6 WHAT'S YOUR ANGLE? Who do you send the most text messages to? What kind of "textspeak" do you use?

WRITING SKILL
Using the right tone in text messages

When you write text messages for friends or co-workers you know well, you can use a casual tone. You can use contractions and abbreviations and leave out the subject, auxiliary verb, and any unnecessary words.

be there in 5 = I'll be there in five minutes.

You can add emphasis (*I'm soooo tired!*), but avoid SHOUTING (writing in capital letters).

When sending a message to a business associate or client, you need to be more professional. It is important to use correct spelling, grammar, and punctuation to appear professional.

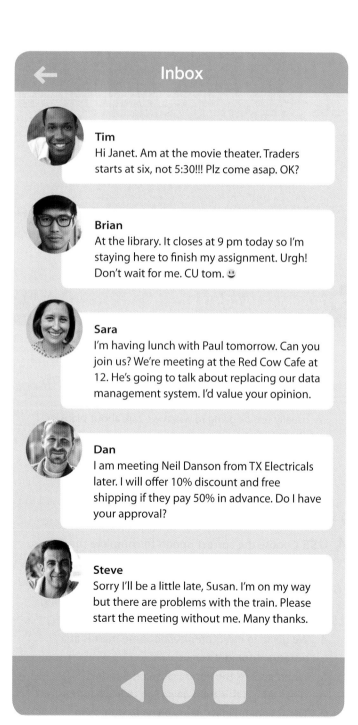

Inbox

Tim
Hi Janet. Am at the movie theater. Traders starts at six, not 5:30!!! Plz come asap. OK?

Brian
At the library. It closes at 9 pm today so I'm staying here to finish my assignment. Urgh! Don't wait for me. CU tom. ☺

Sara
I'm having lunch with Paul tomorrow. Can you join us? We're meeting at the Red Cow Cafe at 12. He's going to talk about replacing our data management system. I'd value your opinion.

Dan
I am meeting Neil Danson from TX Electricals later. I will offer 10% discount and free shipping if they pay 50% in advance. Do I have your approval?

Steve
Sorry I'll be a little late, Susan. I'm on my way but there are problems with the train. Please start the meeting without me. Many thanks.

Inbox

Kim
I'm on my way to the airport. Please don't forget to upload the sales figures for my presentation tomorrow. Put the file on the O drive so I can check it when I get in. Thanks!

Lorraine
Guess what, Chloe? Just saw a really great pair of running shoes in Sports First. Perfect for you! Are you coming into town with mom after work?

Beth
Hi Joanne. I'm playing tennis with Chris at 4 pm, at Fitness4U. RU coming?

Jenny
Did you submit your expense report for last month? I don't seem to have it. I'm going to process these tomorrow morning so please send it asap.

7 ASSESS With a partner, read the messages again. For each message, write *C* (casual) or *P* (professional). Then decide who each person is writing to. Choose from the list.

friend	classmate	co-worker	boss	family member

8 EXPAND Match each example of "textspeak" (1–9) with a meaning (a–i).

Textspeak		English	
1	tom	a	see you
2	Plz	b	your / you're
3	2	c	laughing out loud
4	ur	d	Please
5	CU	e	Thanks
6	min	f	tomorrow
7	LOL	g	to
8	cuz	h	minutes
9	Thx	i	because

9 INTEGRATE Which phrases from Exercise 8 can you find in the messages?

10 APPLY Read the messages below. What do they mean? Write each text message in full sentences.

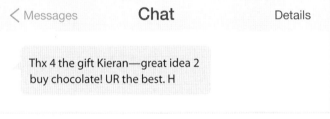

> **⟨ Messages**   **Chat**   Details
>
> Thx 4 the gift Kieran—great idea 2 buy chocolate! UR the best. H

> **⟨ Messages**   **Chat**   Details
>
> Soooo happy u passed ur driving test! CU tom to celebrate!

11 PREPARE Read the situations. For each one, prepare to write a short text message.

- What is the context? (personal or business)
- What tone do you need to use?
- Which tenses or structures are appropriate?
- Do you want to add textspeak?

Situation 1

There is a new Greek restaurant near your home. You want to invite your friend to have dinner there next week.

Situation 2

Your boss has asked you to finish a report before you leave work, but you feel sick and want to go home.

Situation 3

You are waiting for a co-worker to send you an important document. You think the co-worker could be in a meeting, but you need the document urgently.

12 WRITE Write your texts.

13 IMPROVE Read your classmates' text messages. Are the tone and language appropriate? Are all the tenses and structures used correctly? Suggest improvements where possible.

14 WHAT'S YOUR ANGLE? Send a text message to a friend in English using what you have learned.

A man uses his smartphone in Ho Chi Minh City, Vietnam

1 ACTIVATE Complete the questionnaire. Then ask and answer the questions with a partner. Discuss your answers and give examples.

Store manners	Yes	Sometimes	No
Do you ever talk on your cell phone when you're paying?			
Is it rude if someone calls an order over your shoulder?			
Do you say *please* and *thank you* when buying something?			
Should you wait to be asked before you order at a coffee shop?			
If you are in a hurry, do you ever try to get ahead of other people?			
Do you say *hello* and *goodbye* to the workers at the store?			

REAL-WORLD ENGLISH Being a customer

Being a customer usually involves a greeting, an offer of service, a request, and ending the conversation. It is common to say *hi* and ask how the other person is. Normally, you need to wait to be asked for your order.

A: Hi. How's it going? (greeting)
B: Great! And you? How can I help you? (offer of service)
A: I'll have a… (request)

When you order, you often say things like *I'll have a…* or *Could I get…, please?* People usually say *please* and *thank you*. To finish, let the person know that you don't need anything else and thank the person.

B: Can I get you anything else?
A: No, thanks.

2 INTERACT How direct are people in your country? Do people usually say *please* and *thank you* when asking for things? Discuss with a partner.

ENGLISH FOR REAL

3 ▶ **ANALYZE** Watch the video and choose your answers.

	Andy	Customer	Max
1 Who smiles when paying for his order?	☐	☐	☐
2 Who greets Sarah but doesn't ask how she is?	☐	☐	☐
3 Who doesn't wait to be asked for his order?	☐	☐	☐
4 Who says *please* and *thank you*?	☐	☐	☐
5 Who signals that he is in a hurry?	☐	☐	☐

4 ▶ **IDENTIFY** Watch the video again. Complete the expression each person uses to place his order.

1 Andy: _____ a green tea, and a medium coffee, please.

2 Customer: Green tea, _____.

3 Max: _____ green tea, please?

5 **APPLY** Read this extract of the conversation between Andy and Sarah. Label the parts of the conversation.

confirmation of order	greeting
request for service	thanks / finish

1 Sarah: Hey. How's it going?
   Andy: Hey, Sarah. I'm good, thanks.
   Sarah: Great. What can I get you?

   _____

2 Andy: Uh, I'll have a green tea, and a medium coffee, please.

   _____

3 Sarah: Green tea and a coffee. Anything else?

   _____

4 Andy: No. That's all. Thank you.

   _____

6 ◀)) **INTEGRATE** Listen to a different conversation. Complete the missing words.

Server: Hello. ¹_____ I help you?

Customer: Er, yes. ²_____ I ³_____ a large black coffee and a muffin, please?

Server: Certainly. One large black coffee and a muffin. ⁴_____ you ⁵_____ anything else?

Customer: Er. No, thank you. That's ⁶_____.

7 **ANALYZE** Compare the two conversations in Exercises 5 and 6. What differences do you notice?

8 **INTEGRATE** With a partner, choose one location and prepare to role-play a conversation between a customer and a service assistant. Use the questions below to help you.

at a train station	in a restaurant	in a travel agency
at a hotel	in a coffee shop	

■ Where are you?
■ Who are you speaking with?
■ What is your relationship? Do you know the server?
■ What do you want?
■ What language is appropriate?

9 **INTERACT** Role-play your conversation to the class. Can your classmates answer the questions in Exercise 8? Do they agree the language is appropriate for the context?

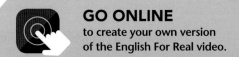

GO ONLINE
to create your own version
of the English For Real video.

4.5 You Might See Whales!

1 ACTIVATE Discuss these questions with a group.

1 Is your hometown popular with tourists?
2 What can visitors see and do there?
3 What's the best way to get around?

SPEAKING Asking for and giving directions

The best way to ask someone on the street for directions is to get their attention first and then ask them.

Excuse me, do you know where Settler's Park is, please?
Sorry, can you tell me where the station is?

When you give directions, use the imperative.

Go straight ahead. Then turn left at the lights.
Take the first street on the right, walk for five minutes, and it's on the left.

You can give more information using *will*.

You'll pass the train station first, and the park is after that.
You'll see a supermarket and a bank, and then the station.

2 IDENTIFY James is visiting Port Elizabeth, South Africa. Listen to him asking for directions. Which three tourist attractions are mentioned?

A Settler's Park, Nelson Mandela Metropolitan Art Museum, Humewood Beach
B Settler's Park, Nelson Mandela Metropolitan Art Museum, Algoa Bay
C Nelson Mandela Metropolitan Art Museum, Algoa Bay, Addo Elephant National Park

3 EXPAND Listen again. What is James going to do in each place?

PRONUNCIATION SKILL
Intonation for asking for and giving directions

When you ask for directions, begin with *Excuse me* and finish with *please*. Be sure to stress the location you are asking for. Listen and notice the intonation.

*Excuse me. Do you know where the **park** is, please?*

When you give directions, use sequence words and add emphasis to key words (turn *left*, go *straight*) and the names of streets and places. Pause between steps in the directions. When you list several steps, make sure your voice goes up each time and then down for the final step.

*Sure. Go **straight** until **Broadway**. Then turn **left**, and you'll see it on the **right**.*

4 NOTICE Listen to these dialogues. Notice the intonation.

1 A: Excuse me. Where's the Modern Art museum, please?
   B: Turn right onto Green Street, go past the bank, and it's on the left.
2 A: Excuse me. Do you know where the beach is, please?
   B: Go along Park Drive, turn right on Fifth Avenue, and it's in front of you.
3 A: Excuse me. Can you tell me how to get to the train station, please?
   B: Go left at the corner, walk past the bank, and it's across from the library.

5 APPLY Practice the dialogues with a partner.

6 PREPARE Work in pairs. Decide on a city or place with some interesting tourist attractions. Make some notes on where they are and what you can do there.

7 INTERACT In your pairs, act out a conversation between a tourist and a resident. Ask for and give directions and information.

Now go to page 150 for the Unit 4 Review.

5 Home

What makes people feel at home?

Is home a place, a feeling, or a person?

Can people have more than one home?

BEHIND THE PHOTO

REAL-WORLD GOAL

Invite some friends to your home for dinner

1 Close your eyes and think about your childhood home. What do you see? What can you hear? What can you smell? Write notes.

1 sights _____

2 sounds _____

3 smells _____

2 Share your sense memories of home with a group.

5.1 Home Sweet Home

1 ACTIVATE How many homes have you had? Where were you happiest? Why? Tell a partner.

2 IDENTIFY Skim the infographic and choose the best description.

A   Advice on decorating your home.

B   Facts about rooms in a house.

The Secret of a
Happy Home

*Home is a place to rest, relax, and be happy.
Here's how you can make the happiest home.*

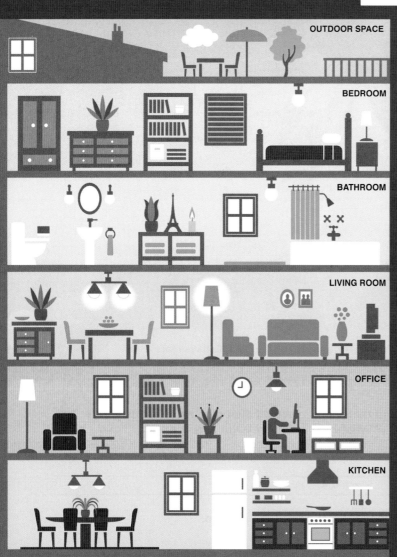

OUTDOOR SPACE

BEDROOM

BATHROOM

LIVING ROOM

OFFICE

KITCHEN

> ### READING SKILL Recognizing cause and effect
>
> Identifying the relationship between causes and effects in a text will help you understand how ideas relate to each other. A cause happens first (*the window was open*) and results in an effect (*I was cold*).
>
> We often use *because, as*, and *since* to introduce a cause. These words can be at the beginning or in the middle of a sentence.
>
> ***Since*** *a clean home gets rid of negative energy, don't make a mess!*
>
> *Put souvenirs around your home* ***because*** *they'll bring back good memories.*
>
> To introduce an effect, we use *so*. This word can only be in the middle of a sentence.
>
> *Make space to store things,* ***so*** *your home is less messy.*

---

1   Try to have somewhere you can connect with nature. You'll feel less stressed than always being indoors.

2   Make space to store things, so your home is less messy.

3   The color blue helps you relax and reduces your blood pressure.

4   Always make your bed! The simplest habits can make you more productive, healthier, and happier!

5   Put souvenirs around your home because they'll bring back good memories.

6   Use candles, so the light will be softer.

7   Keeping everything clean can make a difference. Since a clean home gets rid of negative energy, don't make a mess!

8   Indoor lighting is just as important as natural light. Match your mood, using brighter lights for entertaining and softer lights for relaxation.

9   Display photos of family and friends because seeing people you love every day makes you happier!

10   Green is more relaxing than strong colors, such as red.

11   Always have fresh flowers because they bring positive energy.

12   Put your desk facing the window. Natural light is good for energy levels and helps you concentrate.

13   Be well organized—you'll have a clearer head!

14   Buy a round table as it makes communication easier.

15   Get spider plants since they're great for stopping smells.

3 APPLY Read the Reading Skill. Study the infographic and complete the table.

Cause	Effect	Linking word
fresh flowers	they bring positive energy	because
a round table		
candles		
spider plants		
a family photo		

4 INTEGRATE Cover the infographic. Can you remember the answers to these questions? Discuss your ideas with a partner, and then look again and check.

1 What kinds of houseplants are good to use in the kitchen?

_____

2 Why is it important to make your bed every day?

_____

3 Where is the best place to position your desk?

_____

4 Which color is good to use in the living room?

_____

5 Why is it important to have a clean home?

_____

6 In what way does it help to have an outdoor space?

_____

5 WHAT'S YOUR ANGLE? Which tips for a happier home do you already do? What changes can you make to help your home become a happier place? Tell a partner.

6 VOCABULARY Write these words or phrases next to the correct meaning of each expression with *make*.

space	a mess	an effort	your bed
a difference	sense	changes	

🕮 Oxford 3000™

1 make _____ → seem reasonable
2 make _____ → try, or work hard to achieve something
3 make _____ → cause to be different
4 make _____ → have an effect
5 make _____ → replace sheets and pillows neatly on a bed
6 make _____ → create room for something
7 make _____ → cause to become dirty or untidy

7 USE Complete these sentences using the expression with *make* in Exercise 6.

1 I just cleaned this floor! Take off your shoes, so you don't _____.
2 The colors you use in your home can _____ in your mood and the way you feel.
3 It doesn't _____ to have the lights on when it's sunny.
4 Could you please clean your bedroom and _____ before you come downstairs?
5 You can _____ to your home without spending a lot of money.
6 We need to _____ in the living room for the new table and chairs.
7 Let's _____ to clean up before our guests arrive.

8 WHAT'S YOUR ANGLE? How clean and organized is your home? Is it difficult to make space for all your things? Are there any changes you would like to make?

9 IDENTIFY Study the sentences in the Grammar box and complete the rules.

GRAMMAR IN CONTEXT Making comparisons

We use comparative adjectives (+ _____) to compare people and things with other people and things.
*Green is **more relaxing than** strong colors, such as red. You'll feel less stressed **than** always being indoors.*

We use superlative adjectives (usually with _____) to compare people and things with the whole group.
***The simplest** habits can make you more productive, healthier, and happier!*

We use (_____) as + adjective + as to say that two things or people are equal.
*Indoor lighting is **just as important as** natural light.*

We use not as + adjective + as to say that two things or people are not equal.
*Strong colors such as red are **not as** relaxing **as** green.*

See Grammar focus on page 163.

10 INTEGRATE Find all the examples of comparative and superlative adjectives in the infographic.

11 APPLY Choose the correct option to complete the text.

Throughout history, we built our homes using local materials and carefully positioned them to take advantage of the local weather conditions. Then, in the twentieth century, energy became [1]*cheaper / the cheapest* and [2]*easiest / easier* to get, so we constructed buildings without worrying about the local climate or level of energy use. However, these days energy prices are higher [3]*than / as* in the past, so energy is [4]*more / the most* expensive and not [5]*just / as* available as before. Also, we are [6]*more / as* aware of the environmental cost of global warming. The old traditions of building design are once again [7]*more / just as* important as before in influencing where and how we build our homes and the materials we use.

—adapted from the *Encyclopedia of Climate and Weather*, 2nd ed., edited by Stephen H. Schneider, Terry L. Root, and Michael D. Mastrandrea

12 DEVELOP Read the answers to the question, *What's important to you when choosing a home?* Then complete each statement with one word.

1　A large home is nice, but living close to friends and family is _____ important to me.
2　A good Internet connection is _____ as valuable as good transportation.
3　I love shopping and eating out, so the _____ important thing for me is to be close to local stores and restaurants.
4　These days I work from home a lot, so living near my office is _____ important than it used to be.
5　Because I don't have any children, having a home near a school is the _____ important factor.

13 INTERACT Choose the statements in Exercise 12 that are true for you. Compare your answers with a partner.

14 ASSESS You are going to watch a video about Tinker's Bubble, a small community in England. Look at the photograph. What kind of people do you think live here?

15 ▶ **IDENTIFY** Watch the video. Answer the questions with a partner.

1　What kind of homes do people in Tinker's Bubble have?
_____
2　What materials do people here build their homes from?
_____
3　How do they wash their clothes?
_____
4　How do they get hot water and heat?
_____
5　Why do people choose to live here?
_____

16 INTERACT What are the advantages and disadvantages of having a home in a place like Tinker's Bubble? Make a list with a partner.

17 WHAT'S YOUR ANGLE? Would you be happy living in Tinker's Bubble? Which is more important to you: having a comfortable home or protecting the planet? Share your ideas with the class.

A young girl's room in Belgrade, Serbia

5.2 Perfect for the Beach

1 ACTIVATE When you go on vacation, what type of accommodation do you stay in? Why?

I stay with family or friends.
It's cheaper!

2 IDENTIFY Read the online ads. Choose *A* or *B*.

1   *A / B* is closer to the ocean.
2   *A / B* is cheaper to rent.
3   *A / B* accommodates more people.
4   *A / B* isn't in the center of Brighton.
5   *A / B* has free parking.

A **Rent**Away   Search 🔍

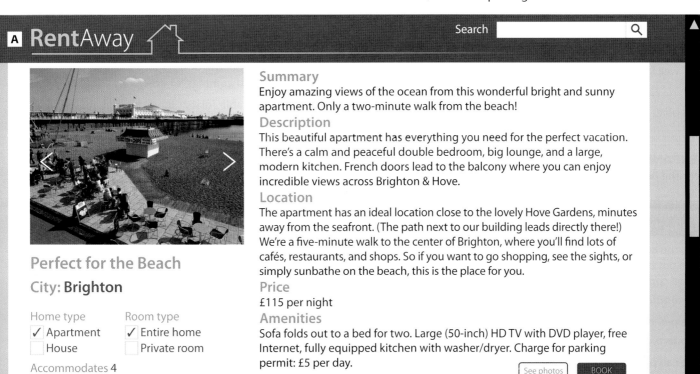

Perfect for the Beach
City: Brighton

Home type	Room type
✓ Apartment	✓ Entire home
☐ House	☐ Private room

Accommodates **4**

Summary
Enjoy amazing views of the ocean from this wonderful bright and sunny apartment. Only a two-minute walk from the beach!

Description
This beautiful apartment has everything you need for the perfect vacation. There's a calm and peaceful double bedroom, big lounge, and a large, modern kitchen. French doors lead to the balcony where you can enjoy incredible views across Brighton & Hove.

Location
The apartment has an ideal location close to the lovely Hove Gardens, minutes away from the seafront. (The path next to our building leads directly there!) We're a five-minute walk to the center of Brighton, where you'll find lots of cafés, restaurants, and shops. So if you want to go shopping, see the sights, or simply sunbathe on the beach, this is the place for you.

Price
£115 per night

Amenities
Sofa folds out to a bed for two. Large (50-inch) HD TV with DVD player, free Internet, fully equipped kitchen with washer/dryer. Charge for parking permit: £5 per day.

[See photos]   [**BOOK**]

B **Rent**Away   Search 🔍

A Home Away from Home
City: Portslade, Brighton

Home type	Room type
☐ Apartment	☐ Entire home
✓ House	✓ Private room

Accommodates **2**

Summary
Stay in this amazing bedroom at the top of our modern, spacious Victorian home. Very private, with your own bathroom, and well located for nearby Brighton. You'll be a short bus ride from this famous seaside city—perfect for a city break!

Description
Your room is on the top floor of our townhouse, so you are separated from the noise of our family and can enjoy a peaceful stay. The room is bright, fresh, and clean with its own bathroom. There is a really comfy king-sized bed, beautiful Egyptian cotton sheets, and fluffy towels.

Location
Portslade is a friendly neighborhood. There is plenty of free parking and great access to public transportation to help you explore easily. There are lots of restaurants, coffee shops, and cafés nearby. We've lived here for ten years and can advise on anything from sightseeing to sports…just ask!

Price
£39 per night

Amenities
TV with 100-plus channels, WiFi, DeLongi coffee machine, free Internet, free bottled water and chocolates

[See photos]   [**BOOK**]

WRITING SKILL Using synonyms

Synonyms are words or phrases that have a similar meaning. We often use synonyms when we want to express similar ideas but without repeating the same words. This variety helps to keep the reader interested. Verbs, adjectives, and adverbs can all have synonyms.

Enjoy amazing views of the ocean from this ~~amazing~~ wonderful apartment.

3 APPLY Look again at the ad "A Home Away from Home." Find synonyms for these words and phrases.

1 wonderful
   amazing

2 well known
   _____

3 quiet
   _____

4 welcoming
   _____

5 without difficulty
   _____

6 locally
   _____

4 EXPAND Find five pairs of synonyms in the ad "Perfect for the Beach."

GRAMMAR IN CONTEXT
Using two or more adjectives

We use adjectives when we describe people or things. We can put two or more adjectives before a noun. We don't use a comma between adjectives of different types.

beautiful Egyptian cotton sheets

We put a comma between adjectives of the same type.

modern, spacious Victorian home

We can put two or more adjectives after a noun + *be*. We use a comma between each adjective, but we put *and* and a comma before the final adjective.

The room is **bright, fresh, and clean**.

When putting adjectives together, follow this order:

opinion size age shape color origin material purpose

See Grammar focus on page 163.

5 IDENTIFY Write each word in the correct column.

leather	glass	wool	round
square	rectangular	tiny	massive
big	lovely	attractive	pleasant

Opinion	Size	Shape	Material
_____	_____	_____	_____
_____	_____	_____	_____
_____	_____	_____	_____

6 APPLY Put the words into the correct order.

1 a / modern / apartment / large
   _____

2 a / new / bed / comfortable
   _____

3 a / round / table / small / wooden
   _____

4 a / mirror / old / square / beautiful / silver
   _____

5 a / leather / big / wonderful / sofa / red / Italian
   _____

7 EXPAND Rewrite the descriptions including the words in parentheses and commas if necessary.

1 a beautiful table (glass / modern / square)
   a beautiful, modern square glass table

2 a new apartment (expensive / small / stylish)
   _____

3 a black sofa (leather / old)
   _____

4 a wooden desk (large / writing)
   _____

5 a small bedroom (neat / pleasant / spare)
   _____

8 WHAT'S YOUR ANGLE? Write three sentences to describe your home and furniture.

VOCABULARY DEVELOPMENT
Nouns and prepositions

Many nouns have specific prepositions that follow them. There is often only one possible preposition that can follow a particular noun. Study these examples.

Nouns followed by *to*: **access, reference**

Nouns followed by *of*: **description, member**

Nouns followed by *for*: **advertisement, demand**

Nouns followed by *in*: **change, interest**

🔑 Oxford 3000™

9 IDENTIFY Find examples of nouns followed by these prepositions in the ads in Exercise 2. (There are multiple correct answers.)

2 x noun + *of* _____ _____

1 x noun + *to* _____

1 x noun + *for* _____

10 BUILD Complete the letter using the noun + preposition combinations from the Vocabulary Development box.

Dear Mrs. Robinson,

I am a ¹_____ the Newberry Residents Association. I am writing in ²_____ your rental property at 201 Lakeside Drive. I understand there is a ³_____ vacation properties in the area, but I'm afraid we have received a lot of complaints from neighbors about noise. They also mention ⁴_____ resident parking spaces is sometimes impossible because of illegal parking by your guests. I am attaching a full ⁵_____ all the problems they have brought to my attention.

I would like to ask you to please remove the online ⁶_____ the property until we can all agree on a way forward. If there is no ⁷_____ the situation, I will contact the police. I have no ⁸_____ causing trouble, but this problem must be resolved.

Yours sincerely

Richard A. Trent

Richard A. Trent

11 PREPARE Imagine you want to rent your home or a room in your home. Prepare to write an ad. Look at the ads in Exercise 2 and make notes of the features you want to advertise.

Title: This is like a headline. Try to grab your reader's attention!

Summary: A short but interesting overview. Focus on two to three important features.

Description: Use lots of adjectives to describe the accommodation in detail. Use synonyms to keep the reader interested.

Location: Give key information about the neighborhood, such as where to eat and how to get around.

12 WRITE Write the ad. Follow the structure in Exercise 11 to help you.

13 DEVELOP Look at the checklist. Find ways to improve your ad.

- ☐ Does the ad include synonyms?
- ☐ Are adjectives in the correct order?
- ☐ Are nouns followed by the correct preposition?
- ☐ Did you use addition linking words?
- ☐ Does the ad have all the parts and give all the information listed in Exercise 11?

14 SHARE Work in groups and read each other's ads. Which ad do you like best? Why? Correct any errors and suggest areas for improvement.

15 IMPROVE Rewrite your ad, using your classmates' feedback to help you.

16 WHAT'S YOUR ANGLE? What are the disadvantages of rental properties? How do they affect the local neighborhood? Would you rent your home to a stranger?

1 ACTIVATE Why do most people need to call somewhere home? How important is having a home to you?

2 VOCABULARY Match each phrasal verb with a phrase.

1 catch up   a   and get married
2 settle down   b   things you don't want
3 figure out   c   on news
4 get rid of   d   the answer to a problem
5 check on   e   so you're not late
6 hurry up   f   someone to make sure they're all right

🔖 Oxford 3000™

3 BUILD Write the number of each phrasal verb (1–6) from Exercise 2 next to the correct definition.

a ___ make sure there is nothing wrong
b ___ try to do something more quickly
c ___ understand
d ___ chat about recent developments
e ___ throw away
f ___ find a home and stop traveling

4 🔊 ASSESS Listen to Nicki, a travel blogger, talking with her brother. Choose the correct words to complete the summary of their conversation.

Nicki and her brother are catching up *before / after* her trip to Paris. *Nicki / Her brother* enjoys traveling for work. Her brother thinks Nicki *should / shouldn't* settle down.

5 🔊 IDENTIFY Listen again and answer the questions.

1 Which country will Nicki visit first on her next trip?
2 Who is she staying with right now?
3 How old is she?
4 Why is she happy about her life?
5 How does she feel about not having a home?

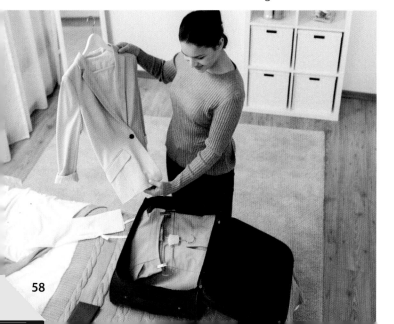

6 WHAT'S YOUR ANGLE? What are the advantages and disadvantages of traveling for work? Do you agree with Nicki or her brother?

> **LISTENING SKILL**
> **Distinguishing levels of formality**
>
> Listening to the way a person speaks can help you understand the level of formality of a situation. Pay attention to the vocabulary, contractions, and sentence structure that speakers use.
>
> In informal situations, people use shorter, simpler sentences. There are often more contractions and informal or idiomatic vocabulary.
>
> *I'm traveling a lot for work, but it's my dream.*
>
> In formal situations, people often use long sentences and more complex language. They avoid contractions and use more standard vocabulary.
>
> *Although the position requires a large amount of travel, I believe deeply in the work.*

7 ASSESS What level of formality do you usually use with each of these people? Put them in the correct column.

a family member	a stranger	a co-worker
a friend	your employer	a client

Formal	Informal

8 🔊 NOTICE Listen to these pairs of sentences. Notice the vocabulary, contractions, and sentence structure. For each sentence, choose *Informal* or *Formal*.

1 A Informal   Formal
   B Informal   Formal
2 A Informal   Formal
   B Informal   Formal
3 A Informal   Formal
   B Informal   Formal
4 A Informal   Formal
   B Informal   Formal
5 A Informal   Formal
   B Informal   Formal
6 A Informal   Formal
   B Informal   Formal

9 🔊 **EXPAND** Listen to Nicki interview Dr. Pierre Dubois from Médecins Sans Frontières. Notice how her language is more formal in this situation. Number the questions in the order you hear them (1–6).

a   Do you mind telling me what your role is? ___

b   Is it correct that MSF is also known as Doctors Without Borders? ___

c   Is having no home a cause of regret for you? ___

d   Could you please start by explaining what MSF does? ___

e   What would you say is the greatest difficulty in your work? ___

f   Does your job require much travel? ___

10 🔊 **ASSESS** Listen again and answer the questions in Exercise 9.

11 **WHAT'S YOUR ANGLE?** Think of jobs that involve a lot of travel. Why do you think some people like to do these jobs? Would you like to have a job that involves a lot of travel?

GRAMMAR IN CONTEXT *-ed* and *-ing* adjectives

We use adjectives ending in *-ed* to talk about a person's feelings. We usually use them after the verb *be*, and they are often followed by a preposition.

*I'm very **pleased** to tell you about the work we do at MSF.*

We use adjectives ending in *-ing* to talk about a quality someone or something has. We can use them after the verb *be* or before a noun.

*My job's **exciting**.*
*That's an **interesting view**.*

See Grammar focus on page 163.

12 **IDENTIFY** Choose the correct option to complete these sentences.

1   Charles was *surprised / surprising* that Nicki's bag was so small.

2   Nicki thinks it's *excited / exciting* to travel to Europe.

3   Her family feels *worried / worrying* about her future.

4   Dr. Dubois has a very *tired / tiring* job.

5   He was very *pleased / pleasing* to talk about MSF.

6   Nicki and Dr. Dubois aren't *disappointed / disappointing* that they don't own a home.

13 **DEVELOP** Choose from the adjectives in Exercise 12 to complete these sentences.

1   We enjoyed the flight, but the meal was _____.

2   Tomorrow's trip to Paris will be great. I'm so _____ I can't sleep!

3   This is a very safe neighborhood, so you shouldn't feel _____ about going out at night.

4   After all day in the hot sun, we returned home _____ and ready for bed.

5   It was _____ that the hotel had rooms available in August.

14 **WHAT'S YOUR ANGLE?** How do you feel before a trip? Are you excited or worried?

15 **EXPAND** Imagine you are leaving home to go on a long trip for work or pleasure. Write five items you would take with you, and note your reasons.

Essential travel items	Reasons

16 **INTERACT** Work in groups. Tell each other what items you want to take, and explain your reasons.

1 ACTIVATE Imagine these people invite you to their home for dinner. Would you bring dessert or some other gift to the dinner?

your boss	a former co-worker	a classmate	a close friend
a new neighbor	a family member	your teacher	

2 INTERACT How often do you invite friends to your home? Tell a partner about the last time. Who did you invite? Why? Did they bring a gift?

3 ▶ IDENTIFY Watch the video and answer the questions.

1   What event does Andy invite Max to?
2   What gift does Andy buy?
3   What does Kevin invite Max and Andy to do?
4   How does Max respond?
5   What gift do Max and Andy take to the party?

REAL-WORLD ENGLISH Making an invitation

When inviting someone to do something, people often begin by asking about a person's availability before bringing up the event indirectly. For example, you might ask if the person is free when the event will happen by saying something like *Are you doing anything tonight?* It's then common to give more information about the event, such as where and when it is before making an invitation.

Ask about availability → *Are you doing anything tonight?*
Introduce the event → *I'm thinking about going to a movie.*
Give more detail → *It starts at eight.*
Invite → *Do you want to go?*

The language you use to invite someone depends on how well you know the person. To invite your employer or someone you don't know well, use longer and more complex expressions: *I was wondering if you would like to come for dinner next Monday.* However, for a friend, a shorter invitation is fine: *Do you want to have dinner next Monday?* Your language may also depend on how big the invitation is. For example, a wedding is a bigger event than having coffee.

4 ▶ IDENTIFY Watch the video again. Complete the sentences each person says.

Andy

1   Phil's having a _____.
2   I can _____.
3   Would _____ come?

Kevin

4   So are you two _____ tonight?
5   There's a good _____ playing at seven.
6   Do _____ go?

5 **IDENTIFY** Write the number of each sentence in Exercise 4 next to the correct function.

Ask about availability ___   Give more detail ___

Introduce the event   ___   Invite   ___

6 **INTEGRATE** Complete the sentences with the words in the box.

want	meeting	free	doing
like	having	be	Thursday

Asking about availability

1 Are you _____ next weekend?

2 What are you _____ tomorrow evening?

Introducing the event

3 I'm _____ a party at my home this Friday.

4 It's my birthday on _____.

More detail

5 We're _____ at the entrance to the mall at noon.

6 I'll _____ 30 years old!

Invitation

7 Would you _____ to join us?

8 Do you _____ to get something to eat later?

REAL-WORLD ENGLISH
Accepting and rejecting invitations

To accept an invitation, confirm and thank the person, and add something positive: *I'll look forward to it*. If necessary, ask for more information, such as what time it is at.

Declining an invitation is more complex. In most situations, it is common to thank the person and say something positive, such as wishing them well. It is also common to apologize and explain why you can't attend. You can suggest an alternative or promise to be available next time.

7 **APPLY** Complete the chart. Write each function next to the correct expressions.

Apologize	Ask for details	Make an excuse
Confirm	Make a promise	Suggest an alternative

Accepting an invitation

1 _____	I'd love to, thanks.
Positive comment	That sounds great. / I look forward to it.
2 _____	Can I bring anything? / Who's coming? / What time?

Declining an invitation

3 _____	I'm (really) sorry.
4 _____	That's very kind of you, but I'm busy then. / I'd love to, but I already have plans.
5 _____	How about Monday instead?
6 _____	Next time for sure.
Say thank you	Thanks very much, though.
Best wishes	I hope you have a great time.

8 ▶ **EXPAND** Watch the video again. Answer the questions.

1 What does Max say to accept Andy's invitation?

2 Who declines an invitation? How?

3 What will Max, Andy, and Kevin do tomorrow evening?

4 What time will they meet?

9 **INTEGRATE** With a partner, prepare to role-play one of the following situations.

Student A: You want to invite your boss to lunch next Thursday. There is something important you want to discuss. What should you include in your invitation? What language is appropriate?

Student B: You are student A's boss. You are busy next Thursday and need to decline the invitation. You don't want to upset Student B. How can you reject the invitation?

Student A: It's your birthday next Tuesday, and you are planning a big party. Student B is an old friend. Invite Student B to your party.

Student B: You are busy next Tuesday evening. You can't go to Student A's party. Reject the invitation without causing offense.

10 **ANALYZE** Work in groups and role-play your conversation to each other. Your classmates will analyze the context and decide if the language you use is appropriate.

GO ONLINE
to create your own version
of the English For Real video.

5.5 Home Is Where the Heart Is

1 ACTIVATE Discuss with a partner the differences between a house and a home. Then complete this sentence in at least five ways.

Home is…

…a warm bed.

…a tasty meal.

…watching TV on the couch.

2 INTERACT Share your ideas of home with a group. How similar or different are your ideas of home?

SPEAKING Describing places

When you want to describe where a place is, use:

in + country/state/city
It's a small town in Wyoming.

close to / *near to* + city/town/famous place
It's very close to Yellowstone National Park.

To say why it's important to you, use:

It's where + *I grew up* / *I went to college* / *my family lives*, etc.
It's where I met my husband, and we bought our first house.

To give a general description, use adjectives and comparative and superlative adjectives:

It's a really beautiful, special place.
It's the biggest city in the state.

To describe specific parts or to say what features it has, use *There is* / *There are* and *It has*:

There are people from all over the world.
It's very cosmopolitan.
There's lots of space.
It has amazing museums and castles and other historical places.

3 ◀) ASSESS Listen to Helen talk about the place she calls home. Where is she talking about, and why does she call it home?

4 ◀) IDENTIFY Listen again and choose the correct answers.

1 Her hometown is *in / near / by* the Rocky Mountains.
2 She thinks it's *an interesting / an exciting / a boring* place.
3 When she was growing up, she enjoyed *outdoor activities / playing games / sports*.
4 The people in California are *just as friendly / less friendly / more friendly*.
5 She *still sees her old friends / only uses social media / doesn't have any old friends*.

5 ASSESS Read the Pronunciation Skill.

PRONUNCIATION SKILL Weak sounds

In English, only the important content words are stressed. Words that are not stressed are reduced or weak. A common weak sound is the schwa /ə/. Listen to this sentence and notice the schwa sounds.

◀) *The air is so fresh there, and there's lots of space.*

Recognizing the schwa will help your listening comprehension, and using it will help your speech sound more natural.

6 IDENTIFY Look at these words. Underline the schwa sound. Some words have more than one schwa sound.

1 condition
2 description
3 memory
4 important
5 about
6 structure
7 similar
8 sentence

7 ◀) NOTICE Listen and check. Then listen and repeat.

8 ◀) APPLY Look at these extracts from Helen's memory of home. Underline the schwa sounds. Then listen and check.

1 For me, the place I call home is Jackson.
2 It's a really beautiful, special place.
3 The air is so fresh there, and there's lots of space.
4 I live in California now, and it's not as lovely as Jackson.
5 Jackson will always be home to me!

9 PREPARE Where do you call home? Make notes in the chart.

Place: _____

Location: _____

Why this is home: _____

Description: _____

10 WHAT'S YOUR ANGLE? Work in groups. Tell your classmates about the place you call home.

Now go to page 151 for the Unit 5 Review.

6 Images

How can we use pictures to shape our image of ourselves?

What makes an image special?

Can an image change the world?

BEHIND THE PHOTO

REAL-WORLD GOAL

Take a selfie and share it with your friends

1 What does the saying *A picture is worth a thousand words* mean? Do you agree? Share your ideas with a group.

I think it means pictures are more important than words. I agree because I think images communicate better than words.

2 What do you take photos of? Think about some photos you have taken recently. Why did you choose to take them?

6.1 The World's Most Famous Photo

 Scientists and Explorers
Episode 26: The Blue Marble

In this episode, we explore a famous photo of the Earth. We hear about where and how it was taken, and why nobody knows who took it!

1 ACTIVATE Read about the podcast and look at the photo. How does it make you feel? Why do you think it has become famous?

2 WHAT'S YOUR ANGLE? Do you think space travel will be popular one day? Tell your partner and explain your reasons.

VOCABULARY DEVELOPMENT Agent nouns

Agent nouns are used for people or things that do a particular activity. Most agent nouns end in: *-er*, *-or*, *-ist*, and *-ian*.

photograph—**photographer**   explore—**explorer**
edit—**editor**   govern—**governor**
art—**artist**   science—**scientist**
music—**musician**   politics—**politician**

♟ Oxford 3000™

3 BUILD Write the agent nouns for these words. Use *-er*, *-or*, *-ist*, or *-ian*.

1 art   _____   4 act   _____
2 library _____   5 perform _____
3 travel   _____   6 support _____

4 USE Work in pairs. Make sentences using the agent nouns from the Vocabulary Development box.

An artist I really like is Van Gogh.

I've always wanted to be a photographer.

5 ASSESS You are going to listen to the story behind the photograph in Exercise 1. Read the sentences. Choose the ones that you think are true.

1 This famous photograph is called the Blue Marble.
2 It is a very recent photograph, taken just a few years ago.
3 A satellite took this photo from space.
4 It's the first photograph of Earth from space.

LISTENING SKILL
Listening for specific information

Listening for specific information is useful when you need to find out important details. Details often include names of places and people, dates, and numbers. Focus on these details as you listen to increase your comprehension.

6 ◀) IDENTIFY Listen to the podcast and check your answers to Exercise 5.

7 ◀) APPLY Read the summary. Then listen to the podcast again. Find and correct the three mistakes.

There were three astronauts on the ship: Eugene Cernan, Ronald Evans, and Harrison Schmitt. About three hours into their flight, they looked out the window and saw the Earth in the sunlight 39,000 kilometers away. Two of them took photographs, even though they knew it was wrong. They used the same camera, so nobody knew which astronaut took the famous photograph!

PRONUNCIATION SKILL Adding focus

🔊 Help your listeners follow your main ideas when you speak by stressing the most important word in each phrase. This also helps to keep your listener interested.

For sentences and *wh-* questions, you stress the focus word by using rising and falling intonation.

*They **looked** out the **window** / and saw this **amazing sight**.*

What did they do?

For *yes/no* questions, you stress the focus words by using rising intonation.

*Did they **follow** the **rules**?*

8 🔊 **IDENTIFY** Listen to these sentences. Find the focus words and decide where the intonation rises and falls.

1 Why is this image so famous?
2 It shows us how beautiful our planet is.
3 It connects us with the universe.
4 Does it help to bring us together?
5 It changed the way we think about ourselves.

9 🔊 **USE** Listen again and repeat the sentences in Exercise 8.

10 **INTEGRATE** Find a photo you like. Write a few sentences about it. Mark the focus words in each phrase, and practice using rising and falling intonation. Then read aloud to your partner.

GRAMMAR IN CONTEXT
Quantifiers: *Both, several, most,* and *all*

We use quantifiers, usually before nouns, to talk about the number of people or things.

We use *both* with a plural noun to talk about two people or things.
***Both** astronauts and satellites have taken photos of Earth.*

We use *several* (+ *of the*) + plural noun to talk about some of the people or things in a group.
*There were 17 Apollo missions to the moon. **Several** missions landed on the moon.*

We use *most* with a plural noun to talk about the majority of the people or things in a group.
***Most** images of Earth weren't as bright or colorful as the Blue Marble.*

We can use *both/several/most/all* + *of* + pronoun to talk about people or things that we have already mentioned.
*There were three astronauts. **All of** them took photographs.*

See Grammar focus on page 164.

Space Food

One of the astronauts on Apollo 17, Eugene Cernan, was also in the earlier Gemini program.

The quality and variety of food for the Apollo astronauts were much better than for astronauts on previous missions. Hot water was available, so they could eat ¹*both / several* freeze-dried foods, and the food was tastier. The astronauts carried special "spoon bowls." ²*Several / All* of the food stuck to the spoon, making eating seem similar to eating on Earth. ³*Both / Several* peas and beans were served in sauce, so they didn't fly away. There was also more choice—100 food items including strawberry and peanut cubes, spaghetti, salmon salad, and 75 drinks. Variety is important because ⁴*both / most* astronauts will get bored of the same menu choices. The astronauts liked ⁵*most of / several of* the food items apart from freeze-dried ice cream. However, visitors can buy this in the NASA gift shop as "space food" and try it for themselves.

Specialists test ⁶*all / all of* new foods for their smell. The smell of food is a big worry. In 1976, a terrible food smell caused one Soviet spacecraft to return to Earth before completing the mission!

—adapted from *The Oxford Encyclopedia of Food and Drink in America*, 2nd ed., edited by Andrew F. Smith

12 **EXPAND** Complete the sentences using the words and phrases in the box.

most	both	several	all of	all

1 On Apollo 11, _____ Neil Armstrong and Buzz Aldrin walked on the moon.
2 When they go to the International Space Station, _____ astronauts can take personal possessions with them. The limit is 5 kilos.
3 In 1972, Apollo 16 astronaut Charles Duke took a photo of _____ his family and left it on the surface of the moon.
4 Although _____ astronauts are men, there are more female astronauts these days.
5 Going into space is dangerous. Over the years, _____ astronauts have died.

13 **WHAT'S YOUR ANGLE?** Imagine you are going to space and you can only take one image with you. What image would you take?

6.2 Express Yourself

1 ACTIVATE Think about your image. What do your clothes and hairstyle say about you? How important is your image to you?

READING SKILL Recognizing prefixes

We add prefixes to the beginnings of words to change their meanings. Recognizing common prefixes can help you guess the meanings of unfamiliar words.

Prefixes such as *un-*, *dis-*, *mis-*, *im-*, and *in-* give the opposite meaning, e.g., *unlike*, *disagree*, *misunderstand*, *impossible*, *informal*.

Here are the meanings of other common prefixes.

anti = against → *anti-smoking*
co = together → *cooperate*
mid = in the middle of → *midtown*
re = do again → *replay*
auto = self → *autofocus*

2 IDENTIFY Read the Reading Skill. Find the prefix in each word.

autobiography	unreal	midlife	unlike	restyle

3 APPLY Guess the meaning of each word in Exericse 2 from its prefix. Then find each word in the article *From Self-Portraiture to Selfie* and check your answers using the context.

1 _____ the middle part of your life
2 _____ the story of a person's life, created by that person
3 _____ not real
4 _____ style again
5 _____ not similar

4 INTEGRATE Read the whole article on selfies and self-portraits. How are they similar?

Home	About	Articles		Search	🔍

From Self-Portraiture to Selfie

In 2013, *selfie* was Oxford Dictionaries' Word of the Year. Does that mean people spend too much time thinking about their image? How many selfies is too many? Do you take a few selfies a week, or a few a day?

Because of social media, anyone can post selfies to show the world who they are and what they do in their daily lives. But is it a good thing to do?

Although taking selfies is a modern activity, the idea of self-portraiture as self-expression is hundreds of years old. But unlike now, the "selfies" of the seventeenth and eighteenth centuries were made by artists, not ordinary people. A good example of this is Rubens, who painted himself to show how rich and successful he was. Lots of people act in a similar way today when they take selfies in front of their new car or house to share on social media. We see few images of people looking unhappy or having a bad day. And we never see how many bad photos they took or how long it took them to restyle their hair or their clothes!

Another common theme in self-portraiture is visual autobiography. The self-portraits of the Dutch artist Rembrandt, for example, follow his life from youth, to the successes of his midlife, to his problems in old age. Similarly, people today post selfies online that act as a digital record of their changing lives.

But do selfies always reveal the truth of someone's life? Some modern artists use self-portraits to ask questions about society and self-identity. For example, Spanish artist Amalia Ulman created a new identity and life story with selfies posted on Instagram. Richard Prince uses other people's selfies in his artworks and sells them for thousands of dollars. Similarly, some people use selfies to make themselves look more successful and their lives more glamorous than they really are.

Today, self-portraits are more popular than ever. Anyone can take a selfie to record a special moment or create an unreal image to make their lives look perfect. Artists have always used the power of the self-portrait; now ordinary people are using self-portraits to express themselves, too.

Van Gogh

Rembrandt

5 **EXPAND** Read the article again. Decide if the statements are true (T), false (F), or not given (NG).

1 The word *selfie* became popular after 2013. ____

2 It's difficult to take a good selfie. ____

3 Artists have created self-portraits for hundreds of years. ____

4 Rubens was a poor artist. ____

5 Rembrandt used painting to show his life story. ____

6 Selfies always reveal the truth. ____

6 **WHAT'S YOUR ANGLE?** Do you think selfies should reveal the truth? What kind of selfies do you take?

7 **APPLY** Choose the correct options.

1 Rembrandt's self-portraits don't have *a little / a lot of* detail in the background.

2 Some people say Van Gogh used *too much / too many* lines of thick paint.

3 *A little / Lots of* self-portraits show a person's status.

4 Only *enough / a few* people can afford to pay an artist to paint their portrait.

5 Do you think too *much / many* people worry about their self-image?

6 Some people spend too *much / many* time posting selfies online.

7 I don't have *too much / enough* skill to take really good photos.

GRAMMAR IN CONTEXT Quantifiers: *Too much/too many, a little/a few, a lot, enough*

We use *too much/too many* to say that the quantity is more than we want or need. Sometimes, this has a negative result.
*Does that mean people spend **too much** time thinking about their image?*

We use *a few* with countable nouns and *a little* with uncountable nouns to describe a small number or amount.
*Do you take **a few** selfies a week, or **a few** a day?*

We use *enough* to say all that is necessary. We use *not enough* to make a negative sentence.
*Rubens put **enough** detail in his self-portraits for people to understand his life.*

We use *a lot of/lots of* with countable or uncountable nouns to describe a large number or amount.
***Lots of** people act in a similar way today.*

See Grammar focus on page 164.

Chinese tourists outside the Colosseum in Rome, Italy

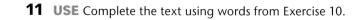

8 BUILD Complete each sentence using the words and phrases in the box.

| too much | too many | a little | a few | a lot | enough |

1 There isn't _____ light to take a good photo in this room. Let's go outside.
2 There are _____ photos in this email. I can't send it!
3 Although you said you aren't good at taking photos, _____ of these are really impressive.
4 You can't print all these photos. It'll cost _____ money!
5 I don't think posting _____ of photos on social media is necessary.
6 Before you take a photo, you need to take _____ time to make sure you include everything you want.

9 INTERACT Find a photo you took that you don't like. For example, you can use a photo on your cell phone. Tell your partner why you don't like it. Use *too much/too many*, *a little/a few*, *a lot*, and *enough*.

10 VOCABULARY Match each phrase with a picture.

landscape photo	photo frame	in focus
use a flash	out of focus	use a **selfie stick**
a view of	a **portrait** of	

🔑 Oxford 3000™

11 USE Complete the text using words from Exercise 10.

Photography Tips

First, decide what you are taking the photo of: Is it ¹_____ a city or ²_____ a friend? If you are taking a photo of a person, get close to them. For a ³_____, stand further away—cities look great if you take the photo from somewhere high like a hill or a tall building. Make sure the image is ⁴_____ before you take the photo. If it's too dark, ⁵_____. If you are taking a picture of yourself, ⁶_____ to get the best result.

12 WHAT'S YOUR ANGLE? What are your three best selfie tips?

1

_____

2

_____

3

_____

4

_____

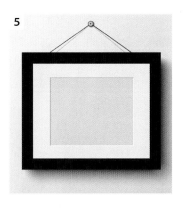

5

_____

6

_____

7

_____

8

_____

6.3 That Looks Just Like a Fish!

1 **ACTIVATE** Describe these buildings with a partner. What does each look like? What do you think each one is called? Which is the funniest?

A

B

C

D

2 **IDENTIFY** Listen and complete the chart.

	A	B	C	D
Name of building:		The Atomium		
Country:			India	
Date:	1986			

69

3 **EXPAND** Read these online posts. Which building in Exercise 1 is each person describing?

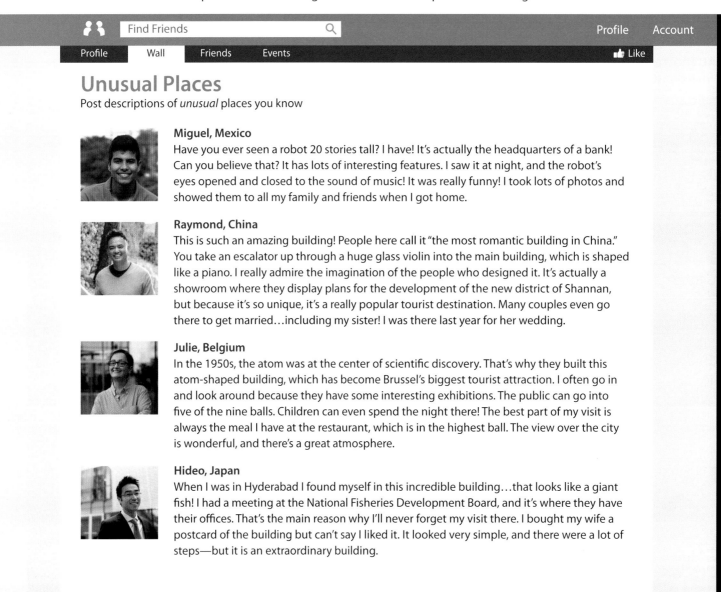

Profile   Wall   Friends   Events   👍 Like

Unusual Places
Post descriptions of *unusual* places you know

Miguel, Mexico
Have you ever seen a robot 20 stories tall? I have! It's actually the headquarters of a bank! Can you believe that? It has lots of interesting features. I saw it at night, and the robot's eyes opened and closed to the sound of music! It was really funny! I took lots of photos and showed them to all my family and friends when I got home.

Raymond, China
This is such an amazing building! People here call it "the most romantic building in China." You take an escalator up through a huge glass violin into the main building, which is shaped like a piano. I really admire the imagination of the people who designed it. It's actually a showroom where they display plans for the development of the new district of Shannan, but because it's so unique, it's a really popular tourist destination. Many couples even go there to get married…including my sister! I was there last year for her wedding.

Julie, Belgium
In the 1950s, the atom was at the center of scientific discovery. That's why they built this atom-shaped building, which has become Brussel's biggest tourist attraction. I often go in and look around because they have some interesting exhibitions. The public can go into five of the nine balls. Children can even spend the night there! The best part of my visit is always the meal I have at the restaurant, which is in the highest ball. The view over the city is wonderful, and there's a great atmosphere.

Hideo, Japan
When I was in Hyderabad I found myself in this incredible building…that looks like a giant fish! I had a meeting at the National Fisheries Development Board, and it's where they have their offices. That's the main reason why I'll never forget my visit there. I bought my wife a postcard of the building but can't say I liked it. It looked very simple, and there were a lot of steps—but it is an extraordinary building.

👍 245 people like this   💬 view all 16 comments

---

4 **INTEGRATE** Answer the questions.

1 How many buildings are government institutions?
2 What can you do at the top of the Atomium?
3 Which building is the head office for a financial organization?
4 What is the main purpose of the Piano House?
5 Which person didn't like the building they are describing?
6 In which building can visitors stay overnight?

5 **WHAT'S YOUR ANGLE?** Which building do you like best? Why? Tell a partner.

GRAMMAR IN CONTEXT Verbs with two objects

Some verbs can have two objects, a direct object and an indirect object.

The direct object usually answers the question *What?*
What did Hideo buy? He bought ***a postcard*** of the building.

The indirect object usually answers the question *Who to/ for?*
Who did he buy it ***for***? He bought a postcard for ***his wife***.

We can put the indirect object before the direct object.
*Hideo bought **his wife** a postcard*.

We can also put the indirect object after the direct object and the preposition *to* or *for*.
*Hideo bought **a postcard** for his wife*.

See Grammar focus on page 164.

6 APPLY Look at the examples. Then rewrite the sentences using *to* or *for*.

1 Miguel showed his family some photos of the Robot Building.
Miguel showed some photos of the Robot Building to his family.

2 I got you a ticket for the concert.
I got a ticket for you for the concert.

3 They gave the architects of the Burj Khalifa in Dubai many awards.
_____

4 Our boss has bought everyone a ticket to see Hurst Castle.
_____

5 Can you bring me back a souvenir of your trip?
_____

6 I mailed you a copy of the guidebook last week.
_____

7 Please could you save me a seat at the lecture?
_____

8 We offered all students a 50 percent discount on admission.
_____

7 DEVELOP Write the words in the correct order. Add punctuation.

1 my friends / unusual photos / to / I often send
_____

2 a free tour / the guide / offered everyone / of the building
_____

3 the architect / I wrote / of complaint / a letter
_____

4 me / to Barcelona / once booked / my family / a surprise trip
_____

5 a copy of / you print / that photo / please can / for me
_____

@ **WRITING SKILL Writing opening sentences**

When posting comments or short messages online, use your opening sentence to get the reader's attention. Asking a question, keeping the reader guessing, or describing the scene will encourage the reader to keep reading. You may also want to surprise your reader.

---

8 ASSESS Read the opening sentences of the online posts in Exercise 3. How does each person start their post? Write the name.

1 starts with a fact _____
2 describes the scene _____
3 asks a question _____
4 keeps the reader guessing _____

9 INTERACT Which person's opening sentence do you think is the strongest? Work in groups. Explain your reasons.

10 PREPARE Prepare to write a short post about something you saw that made an impression on you. Think of a picture that made you laugh or a building that you still remember. Take notes.

What was it?

Where was it?

Why did it impress you?

How did you feel?

11 WRITE Write your post.

12 IMPROVE Review your work. Try to find areas to improve. Use the checklist to help you.

☐ Is your opening sentence effective?
☐ Do any verbs have two objects? Have you used them correctly?
☐ Is it clear how and why this image affected you?
☐ Have you included how the image made you feel?

13 SHARE Work in groups. Read each other's posts. Who has the best opening sentence? Whose post is the most interesting? Which is the funniest?

14 WHAT'S YOUR ANGLE? Think of an image you have seen recently. What is it? Why do you remember it? Tell a partner.

The public library in Nice, France

1 ACTIVATE Look at these topics people often compliment each other on. Match each compliment with a topic.

1	That jacket looks really good on you.	a	home
2	I love your hair!	b	family
3	That's a great report. Well done.	c	possessions
4	Your children are very sweet.	d	clothes
5	Hey. I like your cell phone.	e	work
6	What a beautiful kitchen!	f	physical appearance

REAL-WORLD ENGLISH Giving compliments

To give a compliment in English, you can use simple expressions such as *I really like that sweater* or *I love your shoes*. The most common adjectives people use when giving a compliment are *nice, good, beautiful, pretty,* and *great*. You can add *really* or *very* to most compliments. *Really* is more informal than *very*.

Remember that not all compliments are suitable for everyone. For example, you might say *Your hair looks nice* to a friend but not your employer.

2 INTERACT Do you often give compliments? Who do you give compliments to? What do you compliment them on? How do you accept compliments?

3 ASSESS Study these structures for giving compliments. Write the number of each compliment in Exercise 1 next to the correct structure.

a Your [noun phrase] is/are very [adjective]. ___
b That [noun phrase] looks [adjective]. ___
c I like your [noun phrase]. ___
d What a(n) [adjective] [noun phrase]! ___
e That's a(n) [adjective] [noun phrase]. ___
f I love your [noun phrase]. ___

4 APPLY Work in pairs. Think of at least two more compliments for each structure. Use these adjectives.

nice	good	beautiful	pretty	great

5 ▶ **IDENTIFY** Watch the video. Answer the questions.

1 What does Emma compliment Max on?
2 When will Max give his presentation?
3 What does Max buy before going home?
4 What color does Andy think suits Max?
5 What did Andy loan Max?

REAL-WORLD ENGLISH Accepting compliments

It is common to accept a compliment in English. You can say *thank you* and give more information or ask a question in most situations.

Giving more information develops the conversation.

A: *I really like your sweater!*
B: *Oh, thanks. My sister gave it to me.*

Asking a question encourages the person giving the compliment to explain their reasons.

A: *That's a great hat.*
B: *Really?*
A: *Yeah, it really goes well with your shirt.*

You can also compliment the other person.

A: *I like your shoes.*
B: *Thanks. Yours look nice, too!*

6 **INTEGRATE** Write each expression for responding to this compliment next to the correct strategy.

Do you really think so?	I bought it last week.
So's yours.	Thanks a lot!

That's a beautiful ring!

1 Say thank you.

_____

2 Give details.

_____

3 Ask a question.

_____

4 Return the compliment.

_____

7 ▶ **ANALYZE** Watch the video again. Which strategies for responding to compliments do Max and Andy use, if any?

Who...?	Max	Andy
1 says thank you	☐	☐
2 gives details	☐	☐
3 questions a compliment	☐	☐
4 returns a compliment	☐	☐

8 **EXPAND** Work with a partner. How many different compliments can you think of to use in these situations?

1 Your neighbor has bought a new car.
2 You go to a friend's home for the first time.
3 Your boss at work shows you a photo of her family.
4 A family member is wearing new shoes.
5 A co-worker has a new haircut.

9 **APPLY** Choose one situation from Exercise 8 and role-play the conversation with your partner. Use appropriate expressions and strategies for giving and responding to compliments.

10 **INTERACT** Stand up and interact with as many classmates as you can. Compliment each other on your clothes, possessions, appearance, or something of your choice. Practice different ways of accepting compliments.

A: What a great jacket!
B: Thanks. I got it on sale.

GO ONLINE
to create your own version
of the English For Real video.

6.5 Images with Impact

1 ACTIVATE Discuss this image with a partner. What can you see? What's happening? What do you think is going to happen? How do you think the person feels?

2 **NOTICE** Read and listen to Simon Jones talk about this photo.

"This is a photo my friend Gary took two years ago. We both took lots of photos, but this one is my favorite. We were in the Welsh mountains, on a three-day mountain biking trip. The mountain bike I'm using is new, and I was trying it out for the first time. You can see from the photo the scenery there is amazing. It's so beautiful. Anyway, I really like this photo because it shows the rocky path we rode on, which was…*challenging*—I almost fell a couple of times! Another reason why I like this photo is because about five minutes after Gary took it, the sky went black, and there was this massive thunderstorm. You can see there's nowhere to hide from the rain, so we both got really, really wet. I've been on several biking trips since, but I've never seen rain like that again. It makes me smile just looking at this photo!"

3 IDENTIFY Read the statements and choose your answers.

		True	False	Not given
1	The photo was taken in Wales.	☐	☐	☐
2	He was with a group of cyclists.	☐	☐	☐
3	A professional photographer took the photo.	☐	☐	☐
4	Shortly after, the weather improved.	☐	☐	☐
5	Simon has happy memories of this time.	☐	☐	☐

SPEAKING Giving a presentation using visuals

When you prepare to give a presentation using visuals such as photos, graphs, and charts, think about when and how to use them during your presentation. Give the audience time to study the visual and then describe what you can see, using expressions like *This picture shows…* and *As you can see from the chart*…If you're showing a photo, give details about what's happening and say who took the photo, where, and when.

4 **APPLY** Read and listen to Simon's presentation again. Find the phrases where Simon…

1 gives the audience time to study.
2 describes what you can see.
3 gives details about what's happening.
4 says who took the photo, where, and when.
5 explains why he likes the photo.

5 EXPAND What expressions does Simon use to encourage listeners to look at the photograph?

 6 WHAT'S YOUR ANGLE? Do you like to take photographs? Who or what do you take photos of? Tell your partner.

7 PREPARE Find a photo that you like. You can choose a photo you took, one with you in it, or a photo from a magazine, newspaper, or the Internet. Prepare to talk about it. Make notes and follow the advice in the Speaking box.

Where is the photo from?
What does it show?
What's happening?
Who took it? Where? When?
Why do you like it?

8 INTEGRATE Practice your presentation with a partner. Take turns to present your photograph.

9 IMPROVE Give your partner feedback. How well did they follow the advice in the Speaking box? How could they improve?

10 SHARE Work in groups and give your presentation.

Now go to page 152 for the Unit 6 Review.

7 Predictions

Are you excited about the future?

Why do people try to predict the future?

How can people try to influence the future?

BEHIND THE PHOTO

REAL-WORLD GOAL

Compare the future in two sci-fi movies

1   In groups, discuss the things people may say when they make predictions about these topics.

the weather	political elections
sports results	consumer behavior
financial markets	

2   How possible is it to make accurate predictions? How good are you at making predictions?

1 ACTIVATE How many texts or instant messages do you send each day? Who do you text most often?

 VOCABULARY DEVELOPMENT
Collocations with *get*

Collocations are words that people often use together. There are lots of collocations with *get*.

With *get* + noun, *get* often means "receive."
get an email, get a job, get a chance

With *get* + adjective, *get* often means "become."
get confused, get lost, get ready

In other collocations, *get* has different meanings.
get home = arrive home
get a train = catch a train

Understanding and using collocations will help you communicate more naturally in English.

2 VOCABULARY Complete the sentences with *get* collocations from the Vocabulary Development box. Make sure you use the correct form of *get*.

1 I _____ straight after graduation. Now, five years later, I'm the manager!
2 I was talking on the phone while I was _____, so I didn't realize that my socks didn't match.
3 You'll _____ if you don't ask for directions.
4 I _____ saying I was the winner of a competition I didn't enter. It must be a scam.
5 I normally _____ at six o'clock on weekdays.

3 BUILD Use *get* with the words in the box to complete the sentences. Make sure you use the correct form of *get*.

injured	changed	married	angry
wet	better	invited	

1 My parents _____ when they were in their twenties. I'm 30 and I'm still single!
2 I need to _____ before I go out. These clothes are dirty.
3 Did you _____ to Tina's party? I didn't!
4 I had a horrible cold last weekend, but I'm finally _____.
5 My brother _____ playing football, so he doesn't play any more.
6 The weather forecast is terrible. You better take an umbrella or you'll _____.
7 The customer _____ when the manager told him he couldn't get a refund.

4 INTERACT Work in pairs. Take turns making sentences using collocations with *get*.

This morning I got an email from someone I haven't heard from in ages.

 READING SKILL
Recognizing words with more than one meaning

It is important to know that in English, many words have more than one meaning. Sometimes the meanings are related and do not stop you from understanding. In other cases, the meanings are very different and could cause misunderstandings. For example, the noun *crash* has four different meanings: (1) a car accident; (2) a loud noise; (3) a sudden fall in the value of something; and (4) a sudden computer failure. Use the context to make sure you have the right meaning of a word. If it doesn't make sense, use a dictionary to check other meanings.

5 IDENTIFY Choose the correct meaning of the **bold** word.

1 I want to **see** if James has replied to my text.
   a find out   b watch
2 Sorry, I didn't get your **last** text. Can you resend it?
   a most recent   b only remaining
3 A cube has six **faces**, not four!
   a front of head   b side or surface
4 I like to add **borders** to my digital photos.
   a line between countries   b strip around the edge
5 Press the return **key** after you type your name.
   a piece of metal   b button on computer keyboard

6 APPLY Find these words in the text messages. Use the context to choose the correct meaning.

		Meaning
Conversation 1	plans	A maps
		B arrangements
Conversation 2	bad	A unpleasant
		B rotten
Conversation 3	engaged	A busy
		B agreed to marry someone
Conversation 4	spot	A small mark
		B particular place
Conversation 5	band	A group of musicians
		B strip of material or color

When Texting Goes Wrong!

It's easy to make a mistake when you are texting quickly or on the move. But you know when "autocomplete" tries to predict what you want to type…? I hate that! It's called *predictive texting*, but when the predictions are wrong, people can get confused. Sometimes I look at what I've written and think, *That can't be right*. Then I realize it's the autocorrect. We should get rid of it! Take a look at these examples I found, and see if you agree. If you get a chance, post some of your own.

1

Julie

Hi Simon. Mr. Norris wants to see the plans for the new office. Do you have them?

No, idiot.

Sorry Julie, I meant to say I don't!

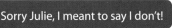

2

Leon

Hi Sarah. Sorry I couldn't come last night. I was sick – I think I ate some bad food.

Oh no, sorry to hear that! ☹ Get week soon!

3

Mateo Sánchez

Hello, is it possible to get an emergency appointment to see the dentist?

I'm sorry, he's engaged all day. What a bit tomorrow at noon?

 CDC

7 IDENTIFY Read the text messages. Find the words where autocorrect makes an incorrect prediction in each conversation. What should it be?

1 Conversation 1: *"No, idiot" should be "No, I don't."*
2 Conversation 2: _____
3 Conversation 3: _____
4 Conversation 4: _____
5 Conversation 5: _____

4

Steve

Hey Susie, I found a nice spot for the picnic on Sunday.

Great, where?

South Park. There's a picnic area by the river wide tables and benches.

5

Eva

Did you see the pics from the wedding? I posted them last night.

Yeah, you look great! The dress is amazing, and I love the hair band!

Soooo sorry you missed it! You shouldn't live so fat away!

Two friends in CapeTown, South Africa

8 EXPAND Read the whole text and answer the questions.

1 Why does the writer think predictive texting is bad?

   a because the predictions are wrong

   b because people get angry

   c because wrong predictions can confuse people

2 What does the writer want to happen?

   a for people to stop using predictive texting

   b for predictive texting to get better

   c for people to be more careful when texting

3 Which conversations are between friends or family members?

   a Conversations 1, 3, and 5

   b Conversations 2, 4, and 5

   c Conversations 2, 3, and 4

4 Which conversation includes a compliment?

   a Conversation 2

   b Conversation 4

   c Conversation 5

5 Which two conversations include a suggestion?

   a Conversations 1 and 3

   b Conversations 3 and 4

   c Conversations 4 and 5

9 WHAT'S YOUR ANGLE? Are you always careful when you send a text? Do you always correct any mistakes you make? Tell a partner.

 GRAMMAR IN CONTEXT *Must*, *have to*, and *can't*: **Deductions about the present**

We use *must* or *has/have to* when we are very sure something is true.

It **must** be the autocorrect.

We use *can't* when we are very sure something is not true. We don't use *mustn't* in this way.

That **can't** be right. ~~That musn't be right.~~

See Grammar focus on page 165.

10 APPLY Choose the correct options.

1 A: Ted still hasn't replied to my text.

   B: His phone *must / can't* be switched off. I just left him a voicemail.

2 A: The keypad on this phone's really small.

   B: That *have to / must* make it difficult to use.

3 A: These aren't my headphones.

   B: Oh. They *have to / can't* be someone else's then.

4 A: I got over 50 texts from friends on my birthday yesterday.

   B: Wow. That's a lot. You *must / can't* be very popular!

5 A: Justin just bought another cell phone.

   B: He *must / mustn't* be crazy. He already has two!

11 EXPAND Complete the dialogue with *can't*, *must*, or *have to*. Multiple answers may be possible.

A: This text [1]_____ be for someone else. I don't know anyone that has this number. It [2]_____ be for me.

B: Did you send a text or give your number to anyone recently?

A: Hmm. Well, actually yes. A friend of my brother, John. I gave him my number last weekend.

B: So it [3]_____ be from him then.

A: Look. Here's another one! I don't understand why…oh, wait a minute. It says J at the end. OK, so they [4]_____ be from him. Mystery solved!

 PRONUNCIATION SKILL Elision

🔊 When the /t/ or /d/ sound comes at the end of a word and the next word starts with a vowel sound, we pronounce the /t/ or /d/. For example:

Please ge͟t i͟n touch by email or sen͟d a͟ text.

However, when the next word starts with a consonant sound, we usually don't pronounce it.

*Can you ge**(t)** my re**(d)** pen from the desk?*

12 🔊 NOTICE Look at the dialogue in Exercise 11 again. Find words ending in /t/ or /d/ and decide if this final sound is pronounced or not. Then listen and check.

13 🔊 APPLY Listen and repeat the sentences from the dialogue that use elision.

14 INTERACT Practice the dialogue with a partner. Be sure to use elision.

15 WHAT'S YOUR ANGLE? When is it better to call someone rather than text? Are there things you don't like to say as a text message?

7.2 Changes Ahead

A hologram

A medical pod

1 ACTIVATE Look at the images. Is this how you imagine the future? What do you think the world will be like in 50 years' time?

GRAMMAR IN CONTEXT
Will and *might*: Predictions

We use *will* or *won't* to make guesses or predictions about the future.

What will life be like in the future?

We often use *I think/believe…* or *I don't think/believe…* to introduce a prediction.

I don't believe driverless cars will be popular.

We can use *will* + *probably* or *probably* + *won't* to make the prediction a little less certain. *Definitely* makes a prediction more certain.

People will probably live longer.
There probably won't be 3D-printed food.
Cities will definitely be much bigger.

We can use *might* or *might not* to make predictions we are less sure about.

People might travel less in the future.
Cars might not need drivers.

See Grammar focus on page 165.

2 APPLY Write the phrases in the correct order to find ten predictions.

1 holograms to attend / We will use / meetings without / leaving home.
2 and Mars on / vacation. / to the moon / People will go
3 in 3D-printed houses / We will live / 3D-printed furniture. / and use
4 they can download / 3D-printed food / Everyone will eat / in minutes.
5 Medical pods / health information. / very accurate / will help to provide
6 entire cities. / giant skyscrapers / There will be / the size of
7 People will live / buildings up to / in huge underground / 25 levels deep.
8 the oceans. / Huge underwater / cities will / be built in
9 will replace / Personal flying drones / cars.
10 be over / Most people / 100 years old. / will live to

3 EXPAND Complete the sentences using *will*, *won't*, *might*, or *might not*.

A: If you ask me, people ¹_____ be able to travel back in time. That's impossible!

B: I agree. And I don't think people ²_____ live on other planets, either.

A: Really? I'm not sure. We ³_____ have a choice, you know!

B: What do you mean?

A: Well, there are more and more people in the world. One day we ⁴_____ definitely have a problem. We ⁵_____ need to find somewhere for everyone to live.

B: Yes, but that ⁶_____ be on another planet. It's too difficult! We ⁷_____ probably live underwater, here on Earth. It's easier to build under the sea!

A: Maybe, but you never know. Space travel ⁸_____ become more common than you think!

4 INTERACT Which of the ten predictions from Exercise 2 do you think will come true? Why or why not? Discuss your ideas with a partner. Give your opinion using *will* or *might* and the phrases in the Grammar box.

I don't think people will eat 3D-printed food. It probably won't taste good.

I agree there might be underwater cities one day. There won't be anywhere else to live!

5 VOCABULARY Read the questionnaire. Then complete it with your own answers.

6 WHAT'S YOUR ANGLE? Work in pairs. Compare your answers. Do you share similar views of your future?

7 VOCABULARY Complete the collocations with the words and phrases in the box.

accurate	for certain	confident
doubt	evidence	as far as

Oxford 3000™

1 seriously _____ something
2 examine the _____
3 _____ I know
4 make an _____ prediction
5 know _____
6 be _____ that something is true

How Will
TECHNOLOGY Change Our Lives?

Bill Gates said, "We don't have the option of turning away from the future. No one gets to vote on whether technology is going to change our lives." While no one knows for certain what the future will bring, technology will definitely cause change. But how? Answer the questions to share your vision of the future.

1 We _____ vacation in space.
   a will   b probably won't   c won't

2 Robot doctors _____ be better than human doctors.
   a will   b might   c won't

3 Spaceships or flying cars _____ replace cars.
   a will   b might   c won't

4 We _____ live in houses anymore.
   a will   b probably won't   c won't

5 We _____ discover evidence of life on other planets.
   a will   b might   c won't

6 Which prediction do you doubt the most? Why?

7 Which prediction are you most confident about? Why?

8 BUILD Use words and phrases from the box in Exercise 7 to complete these sentences.

1 I really hope we'll find _____ of life on other planets. I definitely think there is life out there!

2 I'm _____ that medication will be more effective and equipment in hospitals will be more advanced.

3 I know people think we'll all have spaceships, but _____ I'm concerned, there's nothing that can replace the car.

4 I think it might be possible to go to the moon for a short time, but I _____ I'll be able to afford it because it will be very expensive.

5 I think technology will definitely become more important for our health. We will all carry tiny computers that will record everything we do and keep _____ information about us.

6 Well, I can't say _____, but I hope I'll have a nice house in the country. There might be huge skyscrapers, but I don't want to live in one!

WRITING SKILL Checking your work: Punctuation

Punctuation shows the reader the structure of the sentence and makes it easier for readers to understand your writing. Making mistakes with punctuation looks unprofessional and gives a bad impression.

---

9 IDENTIFY Study the first paragraph of the questionnaire in Exercise 5 and notice the use of punctuation. Which punctuation features can you find?

"" quotation marks   .   period

!   exclamation point   ,   comma

?   question mark   A   capital letter

10 ASSESS Write each punctuation feature next to the correct use.

1 To mark the beginning of a sentence: _____

2 To mark the end of a sentence: _____

3 To mark the beginning and end of a quote: _____

4 To mark pauses in a sentence: _____

5 To signal a question: _____

6 To signal emotion: _____

11 IDENTIFY We also use capital letters for names, titles, cities, countries, and languages. Find the examples of each use in this sentence.

Dr. Jaira Marquez from Puebla in Mexico can speak English, Spanish, and Portuguese.

---

12 APPLY Rewrite these sentences using correct punctuation.

Bad Predictions!

1 in 1943 thomas watson chairman of IBM famously said I think there is a world market for maybe five computers

2 according to a western union memo written in 1876 the telephone has too many disadvantages to be seriously considered as a means of communication

3 when decca recording company rejected the beatles in 1962 they wrote we don't like their sound and guitar music is on the way out

4 a rocket will never be able to function in space predicted the new york times in 1936

5 it will be many years before a woman will become prime minister said margaret thatcher in 1974 she was prime minister of the united kingdom from 1979 to 1990

13 PREPARE How do you think life might be different in the future? Choose one of the topics or your own topic, and note your ideas.

the environment   globalization

future cities   space exploration

your own topic:

14 PLAN You are going to write a short questionnaire to find out about people's attitudes toward the future. Think of a title for your topic, and write a short introduction. Use the model in Exercise 5 to help you.

15 WRITE Use your notes in Exercise 13 to make a list of questions to ask. Use *will/might*, and follow the guidance below.

Keep questions simple.

Use a mix of open questions (*wh-* questions) and closed questions (*yes/no, agree/disagree*).

Make sure each question focuses on one point only.

Write six to eight questions.

16 ASSESS Exchange your questionnaire with a partner. Use the checklist to review your partner's work.

☐ Is the punctuation correct?

☐ Is there a mix of different question types?

☐ Does each question focus on only one point?

☐ Are the questions simple?

☐ Are *will* and *might* used correctly?

17 IMPROVE Ask your partner for their feedback. Find ways to improve your questionnaire.

18 SHARE Find out about your attitude toward the future. Complete the surveys of three other students.

19 WHAT'S YOUR ANGLE? Put your questionnaire online and ask your friends to complete it.

7.3 The Future of Language

1 ACTIVATE English is a global language. Why do you think so many people around the world speak English? How many reasons can you think of?

2 INTERACT How popular is English in your country? How do you think English will help you in your life? Share your ideas with a group.

3 EXPAND Read the text. Decide which language each list of loanwords comes from. Compare your answers with a partner.

Arabic	Italian	French	German	Chinese	Dutch

 A loanword is a word that one language takes from another. For example, in English, the word *garage* is from French. Some loanwords keep their pronunciation, grammar, and meaning, but most change their spelling and pronunciation to fit the rules of the language they move to. This process often takes years.

—adapted from *Concise Oxford Companion to the English Language,* edited by Tom McArthur

	broccoli, balcony, pizza, umbrella
	mayonnaise, niece, souvenir, restaurant
	coffee, cola, cotton, sofa
	cookie, cruise, leak, yacht
	delicatessen, frankfurter, hamburger, kindergarten
	ketchup, silk, tea, tofu

4 WHAT'S YOUR ANGLE? Do you use any English loanwords in your language?

5 VOCABULARY Match the words with their definitions.

accent	translation	global	generation
pronunciation	adopt	billion	

Oxford 3000™

1 all the people who were born around the same time (n) ___

2 way of speaking which shows where you are from (n) ___

3 one thousand million = 1,000,000,000 (number) ___

4 the process of changing words in one language to words in another language (n) ___

5 covering the whole world (adj) ___

6 the way in which something is pronounced (n) ___

7 to start using a particular thing or method (v) ___

6 USE Complete the sentences using words from Exercise 5. Change the form where necessary.

1 It's not your _____ that is important when speaking another language; it's your _____. If you pronounce the words correctly, people will understand you.

2 Schools have _____ a new way of language learning that focuses on speaking and communication skills.

3 English is spoken by more than one and a half _____ people in the world.

4 Social media allows us to feel like we're part of a _____ community.

5 There are many English _____ of novels written by authors such as Tolstoy and Flaubert.

6 Languages change over time: people from different _____ sometimes don't understand each other!

LISTENING SKILL Listening for main ideas

It isn't always necessary to understand all the information you hear. Knowing how to listen for the main ideas can help your listening comprehension. To listen for main ideas, focus on the general topics and don't worry about the details.

7 IDENTIFY Listen to the first part of a student's presentation. Choose the two main ideas.

☐ A Languages are always changing.

☐ B There is more than one kind of English.

☐ C Different accents are hard to understand.

☐ D Lots of people speak English, but that might change.

8 🔊 **APPLY** Read the summaries, then listen to the second part of the presentation. Which summary best describes the presentation?

Summary A

The student talks about how the number of languages in the world will decrease in the future. Then he suggests that creating a new language will help global communication.

Summary B

The student predicts that the number of languages will decrease, and Chinese or Arabic might take over. Then he suggests that loanwords can make learning a language and translation easier.

Summary C

The student thinks that English will kill other languages unless we create a new language that is easier to learn and can help international communication.

9 🔊 **EXPAND** Listen to the whole presentation and answer the questions.

1 How many English speakers are there today?
2 What three things can be different from one kind of English to another?
3 How many kinds of English are there in the world?
4 Which is the fastest growing language today?
5 What two Arabic loanwords does the speaker mention?

10 WHAT'S YOUR ANGLE? Discuss these questions.

1 What are the problems with translation?
2 Do you always understand people who speak the same language?
3 Is a single global language a good idea? Why or why not?

GRAMMAR IN CONTEXT
Adverbs: *A little, pretty, much,* and *really*

We can use the adverbs *pretty, a little,* and *really* + adjective after the verb *be*.

*All the Englishes are **a little** different.*
*Both those predictions are **really** worrying.*

We can also use *pretty* and *really* before adjective + noun.

*That's a **pretty** large number.*

We can use *a little* + negative adjective after the verb *be*.

*I'm **a little** concerned about the future of language.*

We can use the adverbs *a little* or *much* + comparative adjective. We often use *than* after a comparative adjective.

*This new language will be **much** easier to learn than English.*

See Grammar focus on page 165.

11 USE Choose the correct answer.

1 Visiting the country is a *really / much* good way to learn a language.
2 Learning a language can be *much / a little* difficult when you are older.
3 It's important to have *a little / a really* good dictionary.
4 Studying vocabulary is much more useful *as / than* grammar.
5 You should make progress quickly if you study *really / a really* hard.
6 Online learning is becoming *much / pretty* popular these days.
7 It's much *more / a little* interesting to study in groups than alone.
8 It's *pretty / little* embarrassing to make mistakes when speaking a foreign language.

12 DEVELOP When you watch a movie in English, do you prefer to watch it with subtitles? Think about the benefits and problems. Write four sentences using *a little, pretty, much,* and *really*.

1 Sometimes I use subtitles because I get really frustrated when I can't understand what the actors are saying.

13 INTERACT Share your ideas with the class. Take a vote to find how many people like subtitles.

14 WHAT'S YOUR ANGLE? Read the quote. What do you think of people you meet who can't speak your language? Do you think everyone should learn a second language?

"If you talk to a man in a language he understands, that goes to his head. If you talk to him in his language, that goes to his heart."

—Nelson Mandela

7.4 I'm Not Sure about That

1 ACTIVATE How open are you to new ideas or other people's opinions? Complete the questionnaire, and then discuss in a group. What do your answers say about you?

	Strongly agree	Agree	Neutral	Disagree	Strongly disagree
1 In a discussion, I do most of the talking.	☐	☐	☐	☐	☐
2 I can express my opinion confidently.	☐	☐	☐	☐	☐
3 I don't usually change my mind.	☐	☐	☐	☐	☐
4 I am always honest about what I think.	☐	☐	☐	☐	☐
5 I often take advice from other people.	☐	☐	☐	☐	☐
6 I listen to others and give them time to talk.	☐	☐	☐	☐	☐

2 INTERACT What do you do when you disagree with someone? Do you always tell them? Why or why not? How do you feel when someone disagrees with you?

3 ▶ IDENTIFY Watch the video and choose your answers.

	Jenna	Sam	Andy	Cathy
1 Who has taken the reading strategies workshop?	☐	☐	☐	☐
2 Who thinks the reading workshop will be boring?	☐	☐	☐	☐
3 Who feels reading strategies are important?	☐	☐	☐	☐
4 Who prefers writing to reading?	☐	☐	☐	☐
5 Who will email to explain their preference?	☐	☐	☐	☐

If you disagree with someone, the topic, situation, and your relationship with the person influence how you choose to disagree. For differences of opinion about a serious topic or a disagreement with your boss, you may try to avoid disagreement by being less direct. Being less direct often means using sentences that are more complex to avoid saying that you disagree directly or suggesting that you are unsure about your position.

I'm not sure if I agree.   *Have you thought about...?*

For simple topics or with someone you know well, you can be more direct by saying that you disagree and using shorter sentences. In those situations, it's common to say *Really?* to show you disagree. In either case, try to show that you understand the other person's opinion before you disagree.

4 **EXPAND** Look at these expressions from the video. Write each expression in the correct place in the chart.

I see what you're saying, but...	I'm not sure about that
Could you explain your thinking?	I don't agree at all.

Function	More Direct	Less Direct
Disagreeing	1	2
	I'm sorry, but I don't see it that way.	Hmm. That's not quite what I think.
Accepting but disagreeing	Yeah, but don't you think...	Really? I agree with that, but...
	Well, that's a good point, but...	3
Asking for an explanation	What makes you think that?	Would you mind saying more?
	Why do you say that?	4

5 **ASSESS** Find these phrases in Exercise 4: *Well, Hmm, What?,* and *Really?* What purpose do they have?

6 ▶ **ANALYZE** Watch the video again. Notice how the strategies and expressions help people to disagree with each other. Who is the most direct: Sam, Andy, or Jenna?

7 **INTEGRATE** Which is more important for you: improving your reading or writing? Tell a partner and explain your reasons. Do you share the same opinion?

8 **INTERACT** Work in groups. For each statement, choose a situation (A or B) and discuss your ideas. When you disagree, use the strategies and expressions you have learned. Be more or less direct according to the situation.

Situation A: You are a group of friends sitting in a coffee shop. You all know each other well.

Situation B: You are a group of employees talking together during a work break. Some people are from a different department, and you don't know them well.

1   We will discover evidence of life on other planets.
2   Scientists will soon develop a cure for cancer.
3   One day people will do all their shopping online.
4   University education should be free for everybody.

GO ONLINE
to create your own version
of the English For Real video.

7.5 I Will, I Might

1 ACTIVATE Are you someone who has lots of goals and ambitions? Do you plan things, or do you let things happen?

2 INTERACT Complete these sentences, so they are true for you. Then compare your answers with a partner. Who is more relaxed about the future, you or your partner?

1 I get worried if I *do / don't* have plans for the weekend.
2 *I'll probably / I'll definitely / I might* get a new job in the next year.
3 I get excited about *planning vacations / going on spontaneous trips.*
4 *I'll definitely / I might / I definitely won't* be busy this evening.
5 I *do / don't* have a plan for my career.

3 **IDENTIFY** Listen to the conversation between a career advisor and a client, Josh. How similar is Josh's attitude to yours?

4 **EXPAND** Listen again and complete the information about Josh.

Westward Careers Center
Client Information Form

Name: Josh Saunders
Age: 24
Occupation: ¹_____
Reason for visit: isn't very good at ²_____
    and needs help making a ³_____
Interests: ⁴_____ –
    Josh would like to be a ⁵_____
Action: Josh is going to do some ⁶_____
    and then come back for more advice.

5 **WHAT'S YOUR ANGLE?** Have you ever seen a career advisor? Who do you speak to when you want advice about work or study?

SPEAKING
Expressing worries, doubts, and problems

To express worries, you can use *I'm worried about +* noun/(*not*) *-ing* verb.
I'm worried about my grades.
I'm worried about not having enough time.

To express uncertainty or doubt, you can use phrases such as *I'm not (really) sure* and *I doubt that + (it) will.*
I'm not really sure it's the best option for me.
I doubt that being a manager will make me happy.

Use *will probably/definitely* and *might* to talk about possible problems.
It will probably be hard to get a good job.
It might not pay very well.

6 PREPARE Is there anything you need help planning? Use the ideas below or think of your own idea.

a vacation or trip	a celebration
career	exam revision
study project	special event (e.g., a wedding)

7 DEVELOP Make some notes on what kind of help you need, possible problems, your worries, and what the timescale is.

I need help with: _____

Possible problems and worries: _____

_____

Timescale (date of event or deadline): _____

8 INTERACT Walk around the class. Find someone who has experience or information that can help you. Ask them questions and complete the form below for your action plan. Be prepared to answer someone else's questions and help them complete their plan.

First step: _____

I need to know: _____

I will do: _____

9 SHARE How many people completed their plans? Who got the most interesting advice? Whose advice was the most helpful?

Now go to page 153 for the Unit 7 Review.

8 Consumption

What kind of consumer is this man?

How do the media and advertising influence us?

In what ways can consumption make people feel disappointed?

BEHIND THE PHOTO

1 Think about the things you spend your money on every month. How much do they cost? Complete the table below and then compare your expenses with a group.

cell phone _____ clothes _____ education _____ electricity _____

entertainment _____ food _____ Internet _____ transportation _____

other: _____

2 Where do you like to do most of your shopping? Explain your reasons in groups.

online from small, local stores at discount stores

from large department stores at designer stores at big malls

8.1 It's the Wrong Size!

1 ACTIVATE When you buy clothes, how important are these things to you? Number these factors in order (1–5).

a Price ___
b Quality ___
c Fashion ___
d Designer ___
e Comfort ___

2 VOCABULARY Match the words and phrases.

1	impress	a	**exchange** something
2	the **latest**	b	and **match**
3	**mix**	c	someone
4	try to	d	fashion
5	follow	e	a refund
6	keep	f	name
7	ask for	g	within **budget**
8	**brand**	h	a **trend**

🍃 Oxford 3000™

3 BUILD Complete these statements using words from Exercise 2.

1 I prefer to buy presents that are from a well-known _____.

2 I never _____ something if I get it as a gift.

3 When I am not happy with a product, I ask for a _____.

4 If I don't have a _____ for clothes and shoes, I spend too much!

5 I try to give presents that will _____ people.

6 I often choose colors that _____ my eyes or hair.

7 _____ is very important to me.

8 One _____ I definitely don't follow is wearing clothes that look old!

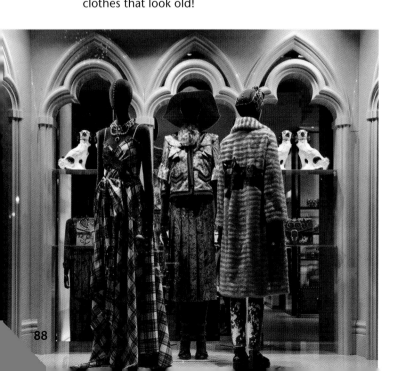

4 USE Choose the statements in Exercise 3 that you agree with. Then compare your answers with a partner.

5 🔊 IDENTIFY Listen to the conversation between a store manager and a customer. What does the customer want and why?

◉ LISTENING SKILL
Recognizing statements used as questions

🔊 Speakers can use intonation to turn statements into questions. Usually, statements have a falling intonation. For example:

It was a present.

When the speaker wants to check that the information is correct, they can use a rising intonation on the final stressed syllable:

It was a present?

If they want to express surprise, they can use a rising intonation at the end of the sentence:

You can't give me a refund?

Listening for the intonation will help you understand when someone is using a statement as a question.

---

6 🔊 NOTICE Listen to each sentence twice. Notice the intonation. Does it fall for a statement or rise for a question? Add a period (.) or a question mark (?) at the end of each sentence.

1 A: You don't have a receipt
  B: You don't have a receipt
2 A: It's the wrong size
  B: It's the wrong size
3 A: It was a present
  B: It was a present
4 A: You're the manager
  B: You're the manager
5 A: That's the store policy
  B: That's the store policy

7 INTERACT Work in pairs. Take turns saying one of the sentences in Exercise 6. Can your partner identify if you are making a statement or asking a question?

We use *can, could,* and *may* to ask for and give permission to do something. To make our requests sound more formal or polite, we use *could*. We use *can / can't* to reply to requests with *could*. One of the most polite or formal ways is with the modal verb *may*.

Requests

Can you help me? Yes, I can.

Could I have a refund? No, I'm sorry you can't. (more polite / formal)

May I see your receipt, please? Yes, you may. (very polite / formal)

Giving permission

You **can** leave your sweater here.

Customers **may not** eat or drink in this store. (more formal)

See Grammar focus on page 166.

8 ◀» **INTEGRATE** Listen to the conversation again and answer the questions.

1 What does the store manager ask to see?
2 How much money does the customer want?
3 Who does the customer ask to see?
4 What does the manager offer instead?
5 Does the customer agree?

9 WHAT'S YOUR ANGLE? Ask and answer the questions with a partner.

1 What do you usually give as gifts?
2 How do you decide what to give people?
3 Are you good at choosing gifts for your friends?
4 Have you ever received a gift that you didn't like? What did you do?

10 ASSESS Decide if the statement is formal (F) or informal (I).

1 Can I have this blue sweater? ___
2 Customers without a receipt may not have a refund. ___
3 Could you show me those brown shoes, please? ___
4 May I help you? ___
5 You can pay by credit card. That's fine. ___

11 EXPAND Correct the mistake in each sentence.

1 In summer, staff may to wear short-sleeved shirts.
2 Couldn't I get a discount?
3 Do I can help you with these bags?
4 A: Can I pay here?
   B: No, sorry you can.
5 A: Can I please try on this sweater?
   B: Yes, you could.

In English, we pronounce the important words, often called content words, more loudly and clearly than other words in the sentence. Content words can be nouns, verbs, adjectives, adverbs, negatives, and longer prepositions and conjunctions. They give the most meaning to the sentence. Stressing these words helps the listener to identify the key information and makes it easier to understand.

12 ◀» **NOTICE** Listen to these sentences from the listening. Identify the words that have stress.

1 May I see your receipt?
2 You can leave your sweater here.
3 You can exchange it for a different size.
4 A friend of mine gave me this sweater as a present.
5 I can't give a refund without a receipt.

13 ◀» **IDENTIFY** Look at these sentences from the listening. With a partner, decide which words have more stress. Then listen and check.

1 What can I do for you?
2 To tell you the truth, it's not my style.
3 May I see the manager?
4 I understand, but I need a receipt to process a refund.
5 You can choose anything from the store of the same value.

14 APPLY Practice saying the sentences in Exercises 12 and 13. Be sure to stress the content words.

15 INTERACT Role-play a conversation between a store assistant and a customer. Use the words and phrases above to help you. Use formal language, and stress the content words.

Student A: You want to return an item. Decide what it is and why you want to return it.

Student B: You work in the store. You do not want to give a refund.

16 WHAT'S YOUR ANGLE? What was the last item you returned to a store? Why did you return it? Did you ask for a refund or an exchange?

8.2 Food Matters

1 ACTIVATE Discuss the questions.

1 What does *healthy eating* mean? How important is eating healthily?
2 Why might some people not get enough to eat?
3 Do you know any food charities? What do they do?

2 ASSESS Read the title and the first paragraph of the food blog. What does the charity do and who does it help?

Home	About		Search

Citymeals on Wheels: My New Heroes

1.4 million elderly people (60+) living in the city – that's over 17% of the city's population

One of the great things about writing this food blog is learning about amazing organizations. Citymeals on Wheels is one of the largest meals-on-wheels programs in the United States. The team there delivers over two million meals by hand every year to more than 18,000 elderly New Yorkers.

Gael Greene, a restaurant critic, and James Beard, cookbook author, started the organization back in 1981. They were shocked to learn that budget cuts meant that many elderly New Yorkers had nothing to eat on weekends and holidays. So they decided to do something. By asking friends and co-workers in the food community, they were able to raise $30,000 to help them give a meal to 6,000 elderly people! Since then, the operation has grown, and the demand is now far greater. The number of elderly people in New York is rising. Most people the organization helps are in their eighties. Thanks to Citymeals delivering a simple meal every day, thousands of elderly people are able to stay in their own homes and neighborhoods even though they can no longer shop or cook for themselves.

I wasn't able to get an interview with Gael or James, but you can find more information on their website. Citymeals is always looking for donations and volunteers, so help if you can.

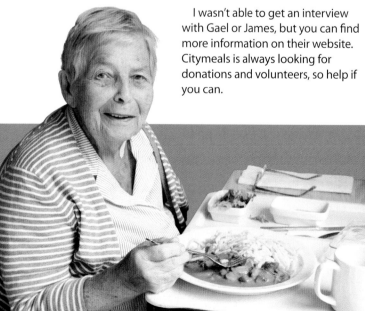

PROGRAM COORDINATION $1,521,299
FRIENDLY VISITING $476,639
WEEKEND MEALS $9,278,166
MOBILE FOOD PANTRY $463,589
HOLIDAY MEALS $259,498
HOLIDAY BOX MEALS $3,183,912
EMERGENCY FOOD PACKAGE MEALS $2,121,032

TOTAL PROGRAM EXPENSES $17,304,135

THE BRONX
MANHATTAN
QUEENS
BROOKLYN
STATEN ISLAND

	MEALS SERVED	MEALS RECIPIENTS
MANHATTAN	598,229	4,356
THE BRONX	315,211	2,677
QUEENS	557,204	4,819
BROOKLYN	660,991	5,273
STATEN ISLAND	83,061	1,289

3 APPLY Read the questions and decide which ones you think will be answered in the text, and which ones in the graphics. Why do you think so?

1 Who is Gael Greene?
2 Why did Gael and James start Citymeals?
3 What are the program's total expenses?
4 Where did they get the money to start the project?
5 How much does Citymeals spend on weekend meals?
6 How many people receive meals from Citymeals in Manhattan?
7 How old is the typical person they serve?
8 What does Citymeals always need?

4 DEVELOP Use the text and graphics to answer the questions in Exercise 3.

5 WHAT'S YOUR ANGLE? Have you ever cooked for an elderly relative or neighbor? What other kind of help might elderly people need?

> **GRAMMAR IN CONTEXT** *Be able to*: Ability and possibility (present, past, and future)
>
> We use *be able to* for abilities and possibilities in the present and past in formal language.
>
> *Thanks to Citymeals, elderly people **are able to** stay in their own homes.*
> *They **were able to** raise $30,000 from the food community.*
>
> We use *be able to*, not *can*, when we are talking about abilities and possibilities in the future.
>
> *Citymeals **will be able to** help more people in the future.*

See Grammar focus on page 166.

6 APPLY Choose the correct options.

1 According to the *Hunger in America* study series, over 46 million Americans *aren't / weren't* able to get enough to eat last year.
2 However, people who do not have enough food *are / will* able to get help from many different organizations.
3 These organizations *will able to / are able to* work together through the Feeding America program to help feed those in need.
4 City Harvest takes food that restaurants and stores *aren't / won't* able to sell and gives these to thousands of community programs around the country.
5 Organizations like these *can / will be able to* help more and more Americans in the years ahead through the Feeding America program.

7 EXPAND Complete the text with the correct form of *be able to*.

Organic Food

Although organic foods are generally more expensive and not everyone [1]_____ afford them, many people choose organic foods as an alternative to factory food production or because they think it's healthier. The organic food business in the United States is worth around $10 billion a year and rising. However, some people worry that in the years ahead, traditional small farms [2]_____ compete with the larger food companies. Major food companies have already bought some traditional organic food businesses because they [3]_____ continue alone. Organic food producers also worry that large multinational companies [4]_____ find ways to break the rules. As the organic food industry grows, local organic producers worry people [5]_____ "think globally and eat locally" anymore.

—adapted from *The Oxford Encyclopedia of Food and Drink in America*, 2nd ed., edited by Andrew F. Smith

8 WHAT'S YOUR ANGLE? Have you ever bought any organic food? Why or why not? Do you think that you are a healthy eater?

9 **INTERACT** How important is food in your life? Ask and answer the questions with a partner. Who is the biggest "foodie"?

Food Quiz

1 Do you like watching cooking shows on TV?

2 When you eat out, do you order something different each time?

3 Have you ever baked your own bread?

4 Do you know more than five recipes by heart?

5 Do you always have fresh ingredients in your fridge?

6 Have you ever taken cooking classes?

7 Do you own any cookbooks?

8 Have you ever eaten raw fish or meat?

9 Which of these kinds of food do you like?
- sweet foods, such as chocolate and cakes
- salty foods, such as potato chips
- spicy foods, such as *chili con carne*
- sour foods, such as lemons and natural yogurt

10 Do you own any expensive kitchen equipment?

Score
Give yourself one point for each "yes" answer.
0-4 points: For you, food is fuel.
5-8 points: You like your food, but you don't live to eat.
9+ points: You are a real food lover, and *foodie* is your middle name!

Oxford 3000™

A customer enjoys food at a restaurant in Ho Chi Minh City, Vietnam

10 **VOCABULARY** Match each word to a definition.

1	eat out	a	items that make up a dish
2	bake	b	flavored with spices
3	recipe	c	eat in a café or restaurant
4	ingredients	d	acidic in flavor
5	raw	e	cook in the oven
6	salty	f	flavored with salt
7	spicy	g	not cooked
8	sour	h	instructions for making a dish

11 **BUILD** Work in pairs. Use the words in Exercise 10 to complete each sentence.

Kitchen Tips Every Cook MUST Know

Here are some great tips from our readers. Try them!

I get all my ^{1}_____ ready before I start cooking. That way I know I have everything that's in the ^{2}_____.
—*Jay*

When you want to ^{3}_____ a cake, don't use too much sugar. A great cake shouldn't be too sweet!
—*Shannon*

Put lemon juice on fruit salad. It stops the fruit from going brown. But don't use too much or it will taste ^{4}_____.
—*Steph*

When you cook a steak, add some soy sauce at the end. The ^{5}_____ flavor makes the steak really tasty!
—*Mike*

When you cook with chili peppers, add a little at a time. You don't want it to be too ^{6}_____!
—*Luis*

And finally...

When all you have in the kitchen are ^{7}_____ potatoes, give yourself a break and ^{8}_____ _____ for once!
—*Margo*

12 **WHAT'S YOUR ANGLE?** What's your favorite dish to cook or bake? Explain how to make it and describe how it tastes!

WHAT IS IMPORTANT TO CONSUMERS?

	15–24	25–34	35–44	45–54	55–64
CLOTHING	🏷️ 👁️ $	🏷️ 👁️ $	⭐ $	⭐ $	⭐ $
CARS	🏷️ 👁️ $	🏷️ ⚙️ $	⚙️ $	🏷️ ⚙️	⚙️ ⭐ $
TECHNOLOGY	🏷️ ⚙️	🏷️ ⚙️	🏷️ ⚙️	⭐ ⚙️	⭐ ⚙️
BEAUTY SUPPLIES	🏷️ $	🏷️ $	$ ⭐	⭐ $	⭐ $

VALUES
- $ Price
- ⚙️ Features
- 🏷️ Brand
- ⭐ Quality
- 👁️ Appearance

1 ACTIVATE Ask and answer the questions.

1 Do you sometimes buy things you don't need because they are new?

2 Are expensive brands better than cheaper ones?

3 Do you ever buy things because you want to impress people?

2 EXPAND Study the infographic. Decide if the statements are true (T) or false (F).

1 When consumers aged 15–24 and 25–34 buy clothing, price is more important than the quality of the product. ___

2 Consumers aged 35–44 value brand less than price when shopping for technology. ___

3 Quality is most important to consumers aged 55–64. ___

4 Consumers aged 15–24 and 25–34 have similar preferences. ___

5 When buying bath and beauty products, quality is important to consumers of all ages. ___

6 For most consumers of all ages, price is important whatever they buy. ___

3 WHAT'S YOUR ANGLE? Are you a typical consumer for your age? Share your opinions in groups.

VOCABULARY DEVELOPMENT Prefixes

A prefix comes at the beginning of a word. Adding a prefix to a word changes the meaning of the word. Study these common prefixes and their meanings:

Prefix	Meaning	Example
anti-	against	anti-consumer
pro-	in favor of	pro-growth
over-	too much	overpriced
under-	not enough	underpaid
post-	after	postmodern
pre-	before	pre-tablet

4 BUILD Complete the sentences using the highlighted words in the Vocabulary Development box.

1 All the things in this store are _____.
2 The government is taking action to stop _____ activities by some businesses.
3 In the _____ days, we all had to carry very heavy laptops.
4 Lots of employees complain they are _____ and overworked.
5 The _____ policies of the government were successful.
6 The works of _____ artists such as Damian Hirst and Jeff Koons sell for millions of dollars.

5 USE Work in pairs. Discuss which of the prefixes in the box can go with these words. Make a sentence to show their meaning.

estimate	eat	use	government
war	graduate	cook	weight

You should not underestimate the importance of saving money.

GRAMMAR IN CONTEXT
May, *might*, and *could*: Possibility

We use *may*, *might* and *could* to talk about possibility in the present and future and to make deductions.

People buy smartphones even though they may not need one. (present)
Smartphones might be essential one day. (future)
Think of the money you could save. (future)

Note: We don't use *could not* to express possibility. We use it when we are certain that something is impossible.

Most people could not imagine life without their smartphone.

Questions about deduction/possibility usually start with an opening phrase or *could*.

Do you think people could live without smartphones? / Could people live without smartphones?

Using *might/may* sounds too formal for most contexts.

See Grammar focus on page 166.

6 IDENTIFY Read these statements. Decide if each statement refers to the present (P) or future (F).

1 Natural resources like oil and coal might run out in my lifetime. ___
2 A simple life may be best, but it's hard to achieve. ___
3 One day the population could become too big for the planet. ___
4 It may not be possible to reduce pollution. ___

7 INTERACT Choose the statements in Exercise 6 you agree with. Then tell a partner.

8 DEVELOP Choose the correct options.

1 Have you ever bought something knowing that you *could not / may* never use it?
2 There *might / may not* be good reasons to trust certain brands.
3 Do you think consumers *may / could not* be influenced by advertising?
4 This *might not / could not* be a good time to think about buying a new car.
5 *Could / Might* the price of smartphones drop soon?
6 Consumers *might not / could not* buy designer clothes if they have low salaries.

WRITING SKILL Giving opinions

When you give your opinion on a topic, it is important to explain the reasons for your opinion and support it with examples. You should also make sure that it is well organized, so each main point is clear for the reader. Doing this will help the reader understand your opinion more easily.

Giving your opinion: *I think / I (strongly) believe / In my opinion*

Supporting your opinion: *For example / For instance / An example of this is…*

Structuring your writing: *Lastly / Finally / In conclusion*

9 NOTICE Read the essay. Find examples of the language in the Writing Skill box.

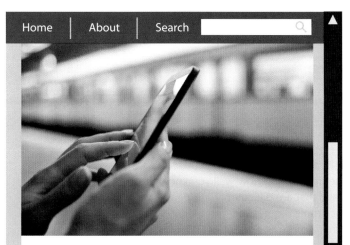

Home	About	Search	

These days, most people could not imagine life without their smartphone. I would like to explore the popularity of smartphones and ask whether we overestimate their importance. A lot of people have them, but do we really need smartphones?

In my opinion, smartphones are simply overpriced fashion accessories. For example, when a new model is available, some people immediately want to buy it. Most smartphone functions are underused because all people really need them to do is check social media and take selfies.

Secondly, a smartphone is expensive to buy, and when the technology goes wrong or it breaks, it is expensive to fix. Think of the money you could save if you didn't have one. In addition, people waste a lot of time on their smartphones texting friends or playing games. How much more work might you be able to do without a smartphone to distract you?

In conclusion, I believe a lot of people buy smartphones even though they may not need them. It is true that smartphones may be essential one day, but that day hasn't arrived yet. Life might be better without them.

10 EXPAND How many reasons for not having a smartphone does the writer give?

11 WHAT'S YOUR ANGLE? Do you agree with the essay? Is having a smartphone necessary, or could you live without one?

12 PREPARE Prepare to write an opinion essay. Choose one of the products below or your own idea. Is it an example of something necessary or unnecessary? Make notes of your opinion, giving examples to support your reasons.

13 WRITE Write an opinion essay of 175–200 words. When you finish, use the checklist below to review your work. Can you improve your essay?

- ☐ Is the essay well organized?
- ☐ Are the points you make clear?
- ☐ Did you give examples to support your opinions?
- ☐ Have you correctly used modals for possibility?
- ☐ Did you use any prefixes?
- ☐ Have your written about 200 words?

14 SHARE Work in groups. Exchange your essay with your classmates, and read each other's work. Who shares a similar opinion to you?

8.4 Is That All Right with You?

1 ▶ **ACTIVATE** Watch the video. Answer the questions.

1   What drinks do Andy and Max ask Kevin to buy for them?
2   How much money does Andy give Kevin?
3   What does Andy ask the student to do?
4   What does Andy ask Kevin to get before he sits down?

REAL-WORLD ENGLISH   Making requests

When you ask someone to do something, the language you use depends on how well you know the person as well as the kind of request you are making. For requests that are difficult or with people you don't know well, soften the request by making it less direct. For simple requests or with people you know well, this is less important. Look at the different ways to ask someone to turn their music down (simple request):

Turn your music down! (very direct)
Could you turn your music down? (direct)
I'm sorry to bother you, but would you mind turning your music down? (less direct)

Making the request a question gives the other person the chance to decide. People also apologize when making a request. It is common to begin a request with *I'm (very) sorry, but….* Using *do you mind* (polite) and *would you mind* (more polite) can soften the request.

2 **ANALYZE** Look at these expressions you can use when you want to ask someone to do something. How direct or polite are they? Choose your answers.

Request form	Direct			Polite
a Could you possibly…?	1	2	3	4
b Could you…?	1	2	3	4
c Would it be possible for you to…?	1	2	3	4
d Do you think you could…?	1	2	3	4
e Would you mind…-ing?	1	2	3	4
f Do you mind…-ing?	1	2	3	4
g Can you…?	1	2	3	4
h Give me…	1	2	3	4

ENGLISH FOR REAL

3 ▶ **IDENTIFY** Watch the video again. Complete the requests.

1 _____ get me a coffee, too?
2 _____ get me a tea?
3 _____ for you to turn the volume down?
4 _____ the sugar from over there.
5 _____ get some milk, too?

4 **ASSESS** Why is Andy's request for sugar different from his request for milk?

5 **ANALYZE** Study the requests in Exercise 3. Which request form is different from the others? Why?

6 **APPLY** Put the words in order to make requests.

a carry these / the car? / help me / can you / bags to
b mind moving / off the table? / do you / your books
c canned tomatoes / where the / show me / are? / could you
d would you / mind / a package / from the / getting / mailroom?
e would it / for you / a taxi / be possible / for five o'clock? / to book

7 **EXPAND** Match each request in Exercise 6 with a situation (a–e).

1 A customer is asking for help from a store clerk.
2 A hotel guest is speaking with a receptionist.
3 A parent and child are walking out of a grocery store.
4 A student is speaking to his roommate.
5 An office worker is speaking with a co-worker.

REAL-WORLD ENGLISH Confirming acceptance

If a person seems hesitant when saying yes, it is a good idea to confirm that the person is willing to accept the request. The way a person responds the first time you ask for something can tell you how willing they are to accept. If the person hesitates or pauses, it could mean that they don't want to accept. Asking again will give them an opportunity to reject the request or add conditions to the request.

(request) *Could you get me a tea?*
(hesitating) *Uh, OK.*
(confirming) *Are you sure?*
(conditions) *Yeah, but do you have any money?*

---

8 ◀ **EXPAND** Listen to three short conversations. How willing is the person to accept the request?

		Willing	Unwilling
1	Two roommates	☐	☐
2	Two co-workers	☐	☐
3	Two family members	☐	☐

9 ◀ **IDENTIFY** Listen again. Which expressions for confirming do you hear?

☐ Are you sure?
☐ Is that OK?
☐ Is that all right with you?
☐ Are you sure that's OK?
☐ Are you sure you don't mind?
☐ Would that be all right?

10 **INTERACT** Work in pairs. Look at the relationships in Exercise 8, and think of a new situation. Prepare a role play.

■ Think of a request. How easy or difficult is it?
■ How willing is the person to agree? Do they have any conditions?
■ What expressions are suitable for the relationship and context?

11 **SHARE** Role-play your conversation for the class.

GO ONLINE
to create your own version
of the English For Real video.

1 ACTIVATE What cell phone plan do you have right now? Compare plans with your classmates.

2 **IDENTIFY** Listen to the conversation. Complete the chart.

Blu Comm:
We're with you for life!

Plan	Minutes	Data	Texts	Cost
Value		1GB	free	$
Smart		___ GB	free	$

3 **IDENTIFY** Listen again and answer the questions.

1 Why is the man calling?
2 Why was his last bill higher than expected?
3 Why is the woman able to offer the man a special deal?
4 Is there a fee to change plans?
5 Does the man change plans?

4 WHAT'S YOUR ANGLE? When was the last time you changed providers for something like your cell phone? How often do you look for a better deal?

SPEAKING Calling customer service

Many companies have customer service departments that you contact by telephone. You might have to call customer service for information, to make a complaint, or to update your account. Be prepared to hear some of the following phrases/questions.

All our representatives are busy right now. Please wait/hold.
Please listen to the following options. If you would like to X, press X.
What's your account number?
I'm going to ask you some security questions. Can you confirm your last name and zip code?

Here is some useful language when speaking to a customer service representative.

I'd like to ask about my latest bill.
Can you tell me how much it would cost to upgrade my phone?
I think my last bill was wrong.
I'm not happy with your service. Reception is really bad when I leave the city.

5 APPLY Complete the dialogue between a customer service representative (R) and a customer (C).

zip code	refund	last bill	security
help	upgrade	account	

R: Hello, how can I ¹_____ you today?
C: Hello. I have a question about my ²_____.
R: OK. I need to ask you some ³_____ questions first. Can you tell me your full name and ⁴_____?
C: It's Maddie Roberts. 80201.
R: Thank you. And your ⁵_____ number? You can find it at the top of your bill.
C: I see it. It's 789-452.
R: Just finding you in our system…OK, Ms. Roberts. What can I do for you?
C: My bill is higher than normal. I think I was overcharged. I didn't make any extra calls.
R: Let's see…Your plan is for $15 a month, and last month you paid $30. Hmm. There's a charge here for a(n) ⁶_____
C: I never asked for that. It must be a mistake.
R: I'm sorry, Ms. Roberts. I'll correct that for you and get you a ⁷_____ now.

6 USE Practice the conversation with a partner.

7 PREPARE Work with a partner. Think of three reasons you might call customer service. Take notes about what both the customer service representative and the customer might ask.

8 INTERACT Work with a different partner. Choose one of your scenarios from Exercise 7 and assign roles. Write a dialogue.

9 SHARE Watch another pair act out their dialogue. Answer the questions.

1 What was the customer calling for?
2 What questions did the customer service representative ask?
3 Did the the customer get what they wanted?
4 What feedback could you give to improve the dialogue?

Now go to page 154 for the Unit 8 Review.

9 Work

| What is hard work? | How can work make us happy? | When do you want to retire, and what do you plan to do? | ▶ BEHIND THE PHOTO |

REAL-WORLD GOAL

Go online and read some job ads in English

1 Take the job quiz. Then discuss your opinions in groups.

Is it better to…?

1 ☐ be an employee
  ☐ be the boss
2 ☐ work from home
  ☐ work at a company
3 ☐ have a well-paid job
  ☐ have a job you love

4 ☐ be bored at work
  ☐ be stressed because you're busy
5 ☐ work with people
  ☐ work with animals
6 ☐ work part time
  ☐ work full time

2 Think of jobs you have had. Which was the best? Which was the worst? Tell your classmates and explain why.

1 **ACTIVATE** Are you good at job interviews? What was the last job interview you had? Were you successful? Tell a partner.

2 **NOTICE** Study these conditional sentences. Then complete the rules in the Grammar box.

Zero conditional:

Look online if you want to find a job!

If you practice interviews, you improve.

First conditional:

You might not get the job if you're nervous in the interview.

If you prepare well, you'll feel more confident.

⊙ **GRAMMAR IN CONTEXT Zero and first conditional**

To form the zero conditional, we use:

If + simple present and _____ or an imperative.

To form the first conditional, we use:

If + simple present and *will* or _____ + infinitive without *to*.

We use the zero conditional to ___ and ___.

We use the first conditional to ___.

a   talk about events and the results that always follow

b   talk about a possible action or situation in the future and the result that follows

c   give instructions

See Grammar focus on page 167.

3 **APPLY** Complete the text using the words in the box. Then identify which sentences are the zero conditional and which are the first conditional.

| don't | might | will | do | are | aren't | won't |

Home | About | Search

Interview Tips and Tricks

1 **Do your homework**

If you research the company and the job in advance, you _____ be better prepared. Take notes and make a list of questions to ask.

2 **Practice**

You'll feel more confident if you _____ a practice interview before the real thing.

3 **Be on time**

If you _____ late, the interviewer might think you are unreliable.

4 **Don't be afraid**

If you _____ sure you understand a question, ask the interviewer to repeat it.

5 **Be polite**

You _____ be successful if you are rude.

6 **Tell yourself to relax**

If you talk too quickly, the interviewer _____ not understand you.

7 **Show you're interested**

Ask questions! If you _____ ask questions, the interviewer might think you don't want the job.

4 **WHAT'S YOUR ANGLE?** Which tips are the most useful for you? Why? Choose three and explain your reasons to a partner. Use the zero or first conditional when you can.

5 **INTERACT** Discuss these questions in groups. Use the zero and first conditional.

1   What will an interviewer think:
   - if you wear nice clothes?
   - if you smile a lot?
   - if your hair is a mess?
   - if you look worried?
   - if your clothes are too casual?

2   How can these things give the interviewer a good or bad impression?
   - looking at the floor or wall
   - speaking very quietly
   - moving your hands a lot
   - looking directly at the interviewer
   - changing position in your seat

If you speak very quietly, people might think…

6 INTERACT Work in pairs. Choose the options you think are correct.

1 Most interviewers *take time / are quick* to decide what they think of someone.

2 Most interviewers look for reasons to *reject / accept* applicants.

3 It is *easy / difficult* to make a negative first impression.

4 There is *some / no* doubt that first impressions count.

5 First impressions have a *small / great* impact on your success in an interview.

6 If the interviewer *talks / doesn't talk* a lot, you have a good chance of getting the job.

7 IDENTIFY Read the article and check your predictions.

READING SKILL Note-taking

Taking notes helps you to understand and remember the important points of a text. You can highlight or underline key information in the text. Then take notes on the main ideas or important details. Keep your notes short. You don't need to write in full sentences.

8 APPLY Read the article again. Notice the important information underlined in paragraphs 1–3. Underline the important information in paragraphs 4 and 5.

9 EXPAND Complete the notes using one word or more in each gap. Then use your notes to summarize the article with a partner.

> **First Impressions Count**
> 1. First impressions form quickly
>   ■ Ex: _____ look intelligent; anxiety causes _____ opinion.
>   ■ Small things create _____ impressions
> 2. Interviewers look to _____ select candidate
>   ■ Need to _____ lots of applicants
>   ■ _____ impressions = hard to change
>   ■ _____ impressions = hard to make
> 3. Interviewer talking a lot = _____ get the job.
>   ■ Pos. interviewer decided
>   ■ Maybe want to _____ candidate
> 4. Nonverbal factors _____ impression
>   ■ Ex: _____
> 5. Improve at interviewing:
>   ■ _____ and experience = _____.
>   ■ Video _____ for feedback on _____

10 WHAT'S YOUR ANGLE? Did any of the information in the text surprise you? Why?

First Impressions Count

Research has shown clearly that people <u>form impressions</u> of each other very <u>quickly</u>. For example, many people think that if someone wears <u>glasses</u>, they are <u>intelligent and thoughtful</u>. Similarly, in an interview, if you are <u>anxious</u>, the interviewer might have a <u>negative opinion</u> of you. Even very <u>small things can create a big impression</u>.

However, did you know that <u>interviewers often look for reasons not to select a candidate</u>? This is understandable because they <u>need to reject most of the applicants</u>, but it means the first impression you give is even more important. Interviewers are <u>quick</u> to reach an early <u>negative impression</u>, and this is <u>difficult to change</u>, whereas an early <u>positive impression</u> is <u>not so easy to make but can change later</u>.

Interestingly, it is clear that <u>if the interviewer talks for a long time</u>, the candidate <u>might get the job</u>. One possibility is that the interviewer has <u>made a quick decision</u> and <u>wants the candidate to be interested in the position</u>.

Nonverbal factors also affect the impression you give. These include your general appearance, clothes, and facial expression as well as eye contact, body movements, and how loud your voice is.

If you want to be good at interviewing, preparation and experience are valuable. Practicing using video can be useful if you want detailed feedback on your weaknesses.

—adapted from *The Oxford Companion to the Mind*, 2nd ed., by Richard L. Gregory

VOCABULARY DEVELOPMENT
Word building: Noun and adjective suffixes

Suffixes are letters added to the end of a word. Some common suffixes for nouns include *-ance*, *-ity*, *-ment*, *-ness*, and *-tion*. Common suffixes for adjectives are *-able*, *-ant*, *ent*, *-ful*, and *-ive*.

11 **BUILD** Find the words below in *First Impressions Count*. Write *n* (noun) or *adj* (adjective) next to each word. Then write the suffixes.

	Part of speech	Suffix
appearance		
thoughtful		
understandable		
movement		
negative		
possibility		
preparation		
useful		
valuable		
weakness		

Oxford 3000™

12 **APPLY** Use the words from Exercise 11 to complete the sentences.

1 Sometimes being good at interviews is more _____ than being well qualified.
2 A(n) _____ impression is hard to change.
3 Do these glasses make me look _____?
4 Her _____ was very professional.
5 He was late for the interview, so it's _____ that he didn't get the job.

6 Did he make a lot of _____ with his hands?
7 I think there is a good _____ that I'll get the job.
8 All the _____ for the interview will pay off.
9 Feedback can help you identify any _____ in your technique.
10 It is really _____ to research the company.

13 **EXPAND** Use the words in the box to complete these questions interviewers often ask job applicants.

leave	tell	weakness	work	hire
see	expect	strengths		

1 Can you please _____ me about yourself?
2 Why do you want to _____ here?
3 What are your _____?
4 Why did you _____ your last job?
5 Why should we _____ you?
6 What is your greatest _____?
7 Where do you _____ yourself in five years?
8 How much do you _____ to earn?

14 **INTEGRATE** Work in pairs. Prepare to role-play a job interview.

Student A: You are the interviewer. Use the questions in Exercise 13 to help you.

Student B: You are the job applicant. Follow the advice in "Interview Tips and Tricks" to give a good performance. Try your best to get the job!

15 **INTERACT** Work in groups. Watch your classmates role-play their interview. What are your impressions? Would you give the candidate the job?

16 **WHAT'S YOUR ANGLE?** Do you decide what someone is like based on first impressions? How accurate are your first impressions?

Small talk at Palazzo d'Orléans in Palermo, Italy

1 ACTIVATE What are the advantages of jobs working with the public, such as a restaurant server, a hotel receptionist, or a taxi driver? What are the disadvantages?

2 ▶ IDENTIFY Watch a taxi driver, Hassan, talk about his job. Which of these topics does he mention?

☐ his family   ☐ work schedule

☐ famous passengers   ☐ car accidents

☐ the traffic   ☐ his taxi

☐ difficult customers   ☐ appearing in movies

3 ▶ EXPAND Watch the video again. Choose the correct answers.

1 He *doesn't mind* / *feels frustrated by* the bad traffic.

2 He *spends* / *doesn't spend* a lot of money on gasoline.

3 His taxi *is* / *isn't* very reliable.

4 He *has* / *hasn't* had a serious accident.

5 He *would* / *wouldn't* like to be an actor.

6 Hassan is a good taxi driver because he is *calm* / *a careful driver*.

4 WHAT'S YOUR ANGLE? Do you think you could do Hassan's job? Why or why not?

5 VOCABULARY Match each adjective with a definition.

1	artistic	a	able to work without help
2	confident	b	strong, never giving up
3	capable	c	not shy or timid
4	enthusiastic	d	excited and eager
5	determined	e	able to do something
6	independent	f	creative and imaginative

Oxford 3000™

6 USE Choose three adjectives from Exercise 5. Write example sentences to show their meaning.

7 INTERACT What personal skills do you think these people need in their jobs? Discuss your ideas in a group.

8 WHAT'S YOUR ANGLE? What personal skills do you have? Use the words in Exercise 5 or talk about other skills you have.

I think I'm hardworking and confident.

My Career Path

Stephania Wadolowska, Poland

I would like to work in the hotel industry one day, perhaps as a hotel manager. The main reason I want to do this is I really like to travel. If I worked for a large hotel group, I'd be able to travel all over the world. It would also be good because I like meeting new people, and I like languages, too. If I worked in a hotel, I'd have lots of opportunities to practice and maybe learn new languages. I'm confident and capable, so I'm sure I'd be good as a receptionist, for example.

I don't think it's a difficult career to get into since tourism is growing all the time. Hotels need staff. The hours are long, but I'm hard-working, so I wouldn't mind.

I'd work for a small hotel first if I was able to choose, in order to get some practical experience. This is because I think I'd be able to get a better job when I want to develop my career.

INTERESTS

Hotel manager. | Travel opportunities. | Meet new people. Learn new languages.

OPPORTUNITIES

Growing industry. Job opportunities. | Get practical experience. | Get a better job!

9 **INTEGRATE** Look at the poster and read the presentation. How many reasons does Stephania give for wanting to work in the hotel industry?

WRITING SKILL Giving reasons

You can support your ideas and opinions with reasons. Phrases for giving reasons are:

The main reason is / *One reason is*

We can use these phrases before *that* clauses; *that* is often left out in informal writing.

The main reason is (that) I want to travel.

Because and *because of*

We use *because* and *because of* when we give the reader new information or a reason they don't know.

because + subject + verb:

I want to be an actor *because I love* performing.

because of + noun / pronoun:

I'd like to be a pilot *because of the travel opportunities*.

As / *Since*

We use *as* / *since* when the reader probably knows the reason already. They are more formal than *because* and are normally used at the beginning of sentences.

As / Since acting is a very glamorous job, it's a very competitive profession.

10 **APPLY** Look at Stephania's text again. Which words and phrases for giving reasons does she use?

11 **USE** Choose the correct option to complete the sentences.

1 Stephania is interested in learning languages *because of* / *because* she likes to travel.

2 *One reason* / *Because* she wants a career in the hotel industry is there are lots of jobs.

3 *Since* / *The main reason* she's hardworking, she doesn't mind the long hours.

4 She's thinking of working for a small hotel first. *The main reason is* / *Because* she needs to get some experience.

5 She'd like to work for a large hotel group *because* / *because of* the better career structure.

GRAMMAR IN CONTEXT Second conditional

We use the second conditional to talk about unlikely events or imaginary situations and their possible results.

If I worked for a large hotel group, I'd be able to travel all over the world.

We form the second conditional with *If* + simple past, *would* / *wouldn't* + infinitive without *to*. We can use either *was* or *were* in the *if* clause after *I, he, she,* or *it*. This use of *were* is sometimes called the subjunctive.

I'd work for a small hotel first if I was able to choose.

See Grammar focus on page 167.

12 **BUILD** Complete the questions using the second conditional.

1 If _____ (you / have) the chance, _____ (you / want) to work abroad?

2 Do you think _____ (you / get) a better job if _____ (you / speak) perfect English?

3 If _____ (you / earn) more money, _____ (you / move) home?

4 _____ (you / apply) for a job if _____ (it / involve) a lot of driving?

5 If _____ (you / not be) happy with your job, _____ (you / try) to make it better or _____ (you / leave)?

13 **INTERACT** Ask and answer the questions from Exercise 12 with a partner.

14 **PREPARE** Prepare to write about a job you would like to have. Read the questions below and take notes on your answers; include your reasons. Then plan a poster to present your ideas. Use the poster on page 104 to help you.

Presentation

■ What job would you like to have?

■ Why do you think you would be good at it?

■ What personal qualities do you have that would be useful?

Poster

■ Focus on the important details.

■ Use pictures to present information.

■ Be clearly organized and easy to read.

15 **WRITE** Write one or two paragraphs about the job you would like to have. Then make a simple poster to support your presentation.

16 **IMPROVE** Use the checklist below to review your work. Can you find anything to improve?

☐ Are your reasons for wanting this job clear?

☐ Did you match your abilities and skills to the job?

☐ Have you used the second conditional correctly?

☐ Are there any examples to support your opinions?

☐ Are the spelling and punctuation correct?

17 **SHARE** In groups, take turns presenting your poster to your classmates.

18 **WHAT'S YOUR ANGLE?** Tell your classmates what your life would be like if you were able to get your dream job!

9.3 You Do What?

1 ACTIVATE Look at the photograph and read the text. What does a Google tricycle mapper do?

2 WHAT'S YOUR ANGLE? Would you leave your current job to be a tricycle mapper or think of becoming one in the future? Why or why not?

3 VOCABULARY Write each word in the correct place.

executive	candidate	employment	qualified

1 potential / unlikely _____
2 temporary / permanent _____
3 fully / highly _____
4 senior / junior _____

🔑 Oxford 3000™

4 USE Complete these sentences using each word in Exercise 3.

1 I am looking for a _____ job, so something just over the summer.
2 Being an airline pilot is a _____ skilled job that requires years of training.
3 The only _____ problem with this candidate is they live overseas.
4 It's a very _____ position, but you should be able to work your way up.
5 After successfully completing your training, you will be a _____ qualified teacher.
6 Martine started the company and is a _____ partner in the business.
7 All _____ employees receive free health care, paid vacations, and sick leave.
8 It is _____ they will offer me the job after that terrible interview.

5 INTERACT Work in groups. Think of at least three examples of each of the following, with reasons why you think so: potential careers for you; unlikely careers for you; temporary jobs you would like to try; jobs you are highly qualified for.

Did you know that Google introduced the Street View Trikes in 2009 to get images of locations that are difficult to reach by car? Would you like to be a tricycle mapper? You have to be in good shape. The Google Trike weighs about 250 pounds and is nine feet high, but you'll earn around $60,000 a year and stay in shape!

LISTENING SKILL Predicting while listening

While you are listening, you can use the information you hear to help you make predictions. Think about what you have already heard, the topic, and the context, and try to guess what you will hear next. Checking if your prediction is correct will help you know if you have understood. If you don't hear what you expect, you may have misunderstood. You can make a new prediction and listen to check if it's correct.

6 ◄)) IDENTIFY You are going to listen to an interview with Annie Hudson about an unusual career. What might the career be? What words might you hear? Why? Listen and check your predictions.

I think the career will be…
I think I might hear…

7 ASSESS What is Annie's job? What kind of information or words and phrases do you think you will hear next? Make predictions for what you might hear in the next part of the interview.

8 🔊 DEVELOP Listen and check your predictions from Exercise 7.

9 ASSESS Make predictions about the next part of the interview: what words, phrases, and information might you hear?

10 🔊 EXPAND Listen to the final part of the interview and check your predictions from Exercise 9.

11 🔊 INTEGRATE Now listen to the complete interview and answer the questions.

1 Why does Annie love her job?
2 Where can you see Annie's work?
3 Who does she work with?
4 How does she travel to work?
5 Where did she train?

12 WHAT'S YOUR ANGLE? Do you ever take photos of food you cook? When? Tell a partner.

GRAMMAR IN CONTEXT Reflexive pronouns

We use reflexive pronouns (*myself, yourself, herself, himself, itself, ourselves, yourselves, themselves*) when the person who does the action (the subject) is also the person affected by the action. The reflexive pronoun is the object of the verb or preposition. It agrees with the subject.

*It's really fun, and we enjoy **ourselves**.*
*I prepare and cook all the food **myself**.*

We sometimes use *themselves* instead of *himself/herself* to talk about a person when we don't say or don't know if the person is male or female.

*Anyone can call **themselves** an expert.*

See Grammar focus on page 167.

---

13 APPLY Complete the list of reflexive pronouns.

Subject pronoun	Object pronoun
I	myself
you (*singular*)	
he	
she	
it	
we	
you (*plural*)	
they	

14 INTEGRATE Complete the sentences with reflexive pronouns.

1 Annie buys all the ingredients _____ for the dishes she makes.
2 I never thought of _____ as having an unusual job.
3 Please help _____ to some more cake.
4 The last time he cooked a meal, Gary burned _____ badly.
5 You have to be very experienced before you can call _____ a food stylist.
6 Anyone who works for _____ has to be prepared to work hard.
7 We grow all the fruit and vegetables we need _____.
8 The oven Annie uses at home can clean _____.

15 EXPAND Put the phrases in order to complete the questions.

1 think of yourself / do you / creative person / as a / ?
2 changing / can you / careers / see yourself / ?
3 or on / by yourself / would you / a team / rather work / ?
4 for yourself / want to work / one day / do you / ?
5 yourself / you see / where do / in a year / ?

16 INTERACT Work with a partner. Ask and answer the questions in Exercise 15.

17 PREPARE Think of an unusual job. Take notes and prepare to talk about it.

Job: _____

Description: _____

18 INTEGRATE Tell the class about the job you chose, but *do not say* what it is. When you finish your description, your classmates can ask questions for more information. Can they guess your job?

19 WHAT'S YOUR ANGLE? Which of the unusual jobs would you like to do? Are there any you *wouldn't* want?

Let Me Get That for You

1 **ACTIVATE** Talk about the pictures with a partner. What's happening? What do you think the people are saying? Who do you think needs help?

2 **INTERACT** Do you always ask for help when you need it? Tell a partner and explain your reasons.

REAL-WORLD ENGLISH Offering to help

When you offer to help, the language you use depends not only on your relationship to the person but also if the person has let you know if they want help. People may not want to ask for help because it can suggest they are not capable. Their facial expressions or body language can sometimes tell you if they want help. You can also say something about the difficulty of the task to let the other person know why you are offering. This gives the other person a chance to let you know if they do or do not want help. People often refuse an offer of help at first but accept if the offer is repeated.

3 ▶ **ANALYZE** Watch the video and answer the questions.

	Andy	Jenna	Sam
1 Who offers to help?	☐	☐	☐
2 Who refuses any offer of help?	☐	☐	☐
3 Who accepts help immediately?	☐	☐	☐
4 Who accepts help in the end?	☐	☐	☐

4 ▶ **IDENTIFY** Watch the video again. Complete the offers you hear. Some offers may be completed in more than one way.

1 Let me…
2 Do you want…
3 Would you like…
4 I can…

a get those.
b this on the table?
c sort those for you.
d get the door.
e me to take one?
f get that for you.
g help you sort?

ENGLISH FOR REAL

5 ASSESS Study the expressions for offering help in Exercise 4. What is the difference in use between them?

REAL-WORLD ENGLISH
Accepting and rejecting offers

The way you accept or reject an offer often depends on the difficulty of the task and your relationship to the person. For accepting help with a difficult task or from someone you don't know, more complex expressions are polite because they show you are grateful. For accepting help with a simple task or from someone you know well, shorter expressions are common. For rejections, the length of the expression also shows politeness, but it is important to pay attention to the tone used. A serious tone can indicate a genuine refusal of an offer.

6 EXPAND Read this extract from the video. What expressions does Sam use to reject Andy's offers? Why do you think he finally accepts?

Andy: Do you want me to take one?

Sam: No…It's OK. Um, I got it.

Andy: Are you sure? I mean…They look…

Sam: It's all right, thank you. I got it.

Andy: Can I help you?

Sam: OK. Thanks.

9 EXPAND For each situation in Exercise 8, imagine you are the person in the picture. Would you accept an offer of help? Tell your partner.

7 INTEGRATE Label the conversation in Exercise 6 with the functions below.

Accept	Offer to help	Refuse again
Comment about the task	Refuse	Offer again

8 ASSESS Work in pairs. Look at the situations. Which people would you offer to help? Tell your partner and explain your reasons. What expressions would you use?

1   You go to the train station to meet a friend. Your friend arrives with lots of baggage.
2   You're at school. You see your teacher carrying lots of books.
3   You're at the bus stop. An elderly man you don't know has dropped his wallet.
4   Your roommate is trying to wrap a gift.

10 INTERACT Role-play each of the situations in Exercise 8 with a partner. Follow the structure below.

Offer to help
↓
Refuse
↓
Comment about the task
↓
Refuse again
↓
Offer again
↓
Accept/refuse

GO ONLINE
to create your own version
of the English For Real video.

9.5 Work Hard, Play Hard

1 ACTIVATE How much free time do you have? What kind of things do you do in your free time?

2 **IDENTIFY** Listen to Ariel and Manish talk about what they do to relax in their free time. Complete the summary.

Ariel has a very ¹*active / peaceful* working life, so in her free time she prefers to ²*relax / see friends*. Manish doesn't get much ³*free time / exercise* in his job, so ⁴*after work / on weekends* he likes to be active. They both like to spend time ⁵*at home / outdoors*.

3 WHAT'S YOUR ANGLE? Are you more like Ariel or Manish? Do you like to relax or play hard in your free time?

SPEAKING Explaining words you don't know

Sometimes when you are talking, you realize that you don't know or remember the word you need to use. To keep the conversation going, let the person you are speaking to know you are looking for a word. They might be able to help you. Try to define the word you need or use a similar word to help them understand. Use these phrases:

What's the word in English? It means "go down."
What's another word for "cook," you know like "cook a cake"?
How do you say it in English?
What's the word I'm looking for? It's part of your car, you put gas in it...Gas trunk? Gas tank? Yes, gas tank!

4 **APPLY** Listen again to Ariel and Manish each explain a word they don't know. Decide who uses each strategy.

		Ariel	Manish
1	uses *you know* to ask for help	☐	☐
2	defines the word	☐	☐
3	takes a guess	☐	☐
4	describes the object	☐	☐

5 EXPAND Decide how you would explain these words if you didn't know them. What language and strategies would you use?

1 anxious (adj) _____

2 client (n) _____

3 congratulate (v) _____

6 INTERACT Work in groups. Choose a word that has been taught in one of the previous units. Explain it to the group. Can they guess the word or understand your explanation?

7 WHAT'S YOUR ANGLE? Are there any words you sometimes forget in English? How can you explain them?

PRONUNCIATION SKILL Linking with /w/ and /j/

 When one word ends in a vowel and the next word begins with a vowel, we link the words with /w/ or /j/.
/w/ *I'm always running from one place to_another.*
/j/ *Templehofer Park used to be_an airport.*

8 **APPLY** Listen to the sentences. Find the /w/ and /j/ sounds.

1 I'll do everything by the end of the week.
2 We are going to Italy on vacation.
3 Who are you meeting in the afternoon?
4 It will be all over before you arrive.
5 Please go and get three extra tickets.
6 I might be able to help you after lunch.

9 **USE** Listen and repeat.

10 PREPARE Prepare to talk about ways your work or school life influences your free time. First, take notes to describe your work/school life.

Is it very busy and stressful, or do you find it boring? Do you sit down a lot or do you get a lot of exercise? Do you see lots of people or are you on your own?

11 DEVELOP Now think about the things you do in your free time. Take notes.

How do you like to relax? Why do you like doing these things?

12 WHAT'S YOUR ANGLE? Can you see any connection between your work or school life and the things you like to do in your free time?

Now go to page 155 for the Unit 9 Review.

10 Information

Where does information come from?

Do we control information, or does information control us?

Do you enjoy living in the Information Age?

BEHIND THE PHOTO

1 How have the ways we get information changed in the past 50 years? Work in groups. Discuss the ways we got information 50 years ago and how we get it today.

2 Which is more important to you? Number these factors in order (1 = most important). Then tell your partner and explain why.

I want to choose who sees information about me. ___

I want to be sure the information I find is accurate. ___

I want to know where the information I find comes from. ___

I want to be able to access information easily and quickly. ___

REAL-WORLD GOAL

Check the Internet for information about yourself

10.1 You Were Hacked!

1 ACTIVATE How safe is your personal information? Ask and answer the questions in the Online Safety Quiz with a partner.

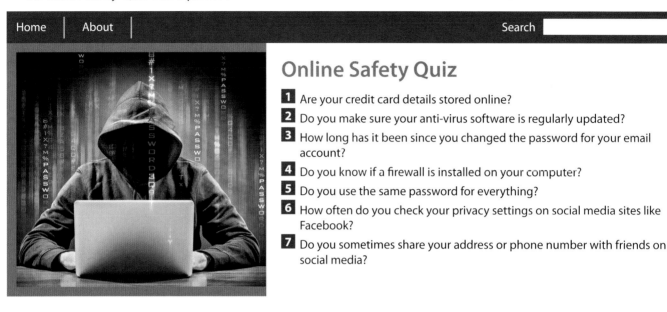

Home	About		Search	

Online Safety Quiz

1 Are your credit card details stored online?

2 Do you make sure your anti-virus software is regularly updated?

3 How long has it been since you changed the password for your email account?

4 Do you know if a firewall is installed on your computer?

5 Do you use the same password for everything?

6 How often do you check your privacy settings on social media sites like Facebook?

7 Do you sometimes share your address or phone number with friends on social media?

2 VOCABULARY Match each idiom with its meaning.

1 After all
2 For instance
3 In case
4 All the time
5 Of course not
6 Right now
7 Too bad

a as an example
b at this moment exactly
c because something might happen
d certainly not
e different to what you expect
f very often, always
g you feel sorry or bad about something

🔑 Oxford 3000™

3 BUILD Complete these statements using the idioms from Exercise 2.

Identity theft is when someone uses your personal information like your name or bank account details without your knowledge or agreement. It's ¹_____, but online identity theft is increasing ²_____, year after year. The Federal Trade Commission in the United States, ³_____, receives about 500,000 complaints of identity theft every year. The chances are that somebody, somewhere, is stealing someone's identity ⁴_____. So does that mean we shouldn't buy anything online? ⁵_____, but it does mean we all need to be aware ⁶_____ we become victims, too. Even if our information is protected, our identity may not be safe ⁷_____. Your personal information is valuable. Identity theft can cost you a lot of money.

4 WHAT'S YOUR ANGLE? Do you know anyone who has been affected by identity theft? Tell a partner.

LISTENING SKILL Focusing on key content words

Content words are the words in a sentence that give the most important information. Knowing how to listen for them will help you focus on key information in a sentence. Content words are usually nouns, verbs, adjectives, and adverbs. When a speaker wants to make a negative sentence or say that something is not true, content words can also be negative words, such as *not* or *never*. Speakers usually stress content words by saying them more slowly and clearly to focus your attention.

5 🔊 **APPLY** Listen to these extracts from a conversation and complete them with the missing key content words.

1 It _sounds_ like you were _hacked_!
2 I _____ we can get a _____.
3 Do you _____ the _____ _____ for _____ _____?
4 I _____ _____ the _____ _____!
5 I _____ _____ if _____ are _____ by a _____ _____.

6 🔊 **IDENTIFY** Listen to the entire conversation. What are they worried about?

7 🔊 **EXPAND** Listen again. Choose *True* or *False*.

		True	False
1	The man bought a washing machine.	☐	☐
2	His credit card is stored on Amazon.	☐	☐
3	The man was hacked.	☐	☐
4	Their anti-virus software was updated recently.	☐	☐
5	The man's passwords are never written down.	☐	☐
6	Numbers are used for letters in passwords.	☐	☐

8 **WHAT'S YOUR ANGLE?** Are your passwords written down? How do you remember them? Do you forget them all the time?

GRAMMAR IN CONTEXT
The passive: Simple present and simple past

We can often say sentences in two ways, in the active or passive.

An active sentence answers the question, "Who does the action?" (Who is the agent?)

I never use the same password.

(The agent here is "I.")

We often use the passive when we don't know who the agent is or when it is obvious or not important.

I hope our information is kept safe.

We form the passive with *be* + past participle.

If we want to say who does an action in the passive, we use the preposition *by*.

*I check if emails are sent **by** a real company all the time.*

Often we don't need to say who does the action.

My card wasn't stolen.

See Grammar focus on page 168.

9 **APPLY** Choose the correct option to complete this summary of a presentation about online safety.

Yesterday, we [1]*attended / were attended* a talk about online safety. We [2]*gave / were given* a lot of good advice by the presenter on how to stay safe online. For example, we [3]*told / were told* not to give out information unless we know who we are giving it to and why it [4]*needs / is needed*. He [5]*explained / was explained* how a strong password [6]*makes / is made*, and he [7]*encouraged / was encouraged* us all to remember our passwords rather than write them down.

10 **EXPAND** Complete the text with the simple past passive or the simple present passive of the verbs in parentheses.

Every time we give out information, it [1]_____ (collect) and it [2]_____ (store) somewhere. Our financial and medical records, the TV shows we watch, the websites we visit, details about our homes, and even our current location [3]_____ (share) with people and companies we do not know about. We can't even walk down the street without cameras identifying us and where we go and who we talk to. What happens to all this information, and is it possible to protect our privacy? The Electronic Privacy Information Center (EPIC) [4]_____ (establish) in 1994. EPIC works to make sure that everyone's personal information [5]_____ (protect) as much as possible. However, when information [6]_____ (exchange) over the Internet, digital footprints, called cookies, [7]_____ (leave) at every point. Since the information [8]_____ (pass) by third parties like Internet service providers, it is very hard to guarantee privacy.

11 **INTERACT** Work in a group and discuss how your personal possessions are protected and why. Which person in the group has the most secure possessions?

1 Your phone
2 Your house
3 Your credit card
4 Your car

My phone is protected with a password in case it is stolen. Then no one can open it.

My phone is protected with face recognition. Phones are stolen all the time, and I don't want someone else to use it.

12 **WHAT'S YOUR ANGLE?** Would you ever close your social media accounts or stop shopping online so that your personal information is protected?

10.2 Do You See What I Mean?

1 ACTIVATE What do you think is the difference between *data, information*, and *knowledge*? Discuss your ideas with a partner.

2 ASSESS Complete the definitions with the words in the box.

data	knowledge	understand	organized	context

¹_____ is a kind of raw material. It comes in many forms: numbers, letters, symbols, even images and sounds. It is not ²_____, and it has no context or meaning.

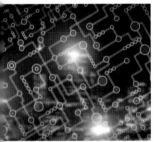

Information is data that we have processed. Information adds ³_____ to data and gives data meaning.

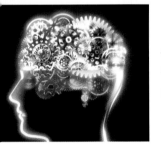

⁴_____ is the ability to ⁵_____ information and to make opinions and decisions.

READING SKILL
Understanding pronoun references

We use pronouns to replace nouns or noun phrases. This avoids repetition. Knowing what a pronoun refers to will help you understand the text better. A pronoun can refer to a noun that comes before or after it. This can be in another sentence.

The expression "I see what you mean" is more accurate now than it's ever been before.

Data is a kind of raw material. It comes in many forms.

---

3 IDENTIFY Read the text. What does Data Cuisine use to represent data?

Home	About	Search	🔍

Can You Taste Data?

Yes, you can taste ¹*it*! Thanks to the inventive people at the Data Cuisine Workshop. ²*They* use meaningful ingredients to create tasty dishes as representations of data. The color, shape, smell, taste, nutrition, and origin of the ingredients can all be important in the final dish. They also do workshops. Participants create their own data menus. Then ³*they* taste them!

This dish, Taste of Migration, represents the non-Finnish nationalities in Finland. ⁴*It* uses typical food from each country to show the different nationalities. For example, salmon for the Swedish and rice for the Chinese. The amount of food on the plate is also important. ⁵*It* represents the number of people of that nationality in Finland: the more of it there is, the more people of that nationality.

4 EXPAND Read the text again. Find the noun each *italicized* pronoun refers to.

5 WHAT'S YOUR ANGLE? How useful is it to present data so you can taste it? Do you think it adds information to the data?

6 INTEGRATE Read the article, "Information is Beautiful." Who or what do these words refer to?

1 this _____
2 These _____
3 them _____
4 it _____
5 him _____
6 them _____

Information Is Beautiful

Did you know that almost all the information we get comes through our eyes? As an artist, I completely agree with [1]*this*. That is why art so deeply impacts us. I recently saw a presentation on data visualization. I hadn't thought of data as art, but I was really excited by what I saw. I think it's extremely likely that data visualizations are the future of knowledge.

The presentation was given by David McCandless. He describes himself as a data journalist and information designer. [2]*These* are new terms for a new 21st-century job; presenting data in easy-to-read charts, maps, and graphs. McCandless strongly believes that visualizations of data help us see patterns and compare [3]*them* in different ways.

What's more, visualizations are often interactive. We can select different sets of data and see how this changes the visualizations. We can also update with real-time data. This makes data come alive. "Data is the new soil. We dig [4]*it*, add to it… and data visualization is like seeing flowers bloom out of the soil," says McCandless.

McCandless and other data journalists like [5]*him* are helping us to make sense of the huge amount of information in today's world. Thanks to [6]*them*, I am absolutely convinced that the expression "I see what you mean" is more accurate now than it's ever been before.

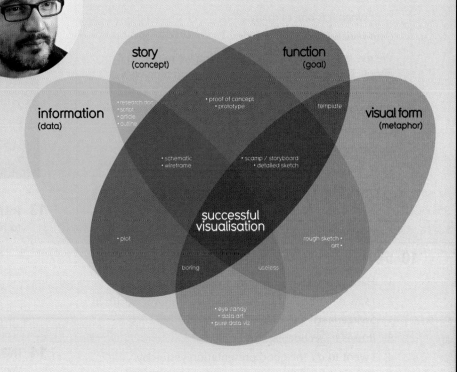

What Makes a Good Visualization?

7 EXPAND Read the article again. Answer the questions.

1 How does most information come to us?
2 Why does the author agree with that?
3 What is David McCandless's job?
4 What does he think visualization helps us see?
5 How are visualizations interactive?
6 Why are data journalists important in today's world?

VOCABULARY DEVELOPMENT
Intensifying adverbs

Intensifying adverbs help to make the word they go with stronger. Common examples are *very* and *really*.

*It's **very** clear. / That report was **really** good.*

Instead of *very* or *really*, you can use other adverbs.

We use *deeply* or *completely* with **emotions**.
*That is why art so deeply **impacts** us.*

We use *extremely* with **probability words**.
*I think it's extremely **likely** that they are the future.*

We use *strongly* or *firmly* with **opinions or beliefs**.
*McCandless strongly **believes** that visualization helps comprehension.*

We do not use use *very* with **adjectives that have extreme meanings** We can use *absolutely* instead.
*I am absolutely **convinced** it's true.*

 Oxford 3000™

8 BUILD Add an intensifying adverb to each of the sentences.

1 I _____ support the idea that images are more powerful than words.
2 It was _____ good to see the presentation finally.
3 It is _____ unlikely that everyone will use data visualization.
4 Wow! That picture is _____ incredible!
5 She was _____ moved by the story behind the image.

9 EXPAND Choose the correct options to compete these sentences.

1 McCandless *strongly / deeply* recommends visualizing data in different ways.
2 I am *absolutely / extremely* certain that this is a skill we should learn at college.
3 It is *extremely / firmly* likely that courses on data journalism will become more popular.
4 I *entirely / very* disagree that there is too much information these days.
5 A lot of companies are *deeply / strongly* concerned about the security of their data.

We use *a/an* when we mention something for the first time…

*David McCandless is **a** data journalist.*

…or when it is one of many.

*Data visualization is **a** hot topic.*

We use *the* when it's clear which thing we're talking about. This is often because it's the second time we've mentioned it…

*Here is **a** graph. **The** graph shows changes in temperature.*

…or when it's the only one.

*Information is everywhere in **the** world.*

There is no article when we talk about plural or uncountable nouns in general.

These days information is all around us.

See Grammar focus on page 168.

10 DEVELOP Choose the correct options.

1 Have you seen *a / the* Data Cuisine website?

2 I saw *a / the* beautiful visualization. It shows wealth in Switzerland.

3 It uses *a / -* chocolate and gold.

4 I went to *a / the* good presentation yesterday.

5 *The / A* person who spoke was David McCandless.

6 There is a lot of data on *the / a* Internet.

7 My college professor was *a / -* great data scientist.

8 What did you study in *- / the* college?

11 APPLY Complete the text with *a/an, the,* or *no article*.

12 WHAT'S YOUR ANGLE? Think of data that you would like to represent. What dish or ingredients would you use?

13 PREPARE Make or describe your dish. Use the checklist to help you.

☐ Is the information easy to understand?
☐ Is the presentation effective?
☐ Is there text? What will it say?
☐ Do the ingredients tell a story?
☐ Is the use of color effective?

14 INTERACT Compare your dishes with a classmate. Who has the most interesting data dish?

 ## Information Theory

Some artists actually create 3D objects to show [1]___ data. Mitchell Whitelaw's *Measuring Cup* is [2]___ small cup-shaped object. It is made of [3]___ series of rings, one on top of the other. The width of each ring is [4]___ average temperature data for each month in Sydney, Australia. The bottom of [5]___ cup starts in 1859. It gives [6]___ physical shape to how global warming has affected the city. The cup is best experienced through touch. As [7]___ cup gets wider toward the top, you can actually feel [8]___ dramatic impact of global warming on [9]___ Sydney's temperatures. This piece of art helps us understand the data in a different way.

—adapted from *Encyclopedia of Aesthetics,* 2nd ed., by Michael Kelly

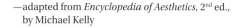

10.3 Everything on the Internet

1 ACTIVATE Read the post. What does *misinformation* mean?

🌐 NEWS

Home | News Watch | World | Technology | Science | Health | Business

Believe It or Not

I read a funny post the other day about misinformation. It gave a great example. Have you heard the quote, "A lie can travel half way round the world while the truth is putting on its shoes"? Everyone thinks Mark Twain, the famous writer, said it. He didn't! It was a different writer, Jonathan Swift. Isn't that funny? I guess we shouldn't trust everything on the Internet.

2 INTERACT Why is the story funny? Can you think of another example of misinformation?

3 WHAT'S YOUR ANGLE? Think about different sources of information like magazines, newspapers, TV, the radio, the Internet, and social media. Which sources do you trust the most? Why?

I trust newspapers more than social media. Anyone can post information on the Internet, so you don't know if it's true!

4 VOCABULARY Match the words and phrases. Then discuss their meaning with a partner.

1	freedom	a	report
2	genuine	b	misinformation
3	accurately	c	of expression
4	spread	d	or fake
5	claim	e	something up
6	trust your	f	proof
7	make	g	judgment
8	look for	h	something is true

🔑 Oxford 3000™

5 BUILD Complete the text with words from Exercise 4.

These days, we can get information from more sources than ever before. But be careful! Because people have the ¹_____ to publish whatever they want, anyone can be a reporter! Someone can easily ²_____ up a story in websites, blogs, and social media and ³_____ it is

true. A fake story can be repeated so often people think it is true. There's nowhere like the Internet for finding fake news. People ⁴_____ misinformation all the time. You need to question the information you find. Always look for ⁵_____ and use your judgment to decide if something is ⁶_____ or fake. Don't ⁷_____ everything you read!

ⓒ GRAMMAR IN CONTEXT
Indefinite pronouns and adverbs

We use *somebody, something*, or *somewhere* in positive sentences to talk about a person, thing, or place when we don't mean a particular one.

***Someone** can easily make up a story.*

We use *everybody, everything*, and *everywhere* in positive sentences and in questions to talk about all people, things, or places.

*Don't trust **everything** you read!*

We use *nobody/no one, nothing*, and *nowhere* with a positive singular verb to mean no person, thing, or place.

*There's **nowhere** like the Internet for finding fake news.*

We use *anybody/anyone, anything*, and *anywhere* in negative sentences and questions.

*I don't know **anything** about it.*

We can also use *any-* in positive sentences when it means "it doesn't matter who/what/where."

*You can post **anything** you want online these days.*

See Grammar focus on page 168.

6 INTEGRATE Choose the correct options.

Research Tips for Finding Reliable Sources

Your guide to separating genuine and false information!

Use a wide range of online sources. Look ¹*everywhere / somewhere*: newspaper websites, journals, blogs, reference sites, etc.

Always ask yourself how reliable the information is. Can ²*anyone / everything* give information here, and can they write ³*anything / nothing* they want?

Find out who wrote information. Can you find their name ⁴*anywhere / everywhere*? Does the writer belong to an organization?

Check all the facts and statistics are accurate and up-to-date. If you can find the same information ⁵*somewhere / nowhere* else, then it might be true. Information that is ⁶*nowhere / nothing* else could be false.

Look in different sources offline, too. Not ⁷*nothing / everything* will be on the Internet. Use books and refer to newspapers or magazines.

7 APPLY Complete these sentences using the words in the box.

anywhere	nothing	everywhere	nowhere
anyone	anything	everyone	someone

1 I've looked _____ , but I can't find that article you mentioned.
2 Does _____ have Gena's phone number? I need to call her.
3 There is _____ on the Internet about yesterday's events.
4 I don't want to read _____ about it. It just makes me angry.
5 I got the same reply from _____ I spoke to. I don't think I trust their answers.
6 There is _____ worse to look for accurate news than the Internet.
7 Is there _____ else we might find more information?
8 Surely there must be _____ who knows what really happened?

8 EXPAND Read this essay on the pros and cons of user-generated content. Can you think of sites that have user-generated content?

User-Generated Content

User-generated content (UGC) refers to any content that users of a website can create or post online. Some examples are videos, blog posts, discussion forums, or social media comments. One well-known example is YouTube. While many people claim we should not trust user-generated content because anyone can post, I believe it is a useful source of information.

One of the biggest advantages of UGC is that it gives everyone a voice. Freedom of expression is important in today's world. Secondly, it allows everyone all over the world to connect with each other. We can learn directly from people anywhere and hear genuine experiences of everything that is covered in the news. In addition, it is easy. It doesn't take long to upload a video or article. This means we have access to even more information.

On the other hand, UGC isn't always controlled. On some sites, anyone can publish anything, so the quality of information can be unreliable. What's more, people are able to change facts to support their view. This makes it difficult to find the truth. Even websites that look good might be spreading fake news or misinformation.

In my opinion, UGC is a valuable source of information because it can report some things more accurately than news sites. There are, however, dangers. You must use your judgment.

9 INTEGRATE Read the article again. Note the advantages and disadvantages of user-generated content. Then complete the chart.

Advantages	Disadvantages
It gives everyone a voice.	

WRITING SKILL Using sequencing words

When you want to write your opinion on a topic, first collect your ideas and organize them into the order you want. Choose the most important points first. Use sequencing words to help your reader follow your argument more easily.

10 APPLY Look at the sequencing words. Write each under the correct heading.

Another important point to consider is…			
Finally	First/Firstly	However	In addition
Lastly	Nevertheless	On the other hand	In conclusion

One of the biggest (dis)advantages (of…) is…
What's more
Second/Secondly

Main point

1 *First/Firstly*
2 _____

Supporting points

3 _____
4 _____
5 _____
6 _____

The opposite view

7 _____
8 _____
9 _____

Concluding points

10 _____
11 _____
12 _____

11 IDENTIFY Look again at the essay "User-Generated Content." How many sequencing words can you find?

12 ASSESS Look at the organization of the essay. Write the number of each paragraph (1–4) next to the correct section.

___ Advantages   ___ Introduction
___ Conclusion   ___ Disadvantages

13 EXPAND Now match the descriptions with the section names from Exercise 12.

a _____ arguments in favor (most important first)
b *Introduction* overview the topic
c _____ give your opinion and overview the main points
d _____ arguments against (most important first)

14 WHAT'S YOUR ANGLE? Do you use any sites with user-generated content? What are the advantages and disadvantages of these sites? If you don't use these sites, why not?

15 PREPARE You are going to write an essay on the advantages and disadvantages of using the Internet for research. Make a list of your ideas using a T-chart.

Advantages	Disadvantages

16 DEVELOP Organize your thoughts into an outline. Follow the organization in Exercise 12. Be sure to put your ideas in order of importance.

17 WRITE Write your essay. Use around 200 words.

☐ Is your essay well organized?
☐ Did you use sequencing words?
☐ Are negative and indefinite pronouns used correctly?
☐ Is your opinion clear?

18 SHARE Work in pairs. Read each other's essays. Can you find any areas to improve? Use the checklist to help you, and give each other feedback.

19 IMPROVE Use your partner's feedback to rewrite your essay.

20 WHAT'S YOUR ANGLE? Research recent news events on the Internet. Can you find any information you don't trust?

People connect to Wi-Fi at El Museo Organico de Romerillo in Havana, Cuba

That's Good to Know

1 ACTIVATE Read the situation. Choose *one* response.

A classmate emails you an essay and asks for your opinion. You read the essay, but it is not very good. Your classmate calls you to ask what you think. What do you do?

☐ Say you didn't have time to read it, but you're sure it's great.

☐ Say you read it and think it's fine.

☐ Change the subject and talk about something else.

☐ Avoid giving an opinion by saying, "As long as you're happy with it."

☐ Tell your classmate you think it could be better.

☐ List all the things you think are wrong and suggest improvements.

2 INTERACT Discuss your answers in groups. Who would do the same? Who would respond differently? Explain your reasons.

REAL-WORLD ENGLISH Giving feedback

The way you give feedback often depends on who you are speaking to and how you think the person will view your comments. You can start by mentioning the things you like and try to be encouraging. When you want to mention weak points, soften criticisms by making them less direct and by using positive adjectives. You can also start with positive comments before giving any negative feedback. This is especially important in formal feedback situations like between a boss and an employee or a teacher and a student. These techniques can make the criticism less direct and more positive.

Start with something positive.

You made lots of great points, but...

Soften negatives by using words like *a little, a bit,* or *some.*

*Some sentences are long. >> Some sentences are **a little** long.*

Try to use positive adjectives rather than negative ones.

*It's difficult to understand. >> It's **not so easy** to understand.*

Use suggestion words like *could* to offer ways to improve and explain how that will make the work better.

*You **could** give more information about the benefits. **That would help people see** how great the project is.*

3 ⏵ **ANALYZE** Watch the video. Compare how Andy and Emma give feedback to Max. Choose your answers.

	Andy	Emma
starts with a positive comment	Yes / No	Yes / No
focuses on negatives	Yes / No	Yes / No
suggests improvements	Yes / No	Yes / No
gives examples of errors	Yes / No	Yes / No
is generally encouraging	Yes / No	Yes / No

4 **ASSESS** Look at your answers to Exercise 3. Who creates a negative situation? Why? Who makes their feedback more positive? How? Discuss with a partner.

5 **INTEGRATE** Change the statements to sound more positive. Use the information in the skill box to help you.

1 It's badly organized.
2 It's difficult to read.
3 It's boring.
4 Your handwriting is terrible.

6 **EXPAND** Look at these comments about a presentation. For each statement, make a suggestion for improvement and explain why it would make the presentation better.

1 Your eye contact isn't very good.
2 Your presentation is too long.
3 There aren't any pictures.
4 The conclusion isn't interesting.

7 **INTERACT** How do you feel when someone gives you negative feedback? What kind of feedback works best for you?

8 ⏵ **ANALYZE** Watch the video again. How does Max respond to the feedback he receives?

	Feedback from Andy	Feedback from Emma
1 Max gives an explanation.	☐	☐
2 Max listens carefully.	☐	☐
3 Max says *thank you*.	☐	☐
4 Max questions the feedback.	☐	☐
5 Max gets upset.	☐	☐
6 Max accepts the criticism.	☐	☐

9 **APPLY** Look at these phrases people use to respond to the feedback they receive. What is the function of each phrase? Use the information in the Real-World English box to help you.

1 What do you mean?
2 Oh, OK. Yes, I can look at that.
3 Could you give me an example?
4 That's a good point. I'll think about that.

10 **INTERACT** With a partner, think about feedback you might receive from the people below. Then think of a situation and what you would say to give and receive feedback. Take turns role-playing the situations. When you finish, give your partner feedback on their performance!

your teacher	your boss	a close friend
a family member	your roommate	a co-worker

GO ONLINE to create your own version of the English For Real video.

121

10.5 Did You Read the Reviews?

1 ACTIVATE Have you ever written an online review? What about? Was it positive or negative?

2 🔊 **EXPAND** Listen to the conversation and answer the questions.

1 What does Mike want to buy and why?
2 What is the problem?
3 How does Mike feel about online reviews?

3 🔊 **INTEGRATE** Listen again and note the similarities and differences between the two items they talk about.

Similarities: _____

_____

Differences: _____

_____

Sony 18.2 Megapixel
Digital Camera

Features:
60x digital zoom
1080p Full HD Video
Wi-Fi
Compact size
Available in black or blue

Reviews: ★★★★★
4.6 stars (344)

Price:
Save $30
Was: $399.99
$369.99

Canon 20.2 Megapixel
Digital Camera

Features:
4x digital zoom
1080p Full HD Video
Wi-Fi
Available in black or silver

Reviews: ★★★★★
4.6 stars (16)

Price:
Save $50
Was: $279.99
$229.99

SPEAKING Comparing and contrasting

If you compare two or more things, you find the similarities in them. When you contrast them, you find the differences between them. We can compare things with phrases such as *both, neither, so does,* and *also.* We can contrast things with phrases such as *on the other hand, yes, but…, while,* and *however.*

Compare: *Facebook is a popular social media site. Twitter also has a lot of users.*

Contrast: *My work computer is well protected. My home PC, however, has a lot of viruses!*

4 🔊 **APPLY** Listen to this extract from the conversation and complete the conversation using comparing and contrasting words and phrases.

Mike: Well, _____ models have the same score from reviewers.

Anne: _____ the Canon has only 16 reviews, _____ the Sony has 344!

Mike: Hmm. They're fairly similar, actually. The Sony has full high-definition video, and _____ the Canon. You can buy them on this site, too, which is good except _____ camera comes with free delivery.

Anne: The Canon looks pretty good to me. It has a bigger discount, and it's cheaper anyway.

Mike: But _____, the Sony has a better digital zoom. That's really useful.

5 EXPAND Work in pairs. Look at the ads and find more similarities and differences between the cameras. Talk about them using comparing and contrasting words and phrases.

PRONUNCIATION SKILL Chunking

When we speak, we use short pauses to divide what we say into chunks, or groups of words. Grouping words into chunks in this way makes it easier for the listener to understand what we say.

6 🔊 **NOTICE** Listen to this extract from the conversation. Notice how the information is grouped into chunks to help understanding.

Anne: Hey Mike. / What are you looking at there?

Mike: Cameras. / Mine's broken / and I want to buy another one.

Anne: Wow! / There are certainly enough choices!

Mike: Yeah. That's the problem. / I don't know which one to get. / I like the look of these two, / but I can't decide which one to buy.

7 🔊 **IDENTIFY** Listen to another extract and divide the conversation into chunks.

Anne: Have you read the reviews? That's what I always do.

Mike: I've read some, but I just don't know who to believe. / Everybody says different things.

Anne: Hmm. Well, you always get people with different opinions, so I just look at the summary to see if they're generally good or bad.

8 APPLY Practice the conversation with a partner. Make sure you group the words into chunks.

9 WHAT'S YOUR ANGLE? With a partner, choose a product you are interested in, like an appliance or a piece of furniture. Go online to a shopping website and find two or three choices that you like. Read the information and customer reviews. Discuss which is best.

Now go to page 156 for the Unit 10 Review.

11 Stories

▼ In what ways do stories take us to different places?

▼ Do you prefer telling stories or listening to them?

▼ What stories do you remember from your childhood?

▶ BEHIND THE PHOTO

1 How can stories change the world we live in? Can you think of any examples of famous works of fiction that have had a big impact on the world we live in?

I heard The Lord of the Rings movies led to a big increase in tourism to New Zealand.

2 Think of a book that has had a big impact on you. How did it influence you, and why? Talk about it in groups.

REAL-WORLD GOAL

Watch a movie in English

1 ACTIVATE You are going to watch a video of Fabio telling a story about something that happened to him on a trip to New York. Before you watch, look at the picture. What do you think happened?

2 ▶ ASSESS Watch the video. Were your predictions correct?

◉▶ LISTENING SKILL
Recognizing linking with consonants

🔊 Linking happens when sounds join together. This helps to make the words sound smooth and flow more naturally. Here are some different ways that linking can happen.

consonant–vowel

When a word ends with a consonant sound and the next word begins with a vowel sound, the consonant sound moves forward and connects to the vowel sound of the next word.

turned around
victim of

consonant–consonant

When a word ends in a consonant sound and the next word begins with the same consonant sound, the consonant sound isn't repeated. Both sounds are pronounced together.

first time
from moving

---

3 🔊 NOTICE Listen and notice the way the words link together in each sentence.

1 I was walking around downtown.
2 It was taken right out from under me.
3 He got away, but he didn't take my passport.

4 🔊 APPLY Study these sentences. Use the information in the Listening Skill box above to identify where the consonants link. Then listen and check.

1 I went after him and just barely kept up.
2 I needed my passport to get back home.
3 He threw it into the air.
4 He had decided to return it. What a surprise!
5 It turned out to be a good day!

5 ▶ IDENTIFY Watch the video again and answer the questions.

1 Why did Fabio put his bag on the ground?
2 What items does he mention were in the bag?
3 What did the thief finally do with Fabio's passport?
4 Why did the thief do that?
5 Why couldn't the police investigate the crime?

6 💬 WHAT'S YOUR ANGLE? Do you think Fabio reacted in the right way? What would you do if somebody stole something from you in the street? Tell a partner.

◉▶ GRAMMAR IN CONTEXT Past perfect

We use the past perfect to talk about an action or an event that happened before something else in the past.

*When Fabio looked down, his bag **had disappeared**.*
(The bag disappeared first, and later he looked down.)

We also use the past perfect to talk about an action or event that happened before a particular time in the past.

*He **had visited** New York several times before. (= before he moved there)*

We form the past perfect with:

*Subject + **had/hadn't** + past participle*

See Grammar focus on page 169.

7 APPLY Complete the text using the verbs in parentheses in the past perfect.

I'll never forget my first flight. It was a disaster! On the morning of my flight, I woke up late. I had a new phone, and I ¹_____ (not / use) the alarm before. When I checked, I realized I ²_____ (forget) to turn up the volume! The bus I wanted to take to the airport ³_____ (leave), so I waited for the next one. The traffic was terrible that day, and the journey took much longer than I ⁴_____ (expect). When I arrived at the airport, the passengers for my flight ⁵_____ (start) boarding the plane! It took ages to get through the passport check. Fortunately, I got to the gate just before it closed. I didn't relax until I ⁶_____ (get) on the plane.

8 INTERACT Think of a funny or disastrous travel experience you have had. Tell your partner about it.

VOCABULARY DEVELOPMENT Verb + particle

In English, many verbs are followed by a particle. The particle can give a different meaning to the verb. Look at the meaning of these particles, and notice how they add more information to the verb.

away = at a distance/in another direction
*I saw a man **running away** with my bag.*

back = the idea of returning
*Please, just **give** me **back** my passport.*

through = from one end to the other
*…so I could **look through** the binoculars.*

9 USE Match the verb phrase with its meaning. Use the particle after the verb to help you.

1	work through	a	escape from a place
2	come back	b	find a solution
3	get away	c	stay at a distance
4	keep away	d	return to a place
5	live through	e	see what is behind you
6	look back	f	survive a hard situation

🔑 Oxford 3000™

10 EXPAND Complete the sentences with the phrases from Exercise 9.

1 It's not easy, but I'm sure we can _____ the problem.
2 The thief _____, but the police hope to find him.
3 We _____ the worst flight we had ever experienced.
4 We hadn't been to New York before, but I'm sure we will _____ soon.
5 To stay safe, I try to _____ from dark streets.
6 Before she entered the train station, she _____ to wave goodbye.

11 INTERACT Use three of the verb + particle phrases in your own sentences. Share them with a partner.

**PRONUNCIATION SKILL
Sound changes with consonants**

🔊 Sometimes sounds can change completely. This is true when a word that ends with a consonant sound comes before a word that starts with a different consonant sound. The first consonant sound changes to make the words easier to pronounce. Here are some examples:

just barely	"jus**p**barely"	/t/ → /p/	before /m/, /b/, or /p/
stolen my	"stole**m**my"	/n/ → /m/	before /m/, /b/, or /p/
just give	"jus**k**give"	/t/ → /k/	before /k/ or /g/
can keep	"ke**ŋ**keep"	/n/ → /ŋ/	before /k/ or /g/

12 🔊 NOTICE Listen to these phrases. Notice how the final sound of the first word changes.

1	light blue	"lieplue"
2	mixed bag	"mixpag"
3	ten minutes	"teminutes"
4	ten past	"tempast"
5	light gray	"likrey"
6	first class	"firsklass"
7	tin can	"tiŋkan"
8	brown glass	"browŋglass"

13 🔊 APPLY Listen to these phrases. How does the sound change for the consonants in bold? Note the sound you hear: /m/, /p/, /k/, or /ŋ/.

1	on Monday	"o___onday"
2	ten pounds	"te___pounds"
3	sit back	"si___ack"
4	sunbathe	"su___bathe"
5	not quite	"no___wite"
6	shortcut	"shor___ut"
7	Great Britain	"gray___ritain"
8	in case	"i___kase"

14 WHAT'S YOUR ANGLE? How do you stay safe when you travel? Discuss in groups.

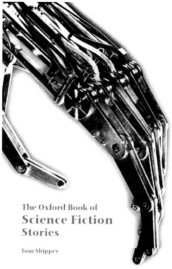

1 ACTIVATE Have you ever read the same book more than once? Why or why not? How important is knowing how a story ends?

2 VOCABULARY Write each type of fiction next to the correct description.

fantasy	romance	fairy tales
historical fiction	science fiction	thrillers
adventure	horror	

Oxford 3000™

3 EXPAND Look at the book covers. What types of fiction are these novels?

4 WHAT'S YOUR ANGLE? Is it harder to predict how some types of fiction end? Do you like predictable endings, or do you want the ending to surprise you?

Types of Fiction

1	If you like reading about fictional worlds with creatures and characters that have magical powers, you'll love these novels!
2	These stories always have a hero and involve lots of action and difficult challenges.
3	This type of fiction is all about two people falling in love and doing whatever it takes to be together.
4	Stories like these, that explore how technology may change our world in the future, are more popular now than ever before.
5	Most people like these exciting "page turners." They're usually about a crime or disaster about to happen!
6	These stories take place in the past and may include real people, events, and places.
7	These are traditional stories told to children, usually to help teach them right from wrong.
8	Stories that scare us and make us feel afraid have always been popular.

The First Stranger

Outside in the heavy rain and darkness, a figure was climbing up the hill from Casterbridge. It was a tall, thin man, about forty years old, dressed all in black and wearing thick, heavy boots.

When he reached the shepherd's* cottage, the rain came down harder than ever. The man left the footpath and went up to the door. He listened carefully, but the music inside had now stopped, and the man seemed unsure what to do. He looked around, but could see no one on the footpath behind him, and no other houses anywhere near.

At last he decided to knock on the door.

"Come in!" called shepherd Fennel. All eyes turned towards the stranger as he entered the warm room.

He kept his hat on, low over his face. "The rain is heavy, friends," he said in a rich, deep voice. "May I come in and rest here for a while?"

"Of course, stranger," replied the shepherd. "You've chosen your moment well, because we're having a party tonight. There's a new baby in the family, you see."

"I hope you and your fine wife will have many more, shepherd," the man answered, smiling politely at Mrs. Fennel. He looked quickly around the room and seemed happy with what he saw. He took his hat off and shook the water from his shoulders.

*shepherd: (noun) a person who takes care of sheep

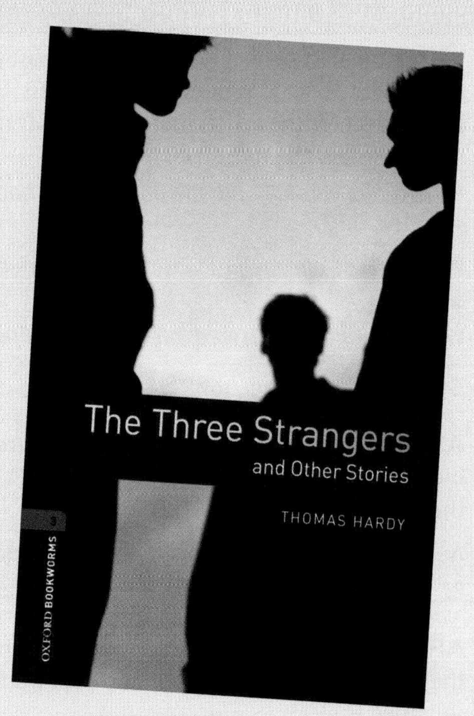

Extract from Oxford Bookworms Level 2 *The Three* Strangers by Thomas Hardy.
Text adaptation by Clare West. © Oxford University Press 2008

5 ASSESS Read this extract from one of Thomas Hardy's best-known short stories, *The Three Strangers*. What type of fiction do you think it is?

6 IDENTIFY Choose the statements that are true.

1 The story takes place at night.
2 The stranger is middle-aged.
3 The shepherd and his wife are alone in the house.
4 They are having a celebration.
5 The stranger decides to leave.

7 WHAT'S YOUR ANGLE? What does the word *stranger* make you think of? Do you trust the stranger in the story?

READING SKILL
Analyzing characters in literary texts

Analyzing a character in a literary text means making conclusions about a character based on direct and indirect descriptions. Direct descriptions often include adjectives and adverbs about the appearance and behavior of the character. Information can also be stated indirectly. For example, descriptions of the scene and how the character fits into it can give indirect information about the character.

8 INTEGRATE Read the text again. How does the author directly describe the stranger? What does the stranger look like? What does he sound like? Take notes.

1 Physical appearance:
_____

2 Clothes: _____
3 Voice: _____

9 EXPAND Think about the indirect descriptions of the two scenes in the story. How does the "heavy rain and darkness" make the stranger seem? How does the "warm room" make the shepherd seem?

10 INTERACT Work in pairs. Find examples in the text that show the character of the shepherd and the stranger. Decide if the adjectives below describe the shepherd, the stranger, or both.

cautious	polite	mysterious	trusting
welcoming	generous	friendly	

A: I think the stranger is cautious because he looked around and "listened carefully" at the door before knocking.

B: I agree. The shepherd isn't! He let a stranger into his house!

GRAMMAR IN CONTEXT
Simple past and past perfect

We use the past perfect with the simple past when we talk about two actions or events in the past. We use the past perfect for the action that happened first. We use the simple past for the most recent action.

*He **listened** carefully, but the music inside **had** now **stopped**.*

We often use *already/just* with the past perfect to say when.

***When** the stranger **arrived**, the party **had already started**.*

See Grammar focus on page 169.

11 ASSESS With a partner, discuss the difference in meaning between this pair of sentences. Pay attention to the order of the actions.

A: When the stranger arrived, the party had started.

B: When the stranger arrived, the party started.

12 APPLY Complete these sentences about the rest of the story. Use the simple past and past perfect in each sentence.

1 The stranger _____ (be) tired because he _____ (walk) a long way.

2 Nobody _____ (see) the stranger before he _____ (come) to the house.

3 He _____ (not / tell) the shepherd why he _____ (leave) Casterbridge so late at night.

4 It _____ (be) cold outside because the temperature _____ (drop) overnight.

5 Another stranger _____ (arrive) soon after the first stranger _____ (sit) down.

6 All the guests _____ (enjoy) the food the shepherd and his wife _____ (prepare).

7 Before the party _____ (finish), a third stranger _____ (knock) at the door.

8 Later, a policeman _____ (say) a prisoner _____ (escape) from a jail nearby.

9 They_____ (look) for the first stranger, but he _____ (disappear).

13 EXPAND Write a short paragraph to continue the story using the simple past and past perfect. Compare your paragraph with a partner's.

14 INTERACT Who were the strangers? How do you think the story ends? Discuss with a partner.

15 EXPAND Who is your favorite fictional character? Make notes and prepare to talk about him/her.

Name:

Description of character:

Plot of story:

Type of fiction:

16 WHAT'S YOUR ANGLE? Describe the character and their story to your classmates. Don't tell your classmates how the story ends.

A private, open-air library in Palermo, Italy

1 ACTIVATE How do you decide what movies to see? Choose your answers, and then tell a partner.

1 ☐ Read the reviews
2 ☐ Ask a friend
3 ☐ Watch the preview
4 ☐ Check the actors
5 ☐ Choose by the type of movie
6 Other: _____

A

B

C

D

E

2 VOCABULARY Use the phases in the box to complete these short movie descriptions.

opening scene	leading role	amusing plot
recent release	real highlight	natural talent

 Oxford 3000™

1 This science fiction movie came out in 2012, so it's not a(n) _____, but it's worth watching if you haven't seen it.

2 The actors in this western have a(n) _____ that makes this one of the greatest movies ever made.

3 There are no surprises in this romantic comedy, but it has a(n) _____ and a few laughs.

4 Hugh Jackman plays the _____ in this outstanding musical based on the famous Hugo novel.

5 Winner of many awards, the _____ of this historical drama is its exciting account of life in thirteenth-century Scotland.

6 This animated movie is a classic. The _____ at the start is very different from the rest of the movie.

3 BUILD Look at the movie posters. Then read the descriptions from Exercise 2 again to match each description with a poster. There is one you won't need.

4 WHAT'S YOUR ANGLE? Have you seen any of these movies? What did you think of them? If you haven't seen them, would you like to? Why or why not? Discuss in groups.

F

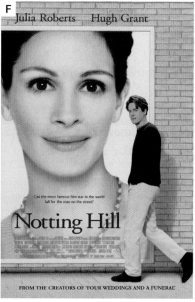

G

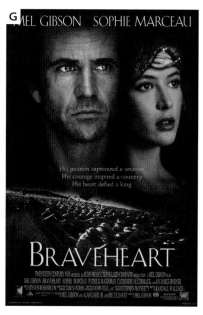

Movie Mad

Finally...

Who hasn't seen *The Hunger Games*? Me! Until last week. I loved the book too much to see the movie! I usually review recent releases, but after finally watching the first movie, I had to write a review. This is a movie that doesn't disappoint from the opening to the final scenes.

The vision of author Suzanne Collins's thrilling science fiction story about the struggle for freedom in a dark future world comes to life thanks to director Francis Lawrence. His use of color is a real highlight of the movie. The actress that plays Katness Everdeen, Jennifer Lawrence, is perfect for the leading role. Her natural talent brings fire to the character. It is a performance that inspires us all to fight for our beliefs.

There are a few weaknesses. For example, the mockingjay pin Katniss wears loses some of its political meaning because she buys it in the movie instead of receiving it as a gift. Also, the action is too fast in some places, and too slow in others.

Despite some weaknesses, this is an exciting movie version of the book with wonderful acting. In my opinion, *The Hunger Games* is one movie you really must see. It is well worth watching and reading.

The Mockingjay pin

5 ASSESS Look at the movie review. Where would you read a review like this?

on a website	in a social media post
in a magazine	in a personal blog
in a newspaper	in a journal

6 IDENTIFY Quickly read the review. What tense is the movie review written in? Why?

7 ASSESS Read the review again. Choose *True* or *False*.

		True	False
1	The movie is based on a novel.	☐	☐
2	Suzanne Collins is the director of the movie.	☐	☐
3	The reviewer was a little disappointed by the movie.	☐	☐
4	Jennifer Lawrence plays her role well.	☐	☐
5	The plot in the movie is exactly the same as the book.	☐	☐

8 INTEGRATE Complete the chart with positive and negative comments about the movie.

Good points	Bad points
The director makes the story come to life.	

9 INTERACT Have you read *The Hunger Games* books and/ or seen the movies? Do you agree with the review? What's the difference between reading a story in a book and watching the same story as a movie? Which do you think is better? Why?

Defining relative clauses tell us which person or thing we're talking about. We use *who/that* to talk about people and *which/that* to talk about things.

The defining relative clause can refer to either the subject or the object of the sentence.

*The Hunger Games is a movie **that/which** doesn't disappoint.* (subject)
*The Hunger Games is one movie **that/which** you really must see.* (object)

We can leave out the relative pronoun when it refers to the object of the sentence.

The Hunger Games is one movie you really must see.

We cannot leave out the relative pronoun when it refers to the subject of the sentence.

*The actress **who/that** plays Katniss Everdeen is perfect for the role.*

See Grammar focus on page 169.

10 IDENTIFY Choose the correct options to complete the text.

The author [1]*which / who* wrote *The Hunger Games* series is Suzanne Collins. There are three books in the series. The first book [2]*that / who* Collins wrote is called *The Hunger Games*. It is a story [3]*which / who* we can admire. It's about a teenage girl [4]*who / which* fights for freedom and refuses to give up. The book [5]*that / who* comes next is called *Catching Fire*. *Mockingjay* is the name of the third book. All three books are now movies, but it is the third book [6]*which / who* is two movies. That's why there are three books, but four movies!

11 ASSESS For each phrase, decide if the relative pronoun is optional (O) or necessary (N).

1 A movie which I really like is… _____
2 Two actors who I think aren't very good are… _____
3 I don't like to watch movies that are about… _____
4 One movie that made me cry is… _____
5 A movie which everyone else loves but I don't like is… _____
6 I can't remember the name of the actor who starred in… _____

12 APPLY Write a sentence to complete each of the phrases in Exercise 11. Then share your ideas with a partner.

To write an effective conclusion, summarize the main points you made and restate your overall opinion so that the reader understands your viewpoint. You can also include a recommendation, clearly stating any actions the reader should take.

13 ASSESS Look at how the movie review is organized. Number these steps in order (1–5).

___ mention the things you enjoy
___ get the reader's attention
___ give a personal recommendation
___ briefly explain the story
___ mention anything you don't like

14 APPLY Look again at the conclusion. How does the reviewer…

1 summarize the main points?
2 restate the overall opinion?
3 give a recommendation?

15 EXPAND How does the conclusion effect your opinion?

16 WHAT'S YOUR ANGLE? What is the last movie you told a friend they should see? Why did you recommend it?

17 PREPARE Make notes to write a review of the movie. Follow the organization in Exercise 13 and refer to the skill box to help you.

18 WRITE Write your review of the movie. Use the checklist to help you improve your review.

☐ Is your review clear and well organized?
☐ Have you used relative clauses correctly?
☐ Did you include movie vocabulary?
☐ Have you used the simple present tense?
☐ Do you mention both positive and negative points?
☐ Did you restate your opinion in the conclusion?
☐ Did you summarize the main points in the conclusion?
☐ Is your recommendation clearly stated in the conclusion?

19 SHARE Exchange your reviews with your classmates. Would you watch the movie based on your partner's review?

Sorry to Interrupt

ENGLISH FOR REAL

1 **ACTIVATE** With a partner, think of reasons why people sometimes interrupt in these situations. Note your ideas. There are multiple options for each situation.

1   in a business meeting   _____
2   in a presentation   _____
3   at a party   _____
4   at a job interview   _____
5   in an English class   _____

2 **INTERACT** What do you do when you want to interrupt someone? For each situation in Exercise 1, discuss with a partner how you would interrupt.

raise your hand

wait for a pause

use eye contact

clear your throat

say "excuse me"

your own idea

3 **EXPAND** Can you think of any occasions when it is *not* acceptable to interrupt?

REAL-WORLD ENGLISH Interrupting a conversation

When you interrupt, you can apologize and ask for permission to speak. How and when you interrupt someone can depend on the situation, the context, and who you are speaking to. For example, for a meeting with co-workers, you can interrupt more directly than with clients. In order to make an interruption more polite, you can use longer expressions for apologizing and asking for permission to speak. Similarly, when speaking with your boss, you need to interrupt less directly than among friends. In less formal situations, you can be more direct by telling the other person to stop speaking and possibly leave out the request for permission.

4 ANALYZE Look at these expressions you can use to interrupt. How direct or indirect are they? Choose your answers.

		Direct	Indirect	
a	Do you mind if I interrupt you for a second?	1	2	3
b	Wait (a minute)! I have to tell you…	1	2	3
c	Can I add something?	1	2	3
d	Hold on!	1	2	3
e	I don't want to interrupt, but…	1	2	3
f	Sorry, can I just say something?	1	2	3
g	Excuse me. Can I interrupt you for a moment?	1	2	3
h	Sorry to interrupt (but…)	1	2	3
i	Wait!	1	2	3

5 ▶ INTEGRATE Watch the video. Which expressions from Exercise 4 do you hear?

_____

_____

_____

6 APPLY Work in pairs. Decide which expressions from Exercise 4 you would use to interrupt in these situations. Write the letter (a–i) of all possible expressions next to each situation.

1 You're in a study group and want to make a point. ____
2 Your boss is chairing a meeting, and you have a question. ____
3 Your teacher has said something you don't understand. ____
4 Two co-workers are talking, and you need to ask for help. ____

7 INTERACT Work in pairs. Practice a short dialogue for each situation in Exercise 6.

8 INTEGRATE Work in groups. Choose one location from Exercise 1 and think of a scenario. Then prepare a role play. Decide your roles and what to say. Who interrupts? How? Why? Use appropriate expressions and follow the advice in the Real-World English box.

9 ANALYZE Take turns role-playing your conversations in front of the class. For each role play you watch, answer these questions.

■ How many interruptions are there?
■ What expressions to interrupt do you hear?
■ Are the expressions suitable for the situation, topic, and relationship between the speakers?

10 WHAT'S YOUR ANGLE? Have you ever interrupted someone and regretted it? Why? What happened?

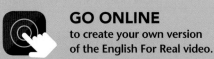

GO ONLINE
to create your own version
of the English For Real video.

11.5 A Person of Influence

1 ACTIVATE Read the text describing a famous person and answer the questions.

1 What did Ernest Hemingway look like?

_____

2 Find examples in the text that support these adjectives to describe his character.

active: _____

hard working: _____

Ernest Hemingway was a powerful, physical man: he stood six feet tall, was very strong, and had a full, black beard. He was a very active man and was always on the move. He traveled a lot, including to Spain where he saw his first bullfight. But like all true writers, Hemingway never stopped writing, even when it appeared he was playing. His enjoyment of the bullfights in Pamplona led to his writing what is thought to be the best book on the subject written by a non-Spaniard, _Death in the Afternoon_ (1932). In addition, his 1933–1934 African safari produced _Green Hills of Africa_ (1935). Both are excellent examples of Hemingway's ability to entertain and instruct through the use of apparently simple nonfiction writing.

—adapted from _The Oxford Encyclopedia of American Literature_, edited by Jay Panini and Philip W. Leininger

SPEAKING Describing people

You might need to describe somebody's appearance to someone who hasn't met them. Physical descriptions of height, hair, eye color, body size, and clothing they often wear are obvious starting points.

She is tall and has short, dark hair.

But personality and behavior descriptions are also useful when you want to give more detail about that person, for example, if someone wants to know how well they might get along with them.

He is very kind and thoughtful, but a bit too serious at times.

Telling a story about the person really brings them to life. This gives a concrete example of what the person is like and helps the listener to get a full picture of the person's character.

2 🔊 IDENTIFY Listen to Nicola describe an important person in her life. Complete the notes.

Relationship → Shirley is Nicola's _____.

Appearance → tall, thin, with _____ dark hair

Character → _____ (example: sends money to buy _____)

Funny (example: she's always _____)

3 🔊 APPLY Listen to Nicola tell a story about her aunt. Which of these character adjectives do you think the story shows best?

adventurous	thoughtful	honest
hard working	easygoing	determined

4 WHAT'S YOUR ANGLE? Have you ever helped to organize a party for a friend or relative? Who? When was it? Has anyone ever organized a surprise party for you?

5 EXPAND Think of some important people in your life. They could be friends, family members, a teacher, or even a famous person you admire. Make a list.

6 PREPARE Choose _one_ person from your list, and make notes of their appearance and character. Give examples to support any character adjectives you use.

1 An important person in my life: _____

2 Relationship to you: _____

3 Appearance: _____

4 Character:

   1 _____ Example: _____

   2 _____ Example: _____

7 DEVELOP Think of a story about this person. Take notes. How does the story show their character?

■ When was it?

■ Where were you?

■ What happened?

8 PRACTICE Practice telling the story to your partner. When you finish, ask your partner for their suggestions and make any necessary changes.

9 SHARE Work in groups. Take turns describing the appearance and character of an important person in your life, and then tell a story about them. Explain how the story shows their character.

10 WHAT'S YOUR ANGLE? Think of a story about you. How does it show your character?

Now go to page 157 for the Unit 11 Review.

12 Emotion

How do you think these people feel?

What affects people's emotions?

What do you do to feel better when you're having a bad day?

BEHIND THE PHOTO

1 **How would you feel in these situations? Discuss your feelings with a partner.**

You're walking in the countryside on a beautiful day.

You are starting a new job.

You're at a party with lots of people.

You dropped your cell phone, and now there is no signal.

The train is delayed, and you're late for a meeting.

2 **What does happiness mean to you? Complete this sentence three ways, and then share your ideas in a group.**

For me, happiness is…

REAL-WORLD GOAL

Write down
something that

12.1   It's All about Attitude

1 ACTIVATE Read the statement. Do you agree? Why or why not?

Your attitude and how you perceive the world influences everything that happens to you.

2 **IDENTIFY** Watch the video of Josh talking about his job. He is a psychologist and motivational speaker, someone who gives talks to encourage and help people to feel more positive. Which three things does Josh think are important?

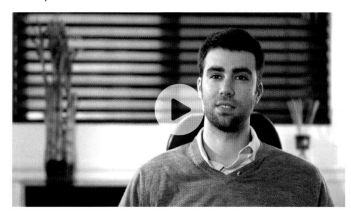

- ☐ Learning from mistakes
- ☐ Doing well at school
- ☐ Having role models
- ☐ Having good time management
- ☐ Laughing at things

3 ▶ **EXPAND** Watch the video again and complete the notes.

Skills Josh Teaches
- problem solving
- how to keep a positive attitude
- how to have ¹_____
- how to build social ²_____
Advice from Josh
Important to learn from ³_____.
Keep a positive ⁴_____.
Don't focus on problems. Focus on ⁵_____ and create a plan.
Don't waste time (texting, ⁶_____, video games).
Find role models.
Get right amount of ⁷_____, healthy food, and exercise.
Find at least one person to ⁸_____.

4 WHAT'S YOUR ANGLE? Do you think your attitude has an influence on people around you?

GRAMMAR IN CONTEXT
Adjective + infinitive / infinitive of purpose

We usually use the *to*-infinitive when a verb follows an adjective.
Josh is **happy to help** people of all ages.

We often use a sentence that starts with *It's…* when we use an adjective + *to*-infinitive.
It's **important to learn** from your mistakes.

We also use the *to*-infinitive to give the reason for doing something. This is called the *infinitive of purpose*.
He gives workshops **to encourage** people to be more positive.

We make negative infinitives with *not* + *to*-infinitive.
It's hard **not to think** about all the work I have to do.

See Grammar focus on page 170.

5 APPLY Choose the correct options.

1   a   It's interesting learn from other people.
    b   It's interesting to learn from other people.
2   a   I've decided to see a motivational speaker.
    b   I've decided see a motivational speaker.
3   a   They were excited to hear his advice.
    b   They were excited heard his advice.
4   a   He was disappointed to not get the job.
    b   He was disappointed not to get the job.
5   a   The company employed him to motivate their staff.
    b   The company employed him motivating their staff.
6   a   It's hard not to play video games all evening!
    b   It's hard not play video games all evening!

6 WHAT'S YOUR ANGLE? Complete these adjective + infinitive sentences to write true statements about yourself.

1   I think I'm fortunate to

_____

2   Recently, I was disappointed to

_____

3   I was surprised to _____

4   I am prepared to _____

5   I hope one day, I will be able to

_____

7 **APPLY** Answer the questions below with a *to*-infinitive.

1 Why is it important to learn English?

It is important to learn English to travel the world, to get a better job, to...

2 How can you save money?

3 Why is it smart to work hard?

4 How can you keep a positive attitude?

5 What can you do to keep healthy?

8 **INTERACT** Work in groups. Compare your ideas. Do you have similar answers?

9 **ASSESS** Read the blog post. Which is the best title for the story?

☐ The day I learned to laugh at myself

☐ The day I learned how to decorate

☐ The day I learned to be more careful with paint

| Home | About | Search | |

The Motivation Man

Today's question: Can you laugh at your mistakes? Tell us about a funny mistake you made and what you learned from it. Post your stories below.

When I moved into my first apartment around a year ago, I was kind of excited. I thought it meant that I was an adult. I decided to paint the place myself to save some money. I had never painted or done things like that before. One weekend, I bought the paint and the brushes and started painting. Things went really well, and after an hour, I had finished one wall. I was feeling sort of tired, so I decided to take a break. I stepped back to admire my work…and put my foot in the can of paint! It went everywhere! I had put newspaper down to protect the floor, but I spent all day trying to clean it up. Eventually, I looked around the room and started laughing. It was a complete mess!

Finally, I called a professional cleaning company. It cost almost $650. I had to throw away a lot of stuff and buy a new pair of shoes. That can of paint only cost $20. I can laugh about it now, but at the time I felt terrible. They say it's important to learn from your mistakes. I'm happy to say I learned never to step on a can of paint! And that being an adult means "paying" for your mistakes.

Kieran O'Brien, Cleveland, USA

10 **EXPAND** Read the text again and answer the questions.

1 Why did Kieran decide to paint the apartment himself?

2 How long did it take him to paint one wall?

3 What was he doing when he had the accident?

4 Who did he call to solve the problem?

5 How does he feel about the accident now?

WRITING SKILL Using narrative tenses

When we describe events or tell a story in the past, we use the narrative tenses: simple past, past continuous, and past perfect.

We use the simple past to describe the main events in the story.

*When I **moved** into my first apartment around a year ago, I **was** kind of excited.*

We use the past continuous for background events or longer actions which are interrupted by shorter actions. We use the simple past for the shorter actions.

*I **was feeling** sort of tired, so I decided to take a break.*

We also use the past perfect to look back to the past before the events of the story.

*I **had never painted** or done things like that before.*

11 **IDENTIFY** Read Kieran's story. How many examples of each tense can you find?

1 Simple past ____

2 Past continuous ____

3 Past perfect ____

12 **APPLY** Choose the correct tense to complete the story.

Yesterday, I met one of my friends for dinner. We [1]*had went / went* to a restaurant we had never been to before. It [2]*rained / was raining* out when I [3]*arrived / was arriving*, so I went inside to wait. Just then, my friend [4]*had sent / sent* me a text. He was running late. I was kind of hungry, so I decided to order something while I [5] *was waiting / had waited* for him. After that, I [6]*texted / had texted* my friend to tell him that I was seated near the entrance. After around ten minutes, my friend [7]*had called / called* me. He said he was at the restaurant and couldn't find me. I [8]*thought / was thinking* that was weird, but we decided to meet at the door. When I got there, he wasn't there! Finally, I [9]*asked / had asked* him what restaurant he was at. He said Green Leaf, which was right. It turns out there are two! He was on the other side of town!

13 WHAT'S YOUR ANGLE? Think of a funny story that happened to you. It could be something from your childhood or more recently. Take notes.

VOCABULARY DEVELOPMENT Vague language

It is not always necessary to use exact words or phrases. You can use vague language, or words and phrases that are not exact. This is more common when writing informally. Look at some vague language you can use.

When it is not necessary to be precise, you can use *about, almost,* or *around.*

*I moved into my apartment **around** a year ago.*

Where you are not certain, you can use *somewhere, something,* or *someone.*

***Someone** told me about The Motivation Man blog; I can't remember who.*

When you do not need to include everything to complete a list, you can use *stuff / things (like that).*

*I had never painted by myself or done **things like that**.*
*I had to throw away a lot of **stuff**.*

When you want to describe feelings, you can use *sort of* or *kind of.*

*I was **kind of** excited.*

14 INTERACT Can you think of any examples of vague language in your language? Discuss in groups.

15 APPLY Make these statements more vague.

1 I was upset when I lost my phone.
2 I spent 20 minutes looking for it.
3 I'd had it in my bag with my wallet when I left for work.
4 I might have lost it on the subway.
5 A new phone will cost me $200.

16 PREPARE Prepare to write an account of your story. Organize your notes according to the following structure.

- What happened?
- How did you feel about it at the time?
- How do you feel about it now?
- What did you learn?

17 WRITE Write your story. Use a variety of narrative tenses.

18 IMPROVE Exchange your work with a classmate. Carefully read each other's story and try to find areas to improve. Use the checklist to help you.

☐ Is it well organized and easy to follow?
☐ Are narrative tenses used correctly?
☐ Can you find examples of the *to*-infinitive?
☐ Is it an amusing story?
☐ Did the writer say what they learned?

19 WHAT'S YOUR ANGLE? Post your story online in a blog or on social media. Encourage your friends to share funny stories about themselves or people they know.

Young women sing at the annual Reed Dance Ceremony in Swaziland

1 ACTIVATE Do you always say how you feel, or do you keep your feelings to yourself? Take the quiz.

1 You are upset with your roommate. Do you…
   a tell them right away and explain why?
   b decide to say nothing?
   c wait and plan to tell them later?

2 Two friends come to visit, but you are working. Do you…
   a let them in and make them feel welcome?
   b ask them to come back when you've finished work?
   c say you need to work and tell them to leave?

3 You don't understand what your homework assignment is. Do you…
   a tell the teacher that you're confused?
   b ask a classmate to explain it?
   c say nothing and decide not to do it?

2 VOCABULARY Write each adjective of emotion in the correct column.

| satisfied | guilty | curious | impatient |
| relaxed | anxious | welcome | |

⚲ Oxford 3000™

Positive	Negative

3 BUILD Work in pairs. Look at the pictures below and discuss how the people feel. How many emotions from Exercise 2 can you identify?

4 USE For each adjective in Exercise 2, think of an example when you feel that way. Tell a partner.

I feel guilty when I don't go to the gym!

PRONUNCIATION SKILL
Adjectives ending in -ed: /t/, /d/, **and** /ɪd/

There are three ways -ed can be pronounced at the end of a word.

/t/ *relaxed* → after unvoiced sounds like *p, k, f, gh, sh, ch, ss, c,* or *x*

/d/ *concerned* → after voiced sounds like *l, n, r, g, v, s, z, b,* or *m*

/ɪd/ *interested* → after /t/ and /d/ sound

---

5 APPLY Put each adjective in the correct column.

amused	delighted	disappointed
embarrassed	excited	impressed
pleased	scared	stressed

/t/	/d/	/ɪd/

6 🔊 NOTICE Listen and check. Then listen and repeat.

7 DEVELOP Work in pairs. Identify the correct pronunciation for each word. Use a dictionary to help you.

amazed	confused	frightened	shocked
bored	delighted	interested	surprised
concerned	determined	relaxed	worried

8 APPLY Work in pairs. Take turns saying a word from the list. Your partner should point to the sound they hear.

/t/   /d/   /ɪd/

9 ASSESS Read the blog post. Is there a phrase in your language that means the same as *l'esprit d'escalier*?

Home	About	Articles	

Wordzone

Joshua Barkley

Did you know there are over 6,000 languages in the world? Not every word and phrase in one language has a direct translation into another. Although some words are easy to translate, others are "untranslatable." For example, there are many words to describe emotions that can't be translated into other languages.

Here's one. Do you know that feeling when someone says something and you want to have a quick and clever response but can't think of one even though you try? Well, the French actually have a phrase for it: *l'esprit d'escalier*, or the "spirit of the stairs." They call it that because it's always when you're leaving or walking away, down the stairs, that you think of the perfect thing to say! Despite the fact that you may never get to say it, it's the perfect reply. We don't have a phrase like that in English. I'd like to find more examples. Do you have any?

Comments

Mauro   We Italians have one: *Abbiocco* means "feeling tired after eating a big meal!"

Fran   Well, there's *Schadenfreude* in German, which is the enjoyment you feel when someone fails or has bad luck.

Joseph   Nice one, Fran. Doesn't that make you feel guilty??

Mathilde   In Denmark, we use *hyggelig* a lot to describe a comfortable, warm, and satisfied feeling. Like relaxing and having a cup of tea with your family.

João   In Brazil, we have *saudade*. It's when you feel pleasure in spite of also feeling pain or sadness…like when you miss someone or something that you love, but you can't hope to get back.

Akiko   In Japan, *mono no aware* is a bitter sweet feeling that beautiful things don't last, so we need to enjoy them while they are alive. We appreciate the beauty of flowers in the spring even though they last only a short time. ☺

10 APPLY Match the contrasting ideas.

1 Why do some people laugh
2 *Although* we were surprised by the election result,
3 *Even though* he said he hadn't broken the vase,
4 I was satisfied with the hotel,
5 *Despite* being in tears just moments earlier,
6 I felt anxious at the interview,
7 *In spite of* the long delay,

a we accepted it.
b none of the passengers was impatient.
c *even though* they don't understand a joke?
d *though* I tried not to show it.
e *despite the fact* that there was no pool.
f the baby was smiling now.
g I could see Tim felt guilty.

11 INTEGRATE Read the blog again and complete the chart.

Phrase	Language	Meaning
		tired after eating a big meal
hyggelig		
l'esprit d'escalier	French	that feeling when someone says something and you want to have a quick and clever reply…but can't think of one
mono no aware		
	Portuguese	
Schadenfreude		

12 INTERACT The Japanese phrase *mono no aware* contrasts how something can make us happy even though it doesn't last. Discuss in groups things that don't last but that make you happy.

I enjoy watching snow fall. It's so beautiful.

I like going on vacation even though a vacation never lasts long enough!

13 WHAT'S YOUR ANGLE? Can you think of a word or phrase to describe a feeling or emotion in your language that has no direct translation to English? Are there words in your language that express the feelings in Exercise 7?

GRAMMAR IN CONTEXT Verb + *to*-infinitive only

We use the *to*-infinitive after verbs for discussing plans and intentions: *agree, decide, hope, plan, promise, want,* and *would like.*

*I'd like **to** find more examples!*

We also use the *to*-infinitive after other verbs, like *need, learn,* and *seem.*

We form negatives by putting *not* before the *to*-infinitive.

*I'm hoping **not to miss** my flight again!*

See Grammar focus on page 170.

14 IDENTIFY Look in the text. How many verb + *to*-infinitive examples from the Grammar box can you find?

15 APPLY Use the verbs in the box to complete the sentences below.

agree to	decide not to	learn to	like to
plan to	promise not to	seem to	want to

1 I'd really _____ visit Florence one day.
2 You must _____ do that again! It's too dangerous.
3 We could see a movie tonight, if you _____.
4 Next year I _____ go on vacation to Egypt.
5 The government might _____ increase taxes this year.
6 Why don't you _____ play the piano?
7 I like the plan, but James will never _____ it.
8 The children _____ like their new school very much.

16 INTERACT Work with a partner. Talk about these topics using verb + *to*-infinitive included in the sentences.

1 Something fun you *would like to* do tonight.
Tonight I'd like to eat out and then watch a movie!
2 Someone you *hope to* meet in the future.
3 Someone special you *plan to* see soon.
4 Something important you *learned to* do when you were young.
5 Someone you *need to* speak to later.
6 Somewhere exciting you *want to* go one day.

17 INTERACT Compare your answers with a partner. How similar or different are you?

1 ACTIVATE Read the text. Have you heard of the Prisoner's Dilemma before?

The Prisoner's Dilemma

The Prisoner's Dilemma is a famous example of game theory. The police have two men who they think have committed a crime. However, the police don't have any evidence. The men are separated and cannot talk to each other. Each man is told: if they both admit the crime, they will get eight years in prison; if one man admits the crime, he will go free but his partner will go to prison for 20 years; if they both say they didn't do it, they both go to prison for a year.

—adapted from *Dictionary of the Social Sciences*, edited by Craig Calhoun

2 ASSESS Read the text again and complete the summary.

1 If both prisoners say they are innocent, they will both receive _____ year(s).

2 If both prisoners say they are guilty, they will both receive _____ year(s).

3 If prisoner A says he's guilty and prisoner B says he is innocent,
   → prisoner A will receive _____ year(s) and
   → prisoner B will receive _____ year(s).

3 INTERACT What is the best decision each man should make? Discuss in groups.

4 VOCABULARY Complete the phrases using words from the box.

balance (n)	calculate (v)	convince (v)
risk (n)	thinking (n)	value (v)

♟ Oxford 3000™

1 work and life _____
2 change your way of _____
3 _____ someone's opinion
4 take a _____
5 try to _____ the possibilities
6 _____ someone you're right

5 BUILD Complete the sentences with the words from Exercise 4.

If you have a problem or a difficult decision to make, then it's important to consider all the factors so you can [1]_____ the best way forward. Of course, you should always [2]_____ the advice of people around you. However, there is a [3]_____ that other people may try to [4]_____ you to agree with their way of [5]_____. Always trust your own judgment, and try to find a [6]_____.

6 **IDENTIFY** Listen to the beginning of a podcast. Do you agree with their decision about the Prisoner's Dilemma?

> **LISTENING SKILL**
> **Recognizing intonation in exclamations**
>
> An exclamation is a statement that shows emotion. Recognizing intonation in exclamations helps you understand how the speaker feels. Often exclamations start with *What (a)…!* or *That's/How* (+ adjective)*!* Expressions such as *Wow!* and *No way!* are also exclamations. When you use exclamations in English, the pitch of your voice goes up more obviously, and you also speak more loudly.

7 IDENTIFY Match each exclamation with a meaning.

1	Ha ha!	a	What a relief.
2	Wow!	b	I understand.
3	Ah!	c	I don't understand.
4	Phew!	d	That's funny.
5	Huh?	e	That's amazing.

8 🔊 **NOTICE** Listen to each statement twice. Notice how intonation can change a statement into an exclamation showing emotion.

1 She left. / She left!
2 It's raining. / It's raining!
3 What a day. / What a day!
4 There's Julie. / There's Julie!
5 James is here. / James is here!

9 🔊 **APPLY** Listen again. Write the number of each expression next to the correct emotion.

___ thankful   ___ excited
___ disappointed   ___ angry
___ surprised

10 🔊 **APPLY** Listen to the rest of the podcast. Choose the correct emotion for each exclamation you hear.

1 What?   surprised / angry
2 I see!   interested / bored
3 A third!   amused / disappointed
4 Really?   surprised / bored
5 No way!   amazed / afraid

Featured Podcast
Strange But True

Decisions, Decisions

Jordan Davis

episode number, 6

11 🔊 **IDENTIFY** Listen to the podcast again and answer the questions.

1 When did the Marshmallow Test begin?
2 How old were the children in the study?
3 What did the children have to do to get two marshmallows?
4 How many children didn't eat the marshmallow right away?
5 What did the study prove?
6 What surprising results did the study find later?

12 **WHAT'S YOUR ANGLE?** Think about your children or children you know. Who do you think would "pass" the Marshmallow Test?

🔊 **GRAMMAR IN CONTEXT Verbs with the -ing form**

We use the -ing form after verbs that express likes and dislikes: *enjoy, like, love, hate, can't stand,* and *don't mind.*
*I **hate making** big decisions.*

We also use the -ing form after these common verbs: *finish, go, imagine, keep, mind,* and *stop.*
*Why don't you **stop worrying** and make up your mind?*

We do not use the -ing form after verbs that express plans and intentions. We use the *to*-infinitive with these verbs: *agree, arrange, decide, hope, need, plan, promise, want,* and *would like.*
*I **decided to start** making quicker decisions.*

See Grammar focus on page 170.

13 **EXPAND** Write the correct form of the verb to complete the sentence.

1 I don't mind *waiting / to wait* to make a decision.
2 I can't stop *thinking / to think* about the Marshmallow Test.
3 I promise *making / to make* quicker decisions.
4 I want *knowing / to know* what else influences decisions.
5 I just finished *listening / to listen* to a great podcast.
6 I love *learning / to learn* about the mind.

14 **APPLY** Complete the text with the correct form of the verb.

The Truth about Decisions

Up to 90% of our decisions are based on emotions. Just think about it. Most of us enjoy ¹_____ (buy) things we don't really need, and we all have fears that don't make sense. For example, I can't stand to ²_____ (go) to the garage because I think I'll see a spider. A friend of mine even stopped ³_____ (use) the elevator because he hates small spaces.

Researcher António Damásio found that people who couldn't feel emotions because of a brain injury also found it very difficult to make decisions. Rather than think our emotions keep ⁴_____ (get) in the way, we need to view them as an essential part of our decision making. Can you imagine ⁵_____ (decide) to do something without also ⁶_____ (ask) yourself how you feel about it?

15 **INTERACT** How do your emotions influence the decisions you make? Think of one thing you really enjoy doing and one thing you can't stand doing. Explain your reasons in groups.

I really enjoy…
I can't stand…

16 **WHAT'S YOUR ANGLE?** Who do you ask for advice before you make an important decision?

No Way!

1 ▶ **ACTIVATE** Watch the video and take notes. What news does each person have?

1 Max's news _____

2 Kevin's news _____

3 Dave's news _____

REAL-WORLD ENGLISH Reacting to news

How you react to news depends on if the news is good or bad and the situation. With friends, your language can be more informal than in a meeting with your employer. Part of reacting to news is letting the other person know you want to hear more. You can use short phrases like *Really?* to show this. *Really?* is used in most situations. The tone you use can express excitement, surprise, or sympathy. In formal situations, the tone is often neutral and the expressions people use are usually less idiomatic.

◀)) *Really?* (neutral) = *Is that correct?*
Really? (sympathy) = *I'm so sorry.*
Really? (excitement) = *That's great!*
Really? (surprise) = *I didn't expect that to happen.*

2 ◀)) **APPLY** Listen to Andy's responses from the video. Choose the tone you hear.

1	*Really?*	Sympathy	Surprise
2	*Thanks.*	Neutral	Excitement
3	*Really?*	Neutral	Sympathy
4	*Hey!*	Sympathy	Excitement
5	*No way!*	Surprise	Excitement

3 **IDENTIFY** Look at these expressions from the video. Match each expression with a way you can react to news. Complete the table.

That's awesome.	You must feel relieved!	I'm really happy for you!
You got the grant!	So what happened?	

Reactions	Informal
Repeat the key information	
Ask for more information	
Show you understand	
Use *That's* + an adjective	
Say how you feel	

ENGLISH FOR REAL

4 ▶ **EXPAND** Watch the second part of the video again. Complete the expressions each person uses to react to news.

1 To show excitement at Kevin's news:
   Andy says → That's _____
   Max says → That's _____

2 To show sympathy with Max:
   Andy says → That's _____
   Kevin says → Don't _____

3 To show surprise at Dave's news:
   Andy says → You're _____
   Max says → You must _____

5 **ANALYZE** Study this formal conversation between two co-workers in the office kitchen. A is one of B's employees. They are both architects. Complete the table.

A: So I won the contract from SK Energy to design their new offices!

B: You won the contract! That's wonderful news!

A: Yes, I'm pleased. I've been working on that for weeks.

B: All the hard work has paid off. I'm happy for you.

A: Thank you. It's three months' work.

B: Really? When do you plan to start?

Reactions	Formal
Repeat the key information	
Ask for more information	
Show you understand	
Use *That's* + an adjective	
Say how you feel	

6 🔊 **DEVELOP** Listen to these expressions you can use to react to news. How would you rate the formality of each expression?

		Informal			Formal	
a	Congratulations! I'm so happy for you.	1	2	3	4	5
b	Wow. How exciting!	1	2	3	4	5
c	Oh, that's too bad.	1	2	3	4	5
d	I'm sorry to hear that.	1	2	3	4	5
e	Good for you. Well done.	1	2	3	4	5
f	That sounds fun.	1	2	3	4	5
g	That's awful. Don't worry about it.	1	2	3	4	5
h	No way! You're kidding.	1	2	3	4	5

7 **INTEGRATE** Complete the dialogues using words from Exercise 6.

1 A: I'm going hiking next weekend.
   B: That _____ fun. Can I come?

2 A: I just heard James is going to move to Australia!
   B: You're _____. I don't believe you.

3 A: Guess what! I passed all my final exams!
   B: _____ for you. That's great.

4 A: I have a terrible cough.
   B: I'm _____ to hear that. Maybe you should see a doctor?

8 **INTERACT** Practice the dialogues in Exercise 7 with a partner. Then think of different expressions to react to the news. Make sure you use the appropriate tone.

9 **EXPAND** Work in pairs. Make conversations from these situations. Use expressions for reacting to news, and follow the information in the Real-World English box to help you.

1 Tell your roommate that your interview went well and they offered you a job.
   A: *Guess what! The interview went really well, and they offered me the job!*
   B: *Really? They offered you the job? Congratulations!*

2 Call your friend to say you have to work late, so you cannot go to their house for dinner tonight.

3 Tell some co-workers you are going on vacation to Hong Kong next month.

4 Explain to your boss you canceled your vacation to Bermuda because you got sick.

5 Your best friend tells you they are getting married next month.

6 Your sister just had a baby boy. You tell your classmates.

7 Tell your teacher you are moving into a new apartment next weekend.

GO ONLINE
to create your own version
of the English For Real video.

I've Had It for Years

1 ACTIVATE Ask and answer the questions with a partner.

1 In what ways do possessions make you happy?
2 Which possession have you had the longest?
3 Do you ever lend things to other people?
4 When you were a child, what possession did you value the most?

2 🔊 EXPAND Listen to Alexander talk about an important possession in his life. What is it called?

3 IDENTIFY Answer the questions.

1 What country is the instrument from?
2 How long has Alexander had one?
3 Who gave it to Alexander?
4 When did he move to the United States?
5 How does he feel when he plays it?
6 Why is it so important to him?

SPEAKING Describing feelings and emotions

When you talk about something, try to avoid very general adjectives. Try to find a more specific word to describe your feelings. For example, instead of *happy*, you can say *optimistic* or *proud*. You can also give a reason to explain why you feel that way.

*I'm **proud** of myself because I've worked hard to learn to play.*

You can use different structures to talk about feelings.

be + adjective
*I **am amazed** that I still have the same one.*

get + adjective
*I **get excited** to play.*

feel + adjective
*I **feel peaceful** when I play it.*

feel like
*I **feel like** it's a part of me.*

If you aren't sure how you feel, you can use *kind of* or *sort of* to show you aren't certain.

*I was **sort of** nervous.*

---

4 🔊 APPLY Listen and choose the emotion that matches the underlined word.

1 I was <u>delighted</u> about it, but worried, too.
   a happy   b afraid
2 I was <u>terrified</u> I would never be as good as him.
   a sad   b afraid
3 I feel <u>peaceful</u> when I play it.
   a calm   b sad
4 I was really <u>anxious</u> because I'm shy.
   a afraid   b angry
5 Now, I get <u>excited</u> to play in public.
   a happy   b angry

5 IDENTIFY Use a dictionary to look up the words. Then complete the sentences with the correct word.

annoyed	cheerful	embarrassed	grateful	thoughtful

1 I get _____ when people use my things.
2 He feels like it's a _____ gift.
3 She feels _____ that she still has it.
4 I was _____ because it was beautiful day.
5 They get _____ to talk in public.

6 PREPARE What is the most important possession in your life? Describe it in the space below. Then take notes to answer each question.

1 My most important possession:
   _____
2 Description: _____
3 Where did you get it?
4 How long have you had it?
5 What do you do with it?
6 Where do you keep it?
7 What do you think of when you use it?

7 EXPAND Write three sentences about how the possession makes you feel. Use a thesaurus or dictionary to find more specific adjectives.

8 SHARE Work in groups. Use your notes to tell each other about a possession that is important to you.

9 WHAT'S YOUR ANGLE? Are there any possessions that you would *never* sell?

Now go to page 158 for the Unit 12 Review.

Unit 1

VOCABULARY

1 Complete the sentences.

1 You might feel a_____ or f_____ when someone shouts at you.

2 You get e_____ from doing things you like.

3 A feeling of c_____ is better for your health than stress.

4 Some people spend their whole lives searching for h_____.

5 Missing someone or losing something important to you can cause s_____.

2 Choose the correct option.

1 He pointed *angry / angrily* at the door.

2 I felt *sadness / sadly* when I waved goodbye to my friend.

3 She stared *happiness / happily* out the window.

4 I hugged my family *enthusiastically / enthusiastic* when I arrived.

5 They *calmly / calm* bowed before I left.

3 Complete the questions using the words in the box.

work	influence	deal	look	keep

1 Of all the people you know, who do you _____ up to most?

2 Do childhood experiences have a(n) _____ on you for the rest of your life?

3 How do you _____ with negative people?

4 Do you prefer to _____ in touch with old friends or make new ones?

5 When you have a problem, can you usually _____ out a solution?

 GO ONLINE to play the vocabulary game.

GRAMMAR

4 Complete each question with *do*, *does*, *is*, or *are*. Then ask and answer the questions with a partner.

1 Who ___ you speak with more: your family or friends?

2 When ___ you speak to your best friend?

3 ___ you a good friend to other people?

4 How often ___ you ask your friends for advice?

5 ___ you often give gifts to other people?

6 ___ your family give you a lot of support?

7 Who ___ the last person you bought a present for?

5 Match each statement with a tag.

1 You're new here,   a don't you?

2 This weather is terrible,   b aren't you?

3 We don't have much time,   c do we?

4 You like working here,   d is it?

5 The meeting isn't in Room 2, e isn't it?

6 Complete the text using the verbs in parentheses in the simple present or present continuous.

Today we ¹_____ (have) more ways than ever before of keeping in contact. People ²_____ (not / need) to meet face to face anymore. The use of smartphones and the Internet ³_____ (become) increasingly popular. In a survey of more than 1,000 young Americans, the top three forms of digital communication were texting, social media, and phone calls. Technology today ⁴_____ (change) the way we connect and what it ⁵_____ (mean) to be friends. However, according to research, it's not the number of people you ⁶_____ (know) that ⁷_____ (matter) but the value of your relationships.

 GO ONLINE to play the grammar game.

DISCUSSION POINT

7 Read the quote. In what ways do you try to be a good friend? Is there anything you *wouldn't* do for a friend?

 "The only way to have a friend is to be one."

—Ralph Waldo Emerson, selected from *Oxford Essential Quotations*, 5ᵗʰ ed., edited by Susan Ratcliffe

 GO ONLINE and listen to a podcast. Then add your comments to the discussion board.

 ZOOM IN

8 What about you?

Task 1 Talk about how you connect with people using technology.

Task 2 Write a paragraph about someone you admire.

Task 3 Find some photos of your friends. Tell your partner about them.

9 Complete the table.

	I did this well	I need more practice
Task 1		
Task 2		
Task 3		

Unit 2

VOCABULARY

1 Complete the sentences using the words in the box.

benefit	decrease	recover	replace	reverse

1 Do you think it is possible to _____ time, and go back in the past?
2 One _____ of managing your time well is it reduces stress.
3 It takes time to _____ from a broken heart.
4 As you get older, you may notice a _____ in the number of hours' sleep you need.
5 After 15 years, I decided it was time to _____ my washing machine.

2 Complete the conversation with a phrase with *time*.

A: Hurry up, or we'll ¹_____ time.
B: Don't worry, I've done this before. ²_____ time I made a web page it was really quick.
A: But the assignment is due in an hour and you're ³_____ time on the title.
B: It's really important to get this right.
A: But we need to ⁴_____ some time on the pictures before it's too late.
B: We will finish it ⁵_____ time. Look—the title's done now. What next?
A: Finally! OK, let's add the pictures. And ⁶_____ time we work together, let's get started earlier!

 GO ONLINE to play the vocabulary game.

GRAMMAR

3 Choose the correct option to complete the sentences.

1 What sports *did / were* you use to play when you were a child?
2 Where did you *use / used* to work before here?
3 How long did Kieran *live / lived* in Nepal?
4 We left the city because *it / there* was a lot of crime.
5 After I *was moving / moved* to the neighborhood, I bought a small apartment.

4 Complete the text using the phrases in the box.

there wasn't	there were	use to
used to	didn't use to	

Before ¹_____ alarm clocks, how did people ²_____ wake up? Well, many people ³_____ worry about time so much because they worked on the land. However, as people started to work in factories, being on time became more important. Because many workers ⁴_____ be late getting to work, factory owners employed a "knocker-upper." This person used a long stick to wake people up by knocking on their bedroom windows. This seems funny now, but back in those days ⁵_____ any other way!

5 Complete the sentences using the verbs in parentheses in the simple past or past continuous.

1 My husband Jeremy _____ (work) in a museum when I _____ (meet) him.
2 While we _____ (travel) around Scotland, we _____ (visit) lots of castles.
3 Last night Tim _____ (come) home, _____ (cook) dinner, and _____ (go) straight to bed.
4 Who _____ (you / wait) for when I _____ (see) you outside the bank?
5 The lecture _____ (be) interesting, but I _____ (not / understand) it all.

 GO ONLINE to play the grammar game.

DISCUSSION POINT

6 Read the quote. Do you think our lives get busier as time goes on? How is your life busier now than in the past?

 "Nobody sees a flower—really—it is so small—we haven't time—and to see takes time."

—Georgia O'Keeffe, selected from *The Oxford Dictionary of American Quotations*, 2nd ed., edited by Hugh Rawson and Margaret Miner

 GO ONLINE and listen to a podcast. Then add your comments to the discussion board.

ZOOM IN

7 What about you?

Task 1 Imagine that you have a time machine. Tell your partner what past event you would like to see.

Task 2 Write about two ways you are different now from when you were younger.

Task 3 Find an old photo of you. Tell a partner about it.

8 Complete the table.

	I did this well	I need more practice
Task 1		
Task 2		
Task 3		

Unit 3

VOCABULARY

1 Match each word with a definition.

1 attend (v)   5 essay (n)
2 certificate (n)   6 presentation (n)
3 degree (n)   7 register (v)
4 educate (v)

- [ ] a document showing a level of achievement in a course
- [ ] the document you receive when you graduate
- [ ] to sign up for a course
- [ ] to give training and instruction at a school or university
- [ ] a short piece of writing on a particular subject
- [ ] to be present at an event or meeting
- [ ] a speech or talk on a subject to an audience

2 Complete the sentences using the verbs in the box.

| announce | perform | recognize | refuse | solve |

1 I didn't _____ my professor at first because she was wearing a hat.
2 The government will _____ plans for more spending on education.
3 There is no quick or easy way to _____ this problem.
4 Teaching assistants should _____ to teach a class on their own.
5 How long will it take to _____ the operation?

3 Complete each word with the correct suffix.

1 How intellig_____ do you think you are?
2 In what ways are you competit_____?
3 Do you have the confid_____ to tell people what you think?
4 What responsibil_____ do you have?
5 What's the most val_____ lesson you've learned?

 GO ONLINE to play the vocabulary game.

GRAMMAR

4 Choose the correct options to complete the text.

In 1950, British scientist Alan Turing [1]*asked / has asked* the question "Can machines think?" He [2]*wanted / has wanted* to test if a machine could trick us so we would think it was human. He [3]*developed / has developed* a test called the Turing test. A person asks questions using a computer and then sees answers from two "people" on a monitor: one is human; the other is a computer. If the questioner can't identify which answers [4]*has / have* come from a machine, then the machine passes the intelligence test. Over the years, many people [5]*tried / have tried*, but nobody [6]*made / has made* a machine that can pass this test...yet!

5 Choose the correct answer.

1 I've ____ turned in my report. I feel great.
   a never   b just   c yet   d ever
2 Have you ____ worked part time?
   a ever   b still   c already   d yet
3 Have you told your boss you're leaving ____ ?
   a yet   b ever   c just   d since
4 Jason's been a student here ____ 2017.
   a for   b already   c since   d never
5 There are ____ things we don't know about the brain.
   a for   b still   c ever   d since

 GO ONLINE to play the grammar game.

DISCUSSION POINT

6 Read this quote. Do you agree that learning and education are the best ways to change the world?

 "Education is the most powerful weapon which you can use to change the world."

—Nelson Mandela, selected from *Oxford Essential Quotations*, 5th ed., edited by Susan Ratcliffe

 GO ONLINE and listen to a podcast. Then add your comments to the discussion board.

ZOOM IN

7 What about you?

Task 1 In what ways has education already helped you? Tell a partner.

Task 2 Write a paragraph about something you have learned that you will never forget.

Task 3 Find a photo of something you want to learn and describe it to a partner.

8 Complete the table.

	I did this well	I need more practice
Task 1		
Task 2		
Task 3		

Unit 4

VOCABULARY

1 Complete the text with a word from the box.

| security | baggage | sights | bargain | reservation |

True story!

Milan Schipper from Holland wanted to travel across Australia. He looked online and found a ¹_____ ticket to Sydney $200 cheaper than all the others. So, he made the ²_____ and looked forward to seeing the ³_____ of Australia's wonderful capital city. When he got off the plane with his ⁴_____ , he realized something was wrong. When he went through ⁵_____ , he discovered he was in the wrong Sydney. He was in Sydney, Nova Scotia—in Canada, not Sydney, Australia!

2 Complete the phrasal verbs with a missing preposition.

1 Can you please pick me _____ from the station when I arrive?

2 Hey. Watch _____! The bus is coming.

3 Why did you decide to go _____ the travel business?

4 I hate to bring this _____, but how much will this vacation cost?

5 I'm pleased we decided to go _____ with the trip.

 GO ONLINE to play the vocabulary game.

GRAMMAR

3 Choose the correct answer to complete each sentence.

1 _____ I leave the office, I'll turn off the lights.
   a As soon as   b After   c Before

2 I'm exhausted! I'll take a bath _____ I get home.
   a if   b as soon as   c before

3 The train will depart _____ the passengers are onboard.
   a after   b before   c if

4 _____ we miss our flight, what will we do?
   a Before   b If   c As soon as

5 _____ you get here, I'll be at the reception desk.
   a If   b As soon as   c When

4 Choose the correct answers to complete these dialogues.

1 A: Have you got the report?
   B: Oh no! I forgot! *I'll / I'm going to* get it now.

2 A: We need some more stamps.
   B: Yes, I know. *I buy / I'm going to buy* some this afternoon.

3 A: Can you go to the bank to exchange these dollars?
   B: *I won't go out / I'm not going out* today. I can do it tomorrow.

4 A: What time *does / is* the travel agency close?
   B: At six, I think.

5 A: James has just passed his driving test.
   B: Has he? OK, *I'll / I* get him a present to celebrate.

5 Complete the text using the simple present or present continuous of the verbs in parentheses.

Next month, ¹_____ (I / go) to Mexico on business. My flight ²_____ (leave) at 8 a.m. on Monday morning, and ³_____ (I / arrive) at 8 p.m. in the evening. ⁴_____ (I / have) meetings there all week, but after my work ⁵_____ (end), ⁶_____ (I / meet) friends and ⁷_____ (we / go) on a road trip.

 GO ONLINE to play the grammar game.

DISCUSSION POINT

6 Read the quote. What motivates you to be active? For example, to travel, to exercise, or to do sports?

"Whenever the urge to exercise comes upon me, I lie down for a while and it passes."

—Robert Maynard Hutchins, selected from *The Oxford Dictionary of American Quotations*, 2ⁿᵈ ed., edited by Hugh Rawson and Margaret Miner

 GO ONLINE and listen to a podcast. Then add your comments to the discussion board.

ZOOM IN

7 What about you?

Task 1 Do you think travel can change people? Has a trip ever changed you?

Task 2 Write a paragraph about your plans for the year ahead. What are you going to do?

Task 3 Find pictures of a place you plan to visit. Tell a partner where it is and what you are going to do there.

8 Complete the table.

	I did this well	I need more practice
Task 1		
Task 2		
Task 3		

Unit 5

VOCABULARY

1 Choose the correct options to complete the questionnaire. Then ask and answer the questions with a partner.

1 When you cook, are you careful or do you make a(n) _____?
   a effort   b mess   c changes

2 Are you making _____ to your home right now?
   a sense   b space   c changes

3 Is your home large, or do you need to make _____ when people visit?
   a space   b difference   c effort

4 Before friends visit, do you make a(n) _____ to clean your home?
   a effort   b mess   c changes

5 What is one thing that would make a _____ to your home life?
   a space   b difference   c space

2 Complete each dialogue with a phrasal verb from the box.

catch up   check on   figure out   get rid of   settle down

1 A: Did you enjoy meeting up with your old college friends?
   B: Yeah. It was great to ¹_____ after all these years.

2 A: Steve said he's going to buy a house in Vancouver.
   B: I guess he finally wants to ²_____.

3 A: I can't ³_____ why our energy bill is so high.
   B: Why don't you call customer service and ask?

4 A: What are all these old plastic bottles for?
   B: I have no idea. You can ⁴_____ them if you want.

5 A: Do you think the kids are asleep yet?
   B: I'll go upstairs now and ⁵_____ them.

 GO ONLINE to play the vocabulary game.

GRAMMAR

3 Complete the statements with the comparative or superlative form of the adjectives in parentheses.

1 Modern houses are comfortable, but they're usually _____ (spacious) than older ones.

2 Buying a home is _____ (big) decision of anyone's life.

3 A garden isn't _____ (useful) as a garage.

4 It's true what they say. City life is _____ (exciting) than life in the countryside.

5 I'm pleased to say my hometown is _____ (safe) now than it was in the past.

4 Add -ed or -ing to the adjectives to complete the text.

Did you know that the colors you use in your home can have a ¹surpris___ influence on the way you feel? Green helps you feel calm, so it's a good color for the bedroom when you feel ²tir___. Blue is also a ³relax___ color, but it helps you think, too, so use it in the office. Red is a strong, ⁴excit___ color, which works well in places for talking, like the dining room. Too much red can look ⁵frighten___ though, so try mixing it with brown, which can be ⁶bor___ on its own.

5 Complete the sentences putting the adjectives in the correct order.

1 How much is that *old / leather / beautiful* chair?

2 What do you think of these *round / silver / small* earrings?

3 We rented this *modern / amazing / huge* apartment.

4 Jim gave me a *glass / huge / rectangular* dish.

5 Outside the house I saw a *red / sports / fantastic* car.

 GO ONLINE to play the grammar game.

DISCUSSION POINT

6 Read the quote. Is home a place or a feeling?

"Some books are so familiar that reading them is like being home again."
—Louisa May Alcott, selected from *The Oxford Dictionary of American Quotations*, 2ⁿᵈ ed., edited by Hugh Rawson and Margaret Miner

 GO ONLINE and listen to a podcast. Then add your comments to the discussion board.

ZOOM IN

7 What about you?

Task 1 Have you ever felt homesick? When? What did you miss about home? Tell a partner about it.

Task 2 Write a paragraph describing a place you once stayed that means a lot to you.

Task 3 Find a photo of your childhood home. Tell your partner your memories of growing up there.

8 Complete the table.

	I did this well	I need more practice
Task 1		
Task 2		
Task 3		

Unit 6

VOCABULARY

1 Fill in the missing letters to complete the sentences.

1 For my friend's birthday, I bought her a f_____ and put a photo of us in it.
2 This photo shows a great v_____ of the pyramids at Giza.
3 If there isn't enough light, use a f_____ when you take photos.
4 A s_____ stick is useful for taking photos of yourself.
5 It's a good photo, although the background is slightly out of f_____.
6 There are lots of p_____ of famous people in the National Gallery.

2 Complete the agent nouns by adding *-er*, *-or*, *-ist*, or *-ian*.

1 As a politic___, I need to have a very clean public image.
2 A good portrait photograph___ shows a person's character, not what they look like.
3 It takes hard work to become a successful scient___.
4 I sent the article to my edit___ for comments.
5 The govern___ of Vermont has a good reputation for protecting rights.
6 People do not expect a travel___ to miss a flight.
7 For an independent music___, image can be as important as music.
8 A digital image special___ can earn a very high salary.

 GO ONLINE to play the vocabulary game.

GRAMMAR

3 Complete the text with these words.

lots	enough	a few
too many	both	too much

I recently visited the Louvre in Paris for the second time. I enjoyed ¹_____ times, but my first visit was more enjoyable. This trip, there were ²_____ people, and I didn't have ³_____ time to see everything I wanted. I took ⁴_____ of photos but, unfortunately, ⁵_____ of them were out of focus. Anyway, I don't mind. I think people give ⁶_____ importance to photographing things. We should spend more time enjoying the experience!

4 Rewrite the sentences with the words in parentheses.

1 My wife and I have digital cameras. (both)
2 I keep my photos online. (all of)
3 My sister posts selfies every day. (several)
4 Children today use cameras more for making videos than taking pictures. (most)
5 Tim painted the paintings at the exhibition. (several of)

5 Choose the correct sentences.

1 a Why didn't you to me send a postcard?
   b Why didn't you send me a postcard?
2 a Please give this picture to James.
   b Please to give James this picture.
3 a I'll show you all the photos from my vacation.
   b I'll to you show all the photos from my vacation.
4 a Joanna brought this poster for me.
   b Joanna bought for me this poster.
5 a They booked an economy class ticket for you.
   b They booked an economy class ticket to you.

 GO ONLINE to play the grammar game.

DISCUSSION POINT

6 Read the quote. Is it always necessary for photographs to tell the truth? When do photographs lie?

 "Photography is truth."
—Jean-Luc Godard, selected from *Oxford Dictionary of Quotations*, 8ᵗʰ ed., edited by Elizabeth Knowles

 GO ONLINE and listen to a podcast. Then add your comments to the discussion board.

ZOOM IN

7 What about you?

Task 1 Who owns an image? Is it the photographer or the person photographed? Discuss with a partner.

Task 2 Write a paragraph about how you think other people see you.

Task 3 Find a photograph of yourself when you were younger. Tell your partner about it.

8 Complete the table.

	I did this well	I need more practice
Task 1		
Task 2		
Task 3		

Unit 7

VOCABULARY

1 Use collocations with *get* to complete the sentences. Make sure you use the correct form of *get*.

1 I'm really not sure I want to _____ in marketing. I'm much more interested in working in fashion.

2 Jared used to be terrible at baseball, but he practiced over the summer and he is _____.

3 Players should wear helmets in order to avoid _____.

4 A: Have you heard the news? James and Michelle are _____!

5 B: Really? I haven't spoken to Michelle for years. I probably won't _____ to their wedding.

6 It's better not to _____ when making a complaint. Polite customers get better service.

7 Alisha _____ after work and then spilled coffee on her clean dress!

2 Write five sentences using collocations in Exercise 1.

3 Complete the missing words.

I really ¹d_____ that we will find intelligent life in the universe. We know a lot about other planets now, but no missions have ever found any ²e_____ of life. As ³f_____ as I know, this is the only planet with life. Of course, that might not be ⁴a_____. The fact is nobody knows ⁵f_____ if there is life out there somewhere, but I feel ⁶c_____ that there isn't.

 GO ONLINE to play the vocabulary game.

GRAMMAR

4 Choose the correct option to complete these sentences.

1 I don't know who left this voicemail, but it _____ be for me. It's in Spanish, and I don't know any Spanish speakers!
   a can't   b must   c has to

2 You've run ten kilometers! That was a big goal for you, wasn't it? You _____ be really pleased.
   a can't   b has to   c must

3 This email _____ be from Simon because that's his address at the top.
   a has to   b can't   c have to

4 They've found water on Mars? You _____ be joking!
   a can't   b have to   c mustn't

5 That's three nights this week Suzie has worked late. She _____ be happy about it.
   a mustn't   b hasn't to   c can't

5 Put the words into the correct order. Add correct punctuation to each sentence.

1 little / are / to / life / hard / some / goals / a / in / achieve

2 useful / learning / pretty / this / is / website / languages / for

3 articles / space / I / interesting / found / really / some / on / travel

4 future / easier / life / today / in / it / is / will / the / be / much / than

6 Make predictions about your future using the words below.

will definitely	will probably	probably won't
might	might not	definitely won't

1 I _____ get married.

2 I _____ move to a new apartment or house in the near future.

3 I _____ be rich or famous.

4 I _____ live and work abroad.

5 I _____ go traveling around the world.

 GO ONLINE to play the grammar game.

DISCUSSION POINT

7 Read the quote. Do you like to prepare for things, or is it better to take life one day at a time?

 "I never think of the future. It comes soon enough."

—Albert Einstein, selected from *Oxford Dictionary of Quotations*, 8th ed., edited by Elizabeth Knowles

GO ONLINE and listen to a podcast. Then add your comments to the discussion board.

ZOOM IN

8 What about you?

Task 1 In what ways could life be easier in the future? Discuss with a partner.

Task 2 Write a paragraph about the life you want to have in five years' time.

Task 3 Find a photo of some places you would really like to visit one day. Show the photos to your partner and explain why you want to visit each place.

9 Complete the table.

	I did this well	I need more practice
Task 1		
Task 2		
Task 3		

Unit 8

VOCABULARY

1 Complete the text.

When we were teenagers, my best friend Zita suddenly became really interested in fashion and famous ¹b_____ names. She had to follow the ²l_____ trends, so she could ³i_____ everyone. My family didn't have as much money as hers, so I had to keep to a tight ⁴b_____. I chose my clothes carefully and tried to ⁵m_____ and ⁶m_____ old and new things. I thought I looked good, but she always complained about my appearance. In the end, we stopped being friends.

2 Complete the text using the words in the box.

sour	salty	bake	spicy	raw	eat out

My son is a really fussy eater. That means there are not many things he likes to eat. We don't often ¹_____ because there are very few restaurants that he likes. He doesn't like Mexican food because they use chili, and that's too ²_____. He doesn't like Chinese food because they use soy sauce and that's too ³_____. He doesn't like French food because they use vinaigrette and that's too ⁴_____. He doesn't like Japanese food because they eat ⁵_____ fish and that's just disgusting!

So what does he like? Well, pizza and pasta. But not pizza that I ⁶_____ myself—no, it has to be from the Italian restaurant down the road!

3 Add the correct prefix to each word to complete the definitions.

1. _____-consumer: not favorable to consumers
2. _____priced: costing more than is fair or reasonable
3. _____-growth: in support of an increase in economic development
4. _____paid: receiving less money than is normal
5. _____-tablet: the world before the tablet computer

 GO ONLINE to play the vocabulary game.

GRAMMAR

4 For each sentence, choose the correct option. Then identify the correct function.

1. We *will / can* be able to reduce spending this year.
   Ability / Permission
2. Sorry, but I *wasn't able / couldn't* find the book you wanted. *Request / Ability*

3. I think that *may / can* be Lisa at the door.
   Possibility / Request
4. *Could / Might* you please wait here for a moment?
   Ability / Request
5. *Will / Can* you be able to exchange it for another size?
   Possibility / Permission

5 Correct the mistakes in these dialogues. More than one answer may be possible.

A: Could I please pay for these now and collect them later?
B: Yes, you could.
A: May I have this last slice of pizza?
B: Yes, you may have.
A: What time can I collect my order?
B: You may to collect it any time after four o'clock.

 GO ONLINE to play the grammar game.

DISCUSSION POINT

6 Think about the world we live in. In what ways are we happier because of the things we consume? Are there any disadvantages of living in the consumer age?

 "We used to build civilizations. Now we build shopping malls."
—Bill Bryson, selected from *Oxford Dictionary of Humorous Quotations*, 4th ed., edited by Ned Sherrin

 GO ONLINE and listen to a podcast. Then add your comments to the discussion board.

 ## ZOOM IN

7 What about you?

Task 1 With a partner, discuss if you agree with this saying: "The customer is always right."

Task 2 Write a paragraph about all the media you "consume" each day. Explain what you use it for and which you use most.

Task 3 Find a photo of something you want to buy. Tell your classmates about it.

8 Complete the table.

	I did this well	I need more practice
Task 1		
Task 2		
Task 3		

Unit 9

VOCABULARY

1 Complete each word with the correct suffix. Then add the part of speech.

| ity | ance | ion | ness | ment |
| ive | ant | ful | ent | |

1 assist___ ___
2 circumst___ ___
3 competit___ ___
4 effici___ ___
5 employ___ ___

6 grate___ ___
7 ident___ ___
8 solut___ ___
9 weak___ ___

2 Complete the conversation with the words in the box.

| fully | highly | junior | permanent |
| potential | senior | temporary | unlikely |

A: Of all the ¹_____ candidates, I think Simone is the best. She is a(n) ²_____ qualified accountant and a very experienced ³_____ executive. None of the other applicants is as ⁴_____ qualified.

B: That's true. But listen…I know Veronica is a(n) ⁵_____ choice, mainly because she's in a more ⁶_____ role right now, but she's a quick learner. I think she'd make a good addition to the team."

A: Well, maybe we could give Simone the ⁷_____ job, and offer Veronica a(n) ⁸_____ position over the summer?

3 Write the missing adjectives.

1 If you are i_____, then you are well organized and able.
2 An a_____ person is someone who is creative and imaginative.
3 Someone who is able to do things is called c_____ .
4 We say someone is e_____ if they are excited and eager.
5 If you are c_____, then you are not shy or timid.
6 A d_____ person is very strong and never gives up.

 GO ONLINE to play the vocabulary game.

GRAMMAR

4 Match the phrases. Then write zero or first conditional.

1 I'll definitely go to Madrid ___
2 Darren won't pass the training course ___
3 The machine stops immediately ___
4 If you need a new tablet computer, ___
5 We will fall behind schedule ___

a ask Human Resources for one.
b if he doesn't study.
c if I take a vacation this summer.
d if you press the red button.
e if we don't finish this project soon.

5 Write the correct reflexive pronouns.

1 Did you write these reports _____, Judith?
2 While he was opening the package, Tim cut _____.
3 I don't see how we can finish all this work _____.
4 I often ask _____ if I'd be happier in another job.
5 Dan and Matt designed this exhibition _____.

 GO ONLINE to play the grammar game.

DISCUSSION POINT

6 Read the quote. Do you agree?

 "The person who knows HOW will always have a job. The person who knows WHY will always be his boss."

—Diane Ravitch, selected from *Oxford Essential Quotations*, 5th ed., edited by Susan Ratcliffe

 GO ONLINE and listen to a podcast. Then add your comments to the discussion board.

ZOOM IN

7 What about you?

Task 1 Talk about how important work or study is to you.

Task 2 Write a paragraph about a job you had.

Task 3 Find a picture of yourself at work. Tell your classmates about it.

8 Complete the table.

	I did this well	I need more practice
Task 1		
Task 2		
Task 3		

Unit 10

VOCABULARY

1 Choose the correct idiom to complete the sentences.

of course not	after all	all the time	too bad	right now

1 A: How was the lecture?
   B: Oh, it wasn't ¹_____.

2 A: My notebook computer is gone. It had all my work files on it!
   B: You should tell your supervisor _____.

3 A: Chris messed up the photocopies again.
   B: Don't be too hard on him. _____, he's just started.

4 A: Do we really want to spend more on data storage?
   B: No, _____. But we have no option.

5 It's really hard to work when you're talking _____.

2 Complete the collocations.

1 Is f_____ of information a human right?

2 It can be hard to tell if news is g_____ or fake.

3 I think news s_____ faster because of social media.

4 Why would you m_____ facts up?

5 Sometimes you just have to t_____ your judgment.

GO ONLINE to play the vocabulary game.

GRAMMAR

3 Choose the correct option to complete the text.

Did you know ¹*an/–* information you post online can have ²*the/–* significant real-life consequences? If ³*an/–* employer finds comments or pictures they don't like on ⁴*an/the* employee's Facebook, Twitter, or Instagram account, ⁵*the/an* employee could lose their job. What's more, one of the first places ⁶*an/–* employers look to find information about job candidates is on ⁷*the/–* social media. So, be careful about ⁸*the/an* information you put online. You never know who's going to see it!

4 Complete the text using the verbs in parentheses in the present simple passive or the past simple passive.

Wikipedia is an online encyclopedia that ¹_____ (start) in 2001. It ²_____ (write) by tens of thousands of unpaid volunteers. These volunteers, who ³_____ (call) contributors, might be international experts, but they also might be people spreading false information. In the past there are examples where false information from Wikipedia ⁴_____ (take) by journalists and academics without

checking the facts. This material ⁵_____ (publish), which was very embarrassing for them! It is therefore a good idea to check the source of information that ⁶_____ (make) available on Wikipedia. Usually, the information ⁷_____ (link) to external sites.

—adapted from *A Dictionary of Journalism*, by Tony Harcup

5 Complete the statements with *any-*, *every-*, *no-*, or *some-*.

1 There isn't _____thing in this file. All the data is gone!

2 You can learn a lot about _____one from social media.

3 _____thing in this article is false. Not one word is true!

4 There was no mention of the robbery _____where in the newspapers.

5 The company's sales fell badly, but _____one accepted responsibility.

GO ONLINE to play the grammar game.

DISCUSSION POINT

6 Read the quote. Will libraries disappear completely one day, or will they once again become a popular place to go for information?

"Google can bring you back 100,000 answers. A librarian can bring you back the right one."

—Neil Gaiman, selected from *Oxford Essential Quotations*, 5ᵗʰ ed., edited by Susan Ratcliffe

GO ONLINE and listen to a podcast. Then add your comments to the discussion board.

ZOOM IN

7 What about you?

Task 1 Is the way information is delivered more important than the information itself? Discuss with a partner.

Task 2 Write a paragraph about a news story you read recently. Why did you read it? How did it affect you?

Task 3 Find an interesting or exciting image you like. Show your partner. What information do you think it gives?

8 Complete the table.

	I did this well	I need more practice
Task 1		
Task 2		
Task 3		

Unit 11

VOCABULARY

1 Choose the correct particles to complete the sentences.

1 There are lots of movies about people coming *away / back / through* to their hometowns.

2 My great grandparents lived *away / back / through* some really difficult times.

3 In horror movies, if a character looks *away / back / through*, you know they're going to get caught!

4 It takes longer to work *away / back / through* some problems than others.

5 In most children's stories, the hero or heroine successfully gets *away / back / through* from the monster.

2 How many collocations can you make?

1 amusing   a highlight
2 feel-good   b movie
3 opening   c plot
4 real   d release
5 recent   e scene

 GO ONLINE to play the vocabulary game.

GRAMMAR

3 Choose the correct options to complete the text.

1 a who   b which   c –
2 a who   b –   c which
3 a which   b –   c who
4 a that   b who   c –
5 a –   b that   c who

Fan Fiction

Stories ¹___ are written for fun, not to make money, and use the work of other writers as a starting point, are called fan fiction. The people ²___ write them are fans ³___ like the stories and characters ⁴___ appear on TV or in books and movies. Though the term is relatively new, the idea that you can take a story you love and continue it or make it go in different directions, is not new: fans of Jane Austen wrote about her characters, and fan fiction ⁵___ features Sherlock Holmes first appeared in the early 1900s. Fan fiction used to be an unusual hobby. However, thanks to the Internet, there are now millions of fan fiction stories.

—adapted from *The Oxford Companion to Children's Literature*, 2ⁿᵈ ed., by Daniel Hahn

4 Use the verbs in the box to complete the sentences in the past perfect.

read   hear   lose   watch   write

1 Simone _____ (not) a horror movie on her own before, so she felt nervous.

2 I didn't want to see the movie because I _____ the book already.

3 We couldn't check to see who _____ the story because the book cover was missing.

4 Everyone said she was a famous author, but I _____ (not) of her.

5 Henry paid $28 because he _____ the books he borrowed from the library.

5 Complete the story using the simple past and past perfect of the verbs in parentheses.

When I ¹_____ (arrive) home last Wednesday, I ²_____ (see) that my roommate Mei Ling ³_____ (prepare) a wonderful Chinese meal. Afterward, Mei Ling ⁴_____ (tell) me it was her birthday. So, I ⁵_____ (buy) a movie online called *One Life*. I ⁶_____ (know) Mei Ling would like it because I ⁷_____ (see) her reading the book earlier in the week.

 GO ONLINE to play the grammar game.

DISCUSSION POINT

6 Read the quote. What makes a good ending for a story? Are there any stories you know where you would like to change the ending?

 "The good ended happily, and the bad unhappily. That is what fiction means."

—Oscar Wilde, selected from *Oxford Dictionary of Quotations*, 8ᵗʰ ed., edited by Elizabeth Knowles

 GO ONLINE and listen to a podcast. Then add your comments to the discussion board.

ZOOM IN

7 What about you?

Task 1 With a partner, discuss whether you agree with this saying: "Fact is stranger than fiction."

Task 2 Think of a fictional character you would like to be. Write a paragraph to explain your reasons.

Task 3 Find an image from your favorite movie. Show your partner, and explain the plot and characters.

8 Complete the table.

	I did this well	I need more practice
Task 1		
Task 2		
Task 3		

Unit 12

VOCABULARY

1 Write about yourself using these adjectives.

satisfied	curious	guilty	impatient	relaxed

2 Match each word with a definition.

1 balance (n)   a   to persuade or influence someone

2 calculate (v)   b   equal or good amounts of different parts

3 convince (v)

4 risk (n)   c   a chance something bad will happen

       d   belief or judgment

5 thinking (n)   e   to estimate or assess

6 value (v)   f   to appreciate or respect

3 Complete the sentences using the phrases below.

kind of	someone like that	around
something like that	somewhere like that	stuff

1 We were so excited we arrived at the concert _____ two hours early.

2 You bought your sunglasses in Singapore or _____, didn't you?

3 To be honest, I was _____ disappointed you didn't call me on my birthday.

4 We should buy some food and _____ for the party on Friday.

5 I think *happy* is *feliz* or _____ in Spanish.

6 I'd love to meet a famous sports star like David Beckham or _____.

 GO ONLINE to play the vocabulary game.

GRAMMAR

4 Choose the *-ing* form or the infinitive to complete the text.

Emotional Appeals

Many advertisements try to influence our feelings towards a brand or product by focusing on our emotions. Some ads hope ¹*to connect / connecting* with the positive emotions we feel towards things like our family, relationships, or the past. However, ads can target negative feelings as well. They want ²*making / to make* us feel fear or guilt, to encourage us to purchase a product. Ads for health and safety campaigns sometimes aim ³*shocking / to shock* us. They use images and music rather than facts to influence us.

Advertisers' choices between emotional and rational appeals depend on whether the product or service has a high or low emotional impact. Bread, for instance, seems ⁴*to have / having* a high emotional impact, so advertisers may decide ⁵*to use / using* emotional appeals (such as the appeal to the past in ads for bread) so we keep ⁶*to buy / buying* a certain brand.

5 Make sentences using the adjectives on the left and the verbs on the right.

surprised to	help
easy to	see
interesting to	make
prepared to	hear
determined to	ask
fortunate to	find
disappointed to	know
	miss

 GO ONLINE to play the grammar game.

DISCUSSION POINT

6 Read the quote. In what ways is it important for people to share their feelings? What are the difficulties?

 "Laugh and the world laughs with you; weep and you weep alone."

—Horace (65–8 BC), selected from *Oxford Dictionary of Proverbs*, 6ᵗʰ ed., edited by Jennifer Speake

 GO ONLINE and listen to a podcast. Then add your comments to the discussion board.

 ZOOM IN

7 What about you?

Task 1 Do you make decisions slowly or quickly? Tell a partner and explain why.

Task 2 Write a paragraph about a time you felt happy.

Task 3 Find some photos of things that motivate you. Show your partner and explain why.

8 Complete the table.

	I did this well	I need more practice
Task 1		
Task 2		
Task 3		

Grammar focus

Unit 1

Simple present and present continuous

FORM

	Subject	auxiliary	main verb	
Simple present				
+	I		leave	at 8 a.m.
	She		eats	at 7 p.m.
–	He	*doesn't*	like	fish.
	We	*don't*	shop	online.
Present continuous				
+	I	*am*	talk*ing*	right now.
	She	*is*	enjoy*ing*	the music.
–	He	*isn't*	eat*ing*	his dinner.
	We	*aren't*	shop*ping*	at the moment.

Simple present questions
"*Do* you enjoy studying?" "Yes, I *do*." / "No, I *don't*."
What does she do?

Present continuous questions
"*Are* you enjoy*ing* the concert?" "Yes, I *am*." / "No, I'*m not*."
What is he do*ing*?

USE

We use the simple present to talk about routines and things that are always true.
  He usually gets home at 7 p.m.   *Penguins eat fish.*
We use the present continuous to talk about things happening now or around now.
  I'm enjoying the music.   *We aren't shopping right now.*

Question forms: *Do, did*, and *be*

FORM

We usually form *yes/no* questions with:
Auxiliary (do, does, did) + subject + infinitive without to.
  Do you drink coffee?   *Does your brother play football?*
We form *wh–* questions with:
Question word + auxiliary (do, does, did) + subject + verb.
  Who does your sister play tennis with?
  How often did you go on vacation as a child?
We also form *yes/no* questions with *be* as the main verb.
  Are you hungry?   *Was Phil at home?*

We also form *wh–* questions with *be* as the main verb with:
Question word + be + subject.
  How old is Tom?   *Why are your friends late?*

USE

We use different question words to ask about different types of information.
  What music do you listen to? (NOT ~~To what music do you listen?~~)
When the main verb in a question is *be*, we change the order of the subject and *be*.
  Are you OK? (NOT ~~You are OK?~~)
We do not use auxiliary verbs in questions with *be*.
  Are you American? (NOT ~~Do you are American?~~)

Tag questions in the present tenses: *Be* and *do*

FORM

We use a negative tag question after a positive statement.

Positive statement	+ negative tag question
The people *are* friendly,	*aren't they?*
He *plays* the guitar,	*doesn't he?*

We use a positive tag question after a negative statement.

Negative statement	+ positive tag question
You aren't cold,	*are you?*
I don't need a visa,	*do I?*

USE

We use tag questions to check information or to ask someone if they agree with us.
  We use tag questions with *be* with statements with *be*.
  The local people are friendly, aren't they?
We also use tag questions with *be* with statements in the present continuous.
  We're staying in a nice hotel, aren't we?
We use tag questions with *do* with statements in the simple present with other verbs.
  Your friends speak English, don't they?
We can reply to a tag question with a short answer.
  "*You don't have Ed's phone number, do you?*" "*No, I don't.*"

 GO ONLINE for the complete grammar reference.

159

Unit 2

Simple past: *Be*

FORM

Was and *wasn't* (*was not*) are the past forms of *is*, *isn't*, *am*, and *am not*. *Were* and *weren't* (*were not*) are the past forms of *are* and *aren't*.

Form statements with subject + *be*:

I/He/She was(n't) in class yesterday.

We/You/They were(n't) in class yesterday.

To form *yes/no* questions, we change the order of the subject and *be*.

Was Tom in class yesterday?

Were they in class yesterday?

Use short answers to respond to *yes/no* questions.

Yes, he was. / No, he wasn't.

Yes, they were. / No, they weren't.

Form *wh-* questions with: **Question word** + **be** + **subject?**

Where was Tom yesterday?

When were they born?

USE

We often use *was/were* with past time expressions, e.g., *last week*, *in 2003*, *500 years ago*, *yesterday*.

They were at school two hours ago.

There was... / There were...

FORM

There was and *There were* are the simple past forms of *There is* and *There are*.

	Singular	Plural	Noncount
+	*There was an* elephant.	*There were some* monkeys.	*There was some* snow.
−	*There wasn't a* tiger.	*There weren't any* bears.	*There wasn't any* snow.
?	Was there a tiger?	Were there any bears?	Was there any snow?

USE

We use *There was/wasn't* to talk about things that existed or didn't exist somewhere in the past.

We use *Was there / Were there* to ask about things in a place in the past.

Simple past and past continuous

USE

We use the simple past for completed actions, repeated actions, and things that happened one after another.

She waited for him for 30 minutes.

We use the past continuous to talk about being in the middle of an action at a time in the past.

At 3 p.m., she was still packing her bags.

We also use the past continuous to describe a scene, especially at the start of a story.

We were driving along the highway and the rain was pouring down.

Simple past and past continuous with *when*

USE

We use the past continuous and simple past with *when* to talk about an interrupted action in the past.

She was walking home when she met an old friend.

We also use *when* with two verbs in the simple past when one event happened straight after another event.

When it stopped snowing, we went outside.

Used to

FORM

We form positive sentences with *used to* + infinitive.

I used to sing in the school choir.

We form negative sentences with *didn't* + *use to* + infinitive.

I didn't use to have a smartphone.

We form questions with: **Did** + **subject** + **use to** + **infinitive?**

*Did you use to play sports in school? "Yes, I **did**." (NOT ~~Yes, I used to.~~)*

USE

We use *used to* + infinitive to talk about regular actions that we did in the past but don't do now.

Kate used to play the cello in the school orchestra.

We also use *used to* to talk about situations that were true in the past but are not true now.

People used to believe the world was flat.

We often use *used to* to compare the past and the present.

People used to travel less than they do nowadays.

We don't use *used to* when the action only happened once or to talk about one period of time or the number of times.

She played in a concert in the town hall once. (NOT ~~She used to play in a concert in the town hall once.~~)

Lisa presented the news for two years. (NOT ~~Lisa used to present the news for two years.~~)

 GO ONLINE for the complete grammar reference.

Unit 3

Present perfect simple with *for* and *since*

USE

We use the present perfect to talk about present activities that started in the past.

We can use the present perfect with *for* to talk about the period of time up to the present, e.g., *for four years*, *for two days*.

> *The company has been in business for four years.*

We can use the present perfect with *since* to talk about the time when an activity started. This can be a date, a day, a month, a time or an event, e.g., *since 1903*, *since yesterday*, *since May*.

> *I've been here since 8 a.m.*

We often use the simple past after *since*.

> *I've had this desk since I started working here.*

We can give a short answer to *How long...?* questions with *for* or *since*.

> "**How long have** you **known** Maya?"   "**For** six years. / **Since** I was twelve."

Present perfect and simple past

USE

We use the present perfect to talk about an action or situation in the past when we don't know the exact time or it isn't important.

> *I've invited Dave and Sue for dinner.*

We use the simple past to talk about a specific time in the past.

> *I wrote to the Admissions Office yesterday.*

We often use the present perfect to start a conversation about our experiences. If we want to ask about or give more details, we use the simple past.

> "**Have** you ever **visited** your cousins in Canada?"   "Yes, we **went** there last year."

Present perfect with *just*, *already*, and *yet*

FORM

We can use the present perfect positive with *just* or *already*:

Subject + **have/has** + **just/already** + **past participle**.

> *I have already visited three universities.*
> *He has just won the tennis match.*

We can use the present perfect negative with *yet*:

Subject + **haven't/hasn't** + **past participle** + **yet**.

> *She hasn't been there yet.*

We can form present perfect questions with *yet*:

Have/Has + **subject** + **past participle** + **yet?**

> *Have you visited your favorite colleges yet?*

USE

We use the present perfect with *just*, *already* and *yet* to talk about recent news and events.

We use *just* in positive sentences to talk about very recent news.

> *Murray has just won the tennis match.*

We use *yet* in questions and negative sentences to talk about news and events happening up to now.

> *Have you visited your favorite colleges yet?*

We use *already* in positive sentences to talk about news and events that happened before now or earlier than expected.

> *I've already visited three universities.*

Present perfect with *ever* and *never*

FORM

We can form the negative of the present perfect with *not* or *never*.

> *He has never watched a horror movie.*

To form questions, we change the order of subject and auxiliary.

> "**Have** you **ever read** a Harry Potter book?"   "Yes, **I have**. / No, **I haven't**."

USE

We can use *ever* and *never* with the present perfect when we talk about life experiences. *Ever* means "at any time in the past" and we use it in questions.

> *Have you ever climbed a mountain?*

Never means "at no time in the past." We use it with a positive verb.

> *I've never read "The Goblet of Fire."*

Present perfect: *Still*

FORM

Still goes between the subject and *haven't/hasn't*.

Subject + **still** + **haven't/hasn't** + **past participle**

> *She still hasn't arrived.*

USE

We use the present perfect with *still* in negative sentences to talk about actions that we expected to happen before now. *Still* looks back at the past.

> *Emma still hasn't arrived. She said that she'd be here at six o'clock. (I expected Emma to arrive before now.)*

 GO ONLINE for the complete grammar reference.

Unit 4

Will and *be going to*: Decisions

USE

We can use both *will* and *be going to* to make decisions. We usually use *will/won't* when we make a decision at the moment of speaking.

> *I'm exhausted. I think I'll go to bed.*

We usually use *be going to* when we have already made a decision. This is often when we are talking about plans and intentions.

> *I'm not going to take my driving test until next year.*

Will and *be going to*: Predictions

USE

We can use both *will* and *be going to* to make predictions about the future.

We usually use *will/won't* to make predictions based on personal feelings or opinions.

> *You'll have a great time on vacation.*

We often say *I don't think…will* for a negative prediction.

> *I don't think people will live in floating cities in the future.* (NOT *I think people won't live in floating cities in the future.*)

We usually use *be going to* when there is some evidence in the present to support the prediction.

> *There isn't a cloud in sight. It's going to be a lovely day.*

Simple present in future time clauses

FORM

Present clause		Future clause
when, **before**, etc.	**simple present**	**will** + infinitive **without to**
As soon as	Max *arrives*,	we*'ll have* lunch.
Before	I *cook*,	I*'ll go* for a swim.
When	we *get* home,	we*'ll have* a cup of tea.
If	the weather *is* nice,	we*'ll eat* outside.
After	I *take* the photo,	I*'ll put* it on the Internet.

USE

We use the simple present to talk about the future after the words *when*, *if*, *as soon as*, *before*, and *after*.

We usually use a future clause with *will* before or after the simple present clause. We add a comma after the present clause when it comes before the future clause…

> *Before we leave, I'll look at the map.*

…but if the future clause comes first, there is no comma.

> *I'll look at the map before we leave.*

If and *when* have different meanings when we are talking about the future. We use *if* when we are not sure that something will happen, and we use *when* if we are sure.

> *If the weather is nice, we'll eat outside. (We are not sure if the weather will be nice.)*
> *When we get home, we'll have a cup of tea. (We are sure that we will get home.)*

When and *as soon as* have a similar meaning when we are talking about the future, but we use *as soon as* to say that something will happen immediately after another thing.

> *As soon as I arrive, I'll call you.*
> *We'll go to the beach when the weather improves.*

Present continuous and *be going to*: Future plans and schedules

USE

We can use the present continuous or *be going to* to talk about future plans. Both forms are often possible and they are very similar.

> *When are they coming home again?*
> *When are they going to come home again?*

When the plan has a fixed time and/or place, we usually use the present continuous. These plans usually include other people.

> *I'm meeting Mike in the cafe at 10 a.m.*

We usually use *be going to* when we talk about plans or intentions with no time or place.

> *I'm going to get a new phone.*

When we talk about schedules, such as bus or train schedules or someone's personal schedule, we use the simple present for future meaning.

> *The bus leaves at 7:30 a.m.*
> *I finish work at 5:00 p.m.*

 GO ONLINE for the complete grammar reference.

Unit 5

Making comparisons

FORM

Most single syllable adjectives have a comparative form ending in *-er*, and a superlative form ending in *-est*. We use *more / most* with longer adjectives.

Type of adjective	Comparative	Superlative
One syllable	long**er**	long**est**
One syllable ending with *-e*	nic**er**	nic**est**
One syllable ending with one vowel + one consonant	hot**ter**	hot**test**
One or two syllables ending with *-y*	happ**ier**	happ**iest**
Two or three syllables	*more* helpful	*most* helpful
	more fantastic	*most* fantastic

There are some exceptions.

> bored → more bored

Some adjectives are irregular.

> good → better → best
> bad → worse → worst
> far → further → furthest

The opposite of *more* is *less* and the opposite of *most* is *least*. *Less/Least* can also be used with short adjectives.

> less tidy (= untidier)
> least shy (= most confident)

USE

We use comparative adjectives (+ *than*) to compare people and things with other people and things.

> My brother is **lazier than** me.
> Children are **more sociable than** adults.

We use superlative adjectives (usually with *the*) to compare people and things with the whole group.

> He's **the most confident** person in the family.

We use *not as* + adjective + *as* to say that two things or people are not equal in some way.

> I'm **not as happy as** Sue. (= Sue is happier than me.)

We use *(just) as* + adjective + *as* to say that two things or people are equal in some way.

> Emma is **just as creative as** Phil. (= They are equally creative.)

Adjectives: Using two or more adjectives

FORM

We put two or more adjectives in the following order before a noun: opinion, size, age, shape, color, origin, material, purpose.

> a **beautiful long silk** dress
> an **exciting young Brazilian** musician
> some **big red Italian** sports cars

USE

We use adjectives when we describe people or things.
We can put two or more adjectives before a noun. We don't use a comma between adjectives of different types.

> She's wearing a **short blue denim** jacket.

We put a comma between adjectives of the *same* type.

> Archaeologists found some ancient **flat, circular** gold coins.

We can put two or more adjectives after a noun + *be*. We use a comma between each adjective, and we put *and* before the final adjective.

> The coins are **ancient, round, and gold**.

Adjectives: *-ed* and *-ing*

FORM

There is a group of adjectives that end in *-ed*, including *interested*, *bored*, *excited*, and *surprised*.
There is another group of adjectives that end in *-ing*, including *interesting*, *boring*, *exciting*, and *suprising*.
Pairs of adjectives such as *interested* and *interesting* have a very similar form but the meaning is different.

USE

We use adjectives ending in *–ed* to talk about a person's feelings. We usually use them after the verb *be*.

> I'm **excited** about my birthday party.

We use adjectives ending in *–ing* to talk about a quality someone or something has. We can use them after the verb *be*...

> The movie's **exciting**.

...or before a noun.

> He's an **interesting** person. He's traveled all over the world.

 GO ONLINE for the complete grammar reference.

Unit 6

Quantifiers: *Both, several, most,* and *all*

USE

We use quantifiers, usually before nouns, to talk about the number of people or things.

We use *both* with a plural noun to talk about two people or things. We can use *both* + ([*of*] *the*) + noun.

> *There are two women. Both women are sitting down.*
>
> *Both the women are wearing colorful clothes.*
>
> *Both of the photos show forms of travel.*

We use *all* with a plural noun to talk about all the people or things in a group. We can use *all* + (*of*) *the* + noun…

> *All the people in the photo are sitting down.*
>
> *All of the children are playing.*

We use *most* + *of the* + plural noun to talk about the majority of the people or things in a group.

> *Most of the houses are painted white.*

We use *most/all* + noun (without *the* or *of the*) to talk about people or things in a general way.

> *Most children like ice cream.*

We use *several* (+ *of the*) + plural noun to talk about some of the people or things in a group.

> *There's a row of stores. Several of the stores are open.*

We can use *both/several/most/all* + *of* + pronoun to talk about people or things that we have already mentioned. We cannot omit *of*.

> *There's a group of people. Several of them are carrying childen, and all of them are smiling.*

We can use *both/several/most/all* without a noun or pronoun when it is obvious what we are talking about.

> *There are two women. Both are smiling.*

Quantifiers: *Too much/too many, a little/a few, a lot, enough*

FORM

The form is:

	Count	Noncount
large quantity	*a lot of/lots of* coins	*a lot of/lots of* money
small quantity	*a few* coins	*a little* money
	not many coins	*not much* money
enough	*enough* coins	*enough* money
more than enough	*too many* coins	*too much* money

USE

We use quantifiers before nouns to talk about the amount or number of things or people.

We use *a lot of/lots of* with countable or uncountable nouns to describe a large number or amount. We can use *a lot of/lots of* in positive or negative sentences and questions.

> *Does the museum have a lot of paintings?*

We use *a few* with countable nouns and *a little* with uncountable nouns to describe a small number or amount. We usually use *a few/a little* in positive sentences.

> *I bought a few gifts.*

We use *much* with uncountable nouns and *many* with countable nouns in negative sentences and questions.

> *Are there many visitors in the winter?*

We use *too much* or *too many* to say that the quantity is more than we want or need. Sometimes, this has a negative result.

> *I did too much shopping yesterday—I have no money left.*

We use *enough* with countable or uncountable nouns to say "all that is necessary." We use *not enough* to make a negative sentence.

> *Do you have enough stamps?*

Verbs with two objects

FORM

Some verbs can have two objects, a direct object and an indirect object:

Subject + verb + indirect object + direct object

> *I wrote Grandma a letter.*

Subject + verb + direct object + preposition + indirect object

> *I wrote a letter to Grandma.*

USE

Some verbs can have two objects, a direct object and an indirect object.

The direct object usually answers the question *What?*

> "***What** did you write?*"   "*I wrote **a letter**.*"

The indirect object usually answers the question *Who to/for?*

> "***Who** did you write a letter **to**?*"   "*I wrote a letter **to Grandma**.*"

We can put the indirect object before the direct object…

> *I wrote Grandma a letter.*

…or we can put the indirect object after the direct object and the preposition *to* or *for*.

> *I'm baking a cake for Ed.*

 GO ONLINE for the complete grammar reference.

Unit 7

Must, have to, and *can't*: Deductions about the present

FORM

We use *must, have to,* and *can't* with a base form.

Subject + must/can't/have to + **base form.**

	Subject	*must/have to/can't*	base form	
+	Someone	*must*	*be*	at home.
	This	*has to*	*be*	your sweater.
	You	*have to*	*be*	joking.
−	This	*can't*	*be*	Karen's coat.
	He		*be*	serious!

With *must* and *can't*, the forms are the same for every subject. *have to* becomes *has to* in the third person (*he/she/it*).

USE

We use *must* when we are very sure something is true.

> *You've been driving all day—you must be tired.*

We can use *have to* with the same meaning as *must*.

> *This has to be the right way—the sign over there says British Museum.*

We use *can't* when we are very sure something is not true.

> *That can't be the right number—you've added the amounts up wrong.*

We don't use *mustn't* in this way.

> *This can't be Karen's coat—it's too big.* (NOT ~~This mustn't be Karen's coat.~~)

Will and *might*: Predictions

FORM

We can make predictions using *will (not)* and *might (not)*. The form is the same for every subject.

Subject + **will (not)/might (not)** + **base form**

> *People will use public transportation more.*
>
> *People might not travel by train anymore.*

To form questions, we change the order of the subject and *will*.

> *How will people travel to work?*
>
> "**Will** planes **fly** without pilots soon?" "Yes, **they will.** / No, **they won't.**"

We don't usually form direct questions with *might* (for example *Might train travel become cheaper next year?*); they can sound unnatural or very formal. Questions with opening phrases are more common.

> *Do you think that train travel might become cheaper next year?*

USE

We use *will* or *won't* to make guesses or predictions about the future. We often use *I think/believe …* or *I don't think/believe …* to introduce a prediction.

> *I think we will all drive electric cars in the future.*

We can use *will + probably* or *probably + won't* to make the prediction a little less certain. *Definitely* makes a prediction more certain.

> *The design of buses definitely won't change.*

We use *might* or *might not* to make predictions we are less sure about.

> *People might live longer, but they might not be healthier.*

Adverbs: *A little, pretty, much,* and *really*

FORM

We can use the adverbs *a little, pretty,* or *really* before an adjective after the verb *be.*

We can use the adverbs *a little* or *much,* before a comparative adjective.

Subject + *be*	adverb	adjective
It's	a little pretty really	expensive. old.
		comparative adjective
	a little much	more expensive. older.

We can use the adverbs *pretty* and *really* before an adjective + noun.

a/an + adverb	adjective	noun
a pretty a really	expensive	restaurant

USE

We can use the adverbs *pretty* or *really* + adjective after the verb *be…*

> *That restaurant is pretty expensive.*

…or before adjective + noun. The adverb may come before or after *a/an*.

> *This is a really interesting book.*

We can use *a little* + negative adjective after the verb *be.*

> *This restaurant's a little expensive. Should we go to a cafe?*

We can use the adverbs *a little* or *much* + comparative adjective. We often use *than* after a comparative adjective.

> *It's much hotter than yesterday.*

 GO ONLINE for the complete grammar reference.

Unit 8

Can, could, and may: Permission and requests

FORM

We use a base form after *can*, *could* and *may*. The form of *can/could/may* is the same for every subject:

Subject + can/could/may (not) + base form

You may not watch TV now.

To form questions, we change the order of *can/could/may* and the subject:

Can/Could/May + subject + base form

Could you hold this, please?

We often use short answers with *can/could/may*.

*"**Can** I **sit** here?" "Yes, you **can**."* (NOT ~~Yes, you can sit.~~)

USE

There are various ways of giving and asking for permission to do something. We use *can* in informal situations. To sound more formal, we use *could*. One of the most polite or formal ways is with the modal verb *may*.

You can borrow up to five books each.

*(more formal) You **may** borrow up to five books each.*

Can I have another drink, please?

*(more formal) **Could** I have another drink, please?*

*(most formal) **May** I have another drink, please?*

Be able to: Ability and possibility (present, past, and future)

FORM

We can use present and past forms of *be* with *able to*. When we are talking about the future, we use *will/won't* and *be able to*.

Subject + (will/won't) be + able to + infinitive.

Present: Young children *are able to learn* quickly.

Past: She *wasn't able to go* to college.

Future: We *will be able to speak* to robots.

To form *yes/no* questions, we change the order of the subject and auxiliary (*be* or *will*).

*"**Are** you **able to attend** the event?" "Yes, I am."*

USE

We use *be able to* to talk about abilities and possibilities in the present and past in formal language.

*Young people **are able to learn** quickly.*

*The doctor **isn't able to see** any more patients today.*

We use *be able to*, and not *can*, when we are talking about abilities and possibilities in the future.

*I **will be able to speak** English better after the course.* (NOT ~~I will can speak English better ...~~)

We also use *to be able to* when we need an infinitive to talk about abilities and possibilities.

*I'd like **to be able to** dance the tango.*

May, might, and could: Possibility

FORM

We use an infinitive without *to* after *may (not)*, *might (not)*, and *could*. The form of *could* is the same for every subject.

Subject + may (not) /might (not) /could + infinitive without to.

*She **could be** the next president.*

To form questions, we change the order and the subject.

***Could** this **be** your purse?*

We often form questions with *may/might/could* with an opening phrase, such as *Do you think ...?*

*Do you think (that) she **could be** the next President of the United States?*

We use *may*, *might*, and *could* to talk about possibility in the present and future and to make deductions.

*Maya's not at work today. She **may be** sick. (about the present)*

*There **might not be** any fish left in the river in ten years. (about the future)*

We don't use *may* in direct question with this meaning.

Could it snow tonight? / Do you think it could snow tonight?

(NOT ~~May it snow tonight?~~)

USE

We use *may*, *might*, and *could* to talk about possibility in the present and future and to make deductions.

*Your keys **may/might/could be** in the front door. (about the present)*

*It **may/might/could snow** this evening, so dress warmly. (about the future)*

We don't use *couldn't* to express possibility. We use it when we are certain that something is not true.

*It **couldn't be** her birthday today—I know she was born in June, not May.*

We don't use *may* in direct question with this meaning.

Could it snow tonight?/Do you think it could snow tonight?

(NOT ~~May it snow tonight?~~)

 GO ONLINE for the complete grammar reference.

Unit 9

Zero and first conditional

FORM

We form conditional sentences with *if* clause + result clause.
The zero conditional uses the simple present in the *if* clause and the simple present or an imperative in the result clause.

  If you mix red and yellow, you get orange.

The first conditional uses the simple present in the *if* clause and *will/might* + infinitive without *to* in the result clause.

  If I study, I'll pass.   If I don't study, I might fail.

  If I don't pass, will you be angry?

USE

We use the zero conditional to talk about events and the results that always follow.

  If you click on the icon, the website opens.

We can sometimes use *when* instead of *if*.

  When you mix red and yellow, you get orange.

We can also use the zero conditional to give instructions.

  If you want coffee, please help yourself.

We don't use a pronoun in the *if* clause when it comes afer the result clause.

  I'll invite Cathy for dinner if I meet her. (NOT *I'll invite her for dinner if I meet Cathy.*)

We use the first conditional to talk about a possible action or situation in the future and the result or effect that follows.
We can put the result clause before the *if* clause when the result is important. We don't use a comma after the result clause.

  We'll reduce global warming if we save energy.

If we aren't certain about the result, we can use *might/might not* instead of *will/won't*.

  We might be late if the traffic's bad.

We can also use the first conditional to give advice.

  If you run, you might fall!

Second conditional

FORM

We form the second conditional with *if* clause + result clause.
We form the *if* clause with *if* + simple past. We form the result clause with *would/wouldn't* + infinitive without *to*.

  If the tickets were more expensive, people wouldn't buy them.

  If we used solar power, would we save money?

We usually use the short form of *would* in spoken English.

  I would → I'd   you would → you'd   he would → he'd, *etc.*

USE

We use the second conditional to talk about unlikely events or imaginary situations and their possible results.

  If more people volunteered, it would make a big difference.

We usually put the *if* clause before the result clause, and we use a comma after the *if* clause.

  If students took fewer exams, they'd have more time.

We can put the result clause before the *if* clause when the result is important. We don't use a comma after the result clause.

  Students would have more time if they took fewer exams.

We can also use the second conditional to say that we believe an event is not likely. Other people might disagree.

  It'd be great if unemployment went down (but I doubt it will).

We can use either *was* or *were* in the *if* clause after *I*, *he*, *she*, or *it*. This use of *were* is sometimes called the subjunctive.

  If I were rich, I'd help the poor.   OR: If I was rich…

Reflexive pronouns

FORM

Subject pronoun		Reflexive pronoun
I	hurt	*myself.*
You		*yourself.*
He		*himself.*
She		*herself.*
It		*itself.*
We		*ourselves.*
You		*yourselves.*
They		*themselves.*

USE

We use reflexive pronouns when the person/animal who does the action (the subject) is also the person/animal affected by it. The reflexive pronoun is the object of the verb or preposition.

  With this math app, you can test yourself.

The reflexive pronoun agrees with the subject.

  She accidentally cut herself on the sharp knife.

But we sometimes use *themselves* instead of *himself/herself* to talk about a person when we don't say or don't know what sex the person is.

  Anyone can call themselves an expert.

There are a few verbs that take a reflexive pronoun when they have a particular meaning.

  The children always behave themselves (= behave well).

  I really enjoyed myself (= had a good time) today.

  Help yourself to (= please take) some more cake.

We can use reflexive pronouns *yourself/yourselves* with the imperative form in wishes.

  Enjoy yourselves at the party!

We can also use reflexive pronouns to mean "without help."

  I can do it myself (= without help).

 GO ONLINE for the complete grammar reference.

Unit 10

The passive: Simple present and simple past

FORM

We form the passive with *be* + past participle:

Present: *Where is the best pasta produced?*

The best pasta is produced in Italy.

Past: *When was the museum built?*

It was built in 2015.

We can answer a *yes/no* question with a short answer.

*"**Are** the **beans** done?"* *"Yes, they **are**. / No, they **aren't**."*

USE

We can often say sentences in two ways, in the active or in the passive. An active sentence answers the question, "Who does the action?" (Who is the agent?)

*My mother **cooks** chicken every Sunday.*

A passive sentence answers the question, "What happens to the person or thing?"

*The chicken is always **served** with potatoes.*

We often use the passive when we don't know who the agent is or when it is obvious or not important.

*The sauce is **made** with honey.*

We use the passive in the simple present to talk about processes and procedures.

*These cars are **made** in Japan.*

We use the passive in the simple past to talk about events and processes in the past.

*America **was discovered** in 1492.*

If we want to say who does an action in the passive, we use *by*.

*All the articles in the magazine **are written by** the students.*

But often, we don't need to say who does the action.

*The oranges **are grown** in Spain.* (NOT ~~The oranges are grown in Spain by Spanish farmers.~~)

A/an, the, and no article

FORM

We use *a/an* with singular countable nouns (e.g., *a car*). We use *an* if the next word (the noun or its adjective) starts with a vowel sound (e.g., *an apple*).

USE

We use *a/an* (the indefinite article) to talk about something when it is one of many…

Did you have a good seat in the stadium?

…or when we mention it for the first time.

My town has a swimming pool and a tennis court.

We use *the* (the definite article) to talk about a particular thing when it's clear which thing we're talking about, often because it's the second time we've mentioned it…

My town has a swimming pool and a tennis court. The tennis court is open only in the summer.

…or when it's the only one.

The clock is in the living room. (There is only one living room in the house.)

There is no article when we talk about plural or uncountable nouns in general.

I love old furniture.

We use no article in some common expressions with *school*, *college*, *church*, *prison*, and *bed* when we talk about the activity that usually happens there.

What did you study in college? *I'm tired. I'm going to bed.*

We use *the* when we talk about the place as a building.

The college is near the church.

Indefinite pronouns and adverbs

USE

We use *somebody/someone*, *something*, or *somewhere* in positive sentences to talk about a person, thing or place when we don't mean a particular one.

Someone called, but they didn't leave their name.

We can also use the *some-* words in questions that are offers or requests.

Will somebody come with me?

We use *everybody/everyone*, *everything*, and *everywhere* in positive sentences and in questions to talk about all people, things, or places.

Is everyone here? *Everything in this store is expensive.*

We use *nobody/no one*, *nothing*, and *nowhere* with a positive singular verb to mean no person, thing, or place.

There's nowhere quite like Venice!

We use *anybody/anyone*, *anything*, and *anywhere* in negative sentences and questions.

I don't know anything about it. *Has anyone called?*

We can also use *any-* in positive sentences when it means "it doesn't matter who/what/where."

Anything could happen!

We can give extra information about these words by adding an adjective…

Let's go somewhere hot for our vacation.

…by adding a *to*-infinitive…

Is there anything to eat?

…or by adding a relative clause.

A receptionist is someone who meets you when you arrive.

When we use any of these words as the subject of the sentence, we use a singular verb.

Everyone hates waiting. (NOT ~~Everyone hate waiting.~~)

 GO ONLINE for the complete grammar reference.

Unit 11

Past perfect

FORM

We form the past perfect with:

Subject + **had / hadn't** + *past participle*
The form is the same for all persons.

Positive and Negative

I *had been* to Europe before.
I *hadn't seen* the Grand Canyon.

Questions

Had you *booked* your flight?
Where *had* you *traveled* before?
We can answer *yes/no* questions with short answers.

> "**Had** you **booked** your flight?" "*Yes, I* **had**."
> "**Had** you **been** there before?" "*No, I* **hadn't**."

USE

We use the past perfect to talk about an action or an event that happened before something else in the past.

> *When we arrived at the station, the train* **had already left**. *(The train left the station first, and then we arrived.)*.

We also use the past perfect to talk about an action or event that happened before a particular time in the past.

> *I* **had stayed** *in the same hotel twice* **before** *(= before the time that I am thinking about)*.

Simple past and past perfect

USE

We use the past perfect with the simple past when we talk about two actions or events in the past.

> *I* **phoned** *the office, but Emma* **had already left**.

We use the past perfect for the action that happened first. We often use *already/just* with the past perfect to say when.

> *I* **phoned** *the office, but my boss* **had just left**.

We use the simple past for the most recent action. We can use *when* + simple past.

> *When I* **got** *there, the train* **had already left**.

We use the past perfect with the simple past to give a reason for a situation. We use the simple past for the situation, and we use *because* + past perfect for the reason.

> *I* **was happy** *(the situation)* **because** *I'd* **gotten** *tickets for the festival (the reason)*.

Defining relative clauses

FORM

	Defining relative clause		Main clause
Subject	**relative pronoun**	**verb phrase**	
The man	*who*	*lives* next door	is kind.
The blog	*which/that*	Kevin *writes*	is really interesting.

USE

Defining relative clauses tell us which person or thing we're talking about. We can't understand what the sentence is talking about without this information.

We use *who* to talk about people.

> *A girl answered the phone. She was very young.*
> *The girl* **who answered the phone** *was very young.*

We use *which* or *that* to talk about things.

> *Kevin writes a blog. It's really interesting.*
> *The blog* **that Kevin writes** *is really interesting.*

The defining relative clause can refer to either the subject or the object of the sentence.

> *One sport* **which is popular all over the world** *is tennis.*
> *Tennis is a sport* **which is popular all over the world**.

> [!TIP]
> **Tip**
>
> We put the defining relative clause immediately after the noun it refers to.
>
> > *The room* **that I sleep in** *is big.* (NOT ~~The room is big that I sleep in.~~)
>
> When a defining relative clause has a subject, we don't add an object pronoun.
>
> > *This is the man* **who I met** *at the wedding.* (NOT ~~This is the man who I met him at the wedding.~~)
>
> We can leave out the relative pronoun when it refers to the object of the sentence.
>
> > *This is the house* **(that) we bought**.
>
> We cannot leave out the relative pronoun when it refers to the subject of the sentence.
>
> > *The poet* **who wrote "Daffodils"** *was Wordsworth.* (NOT ~~The poet wrote "Daffodils" was Wordsworth.~~)

 GO ONLINE for the complete grammar reference.

Unit 12

Adjectives with the *to*-infinitive

FORM

We can use the *to*-infinitive after an adjective.

Subject + *be*	adjective	infinitive
I'm	happy	*to show* you around the school.
Pens are	easy	*to lose.*
It's	nice	*to meet* you.
Is it	necessary	*to show* your passport?

USE

We usually use the *to*-infinitive when a verb follows an adjective.

> We're always **happy to help**.

> I was **surprised to see** him there.

We often use a sentence that starts with *It's…* when we use an adjective + *to*-infinitive.

> **It's easy to make** that mistake.

We make negative infinitives with *not* + *to*-infinitive.

> It's nice **not to work** on the weekend.

Infinitive of purpose

FORM

We can use a *to*-infinitive after another verb.

Subject	verb	*to*-infinitive	
I	*use* my phone	*to listen*	to music.
He	*went* to Spain	*to learn*	Spanish.
Kate	*is going* to the bank	*to change*	some money.

USE

We use the *to*-infinitive to give the reason for doing something.

> He called me **to arrange** a meeting.

We can answer a *why* question with an infinitive of purpose.

> "Why do you bicycle to work?"   "**To keep** fit."

Verbs with the *to*-infinitive

USE

We use the *to*-infinitive after verbs for discussing plans and intentions, such as: *agree, decide, hope, plan, promise, want,* and *would like.*

> We've **decided to visit** Hawaii this summer.

We use the *to*-infinitive after certain other verbs, like *need, learn,* and *seem.*

> You **need to wear** nice clothes to the interview.

We form negatives by putting *not* before the *to*-infinitive

> **Promise not to be late.**

Verbs with the *-ing* form or *to*-infinitive

FORM

We sometimes use a second verb after a main verb. The second verb can be an *ing*-form or a *to*-infinitive.

Subject	main verb	*ing*-form/ *to* infinitive	
I	enjoy	*swimming*	in the morning.

USE

We use the *-ing* form after verbs that express likes and dislikes: *enjoy, like, love, hate, can't stand,* and *don't mind.*

> I **enjoy eating** fish.

We also use the *-ing* form after these common verbs: *finish, go, imagine, keep, mind, stop.*

> Can you **imagine running** a marathon?

We do not use the *-ing* form after verbs that express plans and intentions: *agree, arrange, decide, hope, plan, promise, want,* and *would like.* We use the *to*-infinitive after these verbs.

> You **promised to work** hard.

We also use the *to*-infinitive after the verbs *learn* and *need.*

> He **learned to swim** when he was six.

GO ONLINE for the complete grammar reference.